Library of Congress Cataloging-in-Publication Data:

Developing mathematical reasoning in grades K–12 / Lee V. Stiff, 1999
  yearbook editor, Frances R. Curcio, general yearbook editor.
       p.   cm. — (Yearbook ; 1999)
    Includes bibliographical references.
    ISBN 0-87353-466-2
    1. Mathematics— Study and teaching.   2. Reasoning (Psychology)
I. Stiff, Lee.   II. Curcio, Frances R.   III. Series: Yearbook
(National Council of Teachers of Mathematics) ; 1999.
QA1.N3   1999
[QA11]
510 s—dc21
[510′.19]   99-14117
                                                                  CIP

Printed in the United States of America

Developing Mathematical Reasoning in Grades K–12

1999 Yearbook

Lee V. Stiff
1999 Yearbook Editor
North Carolina State University

Frances R. Curcio
General Yearbook Editor
New York University

National Council of Teachers of Mathematics
Reston, Virginia

CONTENTS

Part 3: Reasoning in the Middle Grades

Part 4: Reasoning in High School

Part 5: Mathematical Reasoning: Charting a Future of Success

Preface

Mathematical reasoning is an ongoing focus of the National Council of Teachers of Mathematics (NCTM). In particular, curricula and instruction that involve students in exploring, investigating, representing, conjecturing, explaining, and justifying mathematics promote the development of students' reasoning abilities. In support of instruction, a variety of assessment techniques can be used to help teachers analyze and evaluate students' reasoning. Each of the NCTM *Standards* documents provides some guidance to understanding and fostering mathematical reasoning. It is my hope that the NCTM 1999 Yearbook, *Developing Mathematical Reasoning in Grades K–12*, will contribute to this body of work in a significant way.

Learners come to school with a wealth of knowledge and skills that provide teachers with a foundation for making instructional decisions. One important decision that each teacher must make is how best to engage students in thinking and reasoning about mathematics. Indeed, what is the interplay among knowledge, skills, and mathematical reasoning? Often, we teachers assume that if students can perform certain number operations, follow established algorithms or procedures, or solve problems, then they must be able to explain or justify their actions. Unfortunately, this is often not the case. If we view this fact in light of the different types of mathematical reasoning that students may be asked to perform (e.g., algebraic, statistical, geometric, probabilistic, inductive, deductive, and so on), it is clear that the effectiveness of the organization and character of the curriculum, the nature of the classroom environment, and the instructional practices of teachers must be addressed.

The 1999 Yearbook addresses these issues and more. The yearbook is divided into five parts. In Part 1, the four articles give different insights into mathematical reasoning. Each author shares a perspective about the nature of reasoning that will, it is hoped, sharpen the reader's view of mathematical reasoning in the schools. Parts 2, 3, and 4 each address such concerns as (*a*) how learners reason with mathematics, (*b*) how teachers gather evidence of students' reasoning, (*c*) what tasks elicit students' reasoning throughout the grades, (*d*) how communication promotes reasoning, and (*e*) which types of justifications, validations, explanations, and convincing evidence students might be asked to demonstrate. Part 2 focuses on the early grades, Part 3 focuses on the middle grades, and Part 4 focuses on high school. In Part 5, issues related to the development of mathematical reasoning in the schools are discussed, concerns related to the professional development of teachers are examined, and curricular approaches that could be profitably explored are presented.

More than eighty manuscripts were submitted to the Editorial Panel for review. Each manuscript made a real contribution to the creation of this yearbook, and I would like to express my deep appreciation to all the authors who submitted articles. I am especially grateful to the thirty-nine authors who have, ultimately, shared their perspectives on developing mathematical reasoning with the reader.

During the past three years, I have had the distinct pleasure of working with outstanding mathematics educators whose expertise, energy, and dedication have been without equal. My sincere gratitude is given to the 1999 Yearbook Editorial Panel:

Michaele F. Chappell	University of South Florida, Tampa, Florida
Frances R. Curcio	New York University, New York, New York
James M. Landwehr	AT&T Bell Laboratories, Murray Hill, New Jersey
Peter D. Lax	New York University, New York, New York
Alan H. Schoenfeld	University of California at Berkeley, Berkeley, California
Linda L. Walker	Leon County Schools, Tallahassee, Florida

I am most indebted to the General Yearbook Editor, Frances R. Curcio. Her support and editorial guidance were unequivocal and constant — thanks, Fran. Many thanks, too, to the editorial and production staff at the NCTM Headquarters Office who transformed "countless" pages of manuscript into a quality yearbook.

The authors of the articles in this yearbook devoted many hours to creating manuscripts that would inform, motivate, and challenge readers. It is my hope that the reader will reflect on the ideas presented in this publication and embrace those elements of the yearbook that benefit all the children we teach.

Lee V. Stiff
1999 Yearbook Editor

1

Mathematical Reasoning in the Elementary Grades

Susan Jo Russell

MATHEMATICAL reasoning must stand at the center of mathematics learning. If I had to choose the most important of the four "cross cutting" Standards from the *Curriculum and Evaluation Standards for School Mathematics* (National Council of Teachers of Mathematics [NCTM] 1989), it would be the Standard on mathematical reasoning. Mathematics is a discipline that deals with abstract entities, and reasoning is the tool for understanding abstraction. From the very beginning, children encounter the abstraction of mathematics—not only five fingers or five rabbits but the *idea* of "fiveness," not just that circular clock or this circular penny but the *idea* of a circle. Reasoning is what we use to think about the properties of these mathematical objects and develop generalizations that apply to whole classes of objects—numbers, operations, geometric objects, or sets of data.

In this article, I want to stress four points about active mathematical reasoning in elementary school classrooms. First, mathematical reasoning is essentially about the development, justification, and use of mathematical generalizations. In the classroom where mathematical reasoning is at the center of activity, the solution of an individual problem is closely linked to the generalizations behind that solution. Second, mathematical reasoning leads to an interconnected web of mathematical knowledge within a mathematical domain. Third, the development of such a web of mathematical understandings is the foundation of what I call "mathematical memory," what we often refer to as mathematical "sense," which provides the basis for insight into mathematical problems. Fourth, an emphasis on mathematical reasoning in the classroom, as in the discipline of mathematics, necessarily

The writing of this article was supported in part by grant no. ESI-9050210 from the National Science Foundation. Opinions expressed are those of the author and not necessarily those of the Foundation. TERC is a nonprofit company working to improve mathematics and science education.

incorporates the study of flawed or incorrect reasoning as an avenue toward deeper development of mathematical knowledge.

REASONING IS ABOUT MAKING GENERALIZATIONS

Katie, a third grader, was working with her partner to find factor pairs for 120. Her class had been working with paper arrays (see fig. 1.1) as well as with a computer game in which students filled in arrays with different dimensions. Katie reported their work to the class as follows: (*Note.* All dialog from students and teachers in this paper is taken verbatim from videotaped classroom sessions in grades K–5 [Russell et al. 1999].)

Katie: Micky and I did three by forty.

Teacher: All right, and did you double-check it? How did you know it would be the same?

Katie: Because, well, actually at first we thought it was three by forty-two, but then on another day ... it was six by twenty, and we thought, well, if we split six in half and we get three, then we would have to double twenty and we got forty, not forty-two.

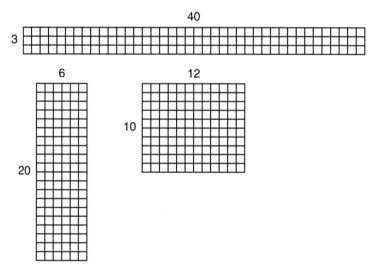

Fig. 1.1. Arrays showing factors of 120

Katie is reasoning from a known relationship (6 × 20) in order to find a new factor pair for 120. Her work gives some insight into what mathematical reasoning is and how it is based on the construction and application of mathematical generalizations. At first glance, it might appear that her work has to do only with the relationship between two small pieces of mathematical information—that 6×20 equals 120 and that 3×40 also equals 120. In fact, her reasoning makes use of several mathematical generalizations.

From her experiences with rectangular arrays, Katie knew that a rectangular array is one way to model the relationship between a product and one of its factor pairs and that by maintaining the area of the rectangle while changing its shape, she could generate new factor pairs (see fig. 1.1). However, as she gives her response about 3×40, Katie seems to be reasoning from the numbers themselves and making use of a new generalization: If you halve one number in a factor pair and double the other, you generate a new factor pair that is equivalent to the first pair and therefore equivalent to the same product. Katie and her partner had miscounted one of the dimensions of a 3×40 paper array, so that they thought the result was 3×42, but they *reasoned* that this must be incorrect because of the logical relationship of this factor pair to 6×20.

Katie's generalization now becomes a building block, a tool in her understanding of factors and products to be used, refined, critiqued, expanded. She may already know that this generalization about halving and doubling will work only for factor pairs that include at least one even factor. However, she has not yet discovered that this generalization is just one instance of a more inclusive generalization, based in associativity: Dividing one number in a factor pair by any of its factors and multiplying the other number in the pair by that same factor will result in a new, equivalent factor pair (e.g., for 15×14, divide 15 by 3 and multiply 14 by 3 to get 5×42 or divide 14 by 7 and multiply 15 by 7 to get 2×105).

Developing and using generalizations happens from the very beginning of mathematical learning in the elementary grades. One unfortunate, oversimplified legacy of Piaget's complex ideas is the belief that students move strictly from "concrete" to "pictorial" to "abstract" thinking. This construct is taken to mean that when young students use concrete materials to develop and test their mathematical ideas, they are not doing abstract thinking. Yet the very nature of mathematics is abstract. As young children learn to count, they are already encountering abstraction. For example, the idea that "one more" can always be applied to a number, no matter how large—that, therefore, the counting numbers must go on forever—is an abstract idea. It is this movement from the individual instance to the generalization that we are striving for in the mathematics classroom—reasoning about a whole class of mathematical objects, such as all whole numbers or all regular polygons.

It is when children "lift off" from the specific instance to consider the general case that they are really doing mathematical reasoning. We may be working on the solution to 6×20, but we are not concerned *only* with the solution to 6×20. In fact, there is nothing very interesting about the solved problem, $6 \times 20 = 120$, if it is understood simply as an individual assertion. Mathematics becomes interesting only as we start to investigate how 6×20 is related to its product, to other factors of 120, to other multiplication expressions. How is the solution to 6 × 20 related to the solution to 6 × 10? How is the solution to 598 × 20 related to the solution to 598 × 10? As students become involved with such questions, they begin to develop mathematical sense and insight, grounded in a web of mathematical generalizations.

The Accrual of Reasoning: A Web of Generalizations

Mathematical reasoning both leads to and builds on a web of mathematical knowledge—a hammocklike structure in which knots are joined to other knots in an intricate webbing. Even if one knot comes undone, the structure does not collapse but still bears weight—as opposed to what might happen if each individual rope was strung only from one point to another, with no interweaving.

It is easy to learn ideas in such a way that each idea is isolated from the others. Once many years ago, I moved to a new town where I lived at the end of a short street off Major Road A. If I went up my street to Major Road A and turned right, it intersected Major Road B. Taking a right again onto Major Road B, I soon passed a Chinese restaurant (see fig. 1.2a). I tried the restaurant, found I liked it, and ate there several times, always traveling up my street and taking the two rights—it took about ten minutes by car. One afternoon I took a walk in the opposite direction down my street, away from Major Road A, took a left, and suddenly found myself virtually on the doorstep of the restaurant (see fig. 1.2b). I had been learning single pathways, but was now beginning to connect pathways into a web that gave me a fuller mental picture of the connections in my neighborhood.

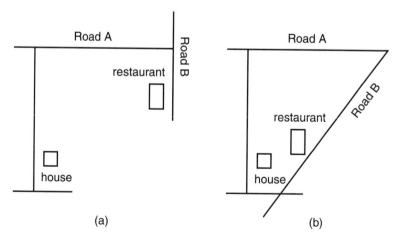

Fig 1.2. Two mental models of my neighborhood

Seeing mathematics as a web of interrelated ideas is both a result of an emphasis on reasoning and a foundation for reasoning further. When Katie found the factor pair 3×40 by using her knowledge about 6×20, she was beginning to weave this web of mathematics. Besides the particular mathematical ideas that she used in her reasoning, she knew something else about mathematics that was important to her thinking: she assumed the existence of logical connections among these ideas. Katie did not view $6 \times 20 = 120$ as an isolated fact she happened to know. Rather, she viewed mathematics as a discipline in which one idea is logically connected to many others.

Experience with reasoning through the use of models, images, and a variety of problem situations in a particular mathematical domain leads to the construction of a web of ideas bound together by rational connections. For example, a fourth-grade class was trying to find all the factors of 300. Although many of the factors were easily found from what students already knew about 300, there were many numbers that students could not immediately decide about. Did they need to test each one of these numbers individually? Eventually, some students began to argue that there were many numbers that could be eliminated as factors of 300. Laurel said:

> I know that between a hundred and a hundred and fifty, none of those can work because a hundred is, goes into three hundred three times, and a hundred and fifty goes in two times, and there's nothing between three and two.

This reasoning is based on a set of definitions and generalizations about factors and products that form a web of ideas about how factors of a number are interrelated. Laurel knows that factors of a number come in pairs, that they must be whole numbers, and that as you increase one factor, you must decrease the other in order to maintain the same product. Thus, an ordered list of factors for 300 begins like this:

$$1 \times 300$$
$$2 \times 150$$
$$3 \times 100$$
$$4 \times 75$$
$$5 \times 60$$

Laurel is reasoning that there can be no other factor pairs in the list between 2×150 and 3×100 because in order for any number between 100 and 150 to be a factor of 300, it would need to be paired with a factor greater than 2 and less than 3. Therefore, assuming that there is a factor between 100 and 150 leads to an impossible condition—the existence of a whole number between 2 and 3. We can find multiplication expressions equivalent to 300 that use numbers between 100 and 150, such as 2.5×120, but they require the use of decimal numbers. By considering the whole set of factors of 300 and the interrelationships among the factor pairs, Laurel has developed a simple proof by contradiction. (A proof by contradiction is a way of proving something cannot be true by assuming it *is* true and showing how that assumption leads to an impossible condition of some kind. Note that her reasoning can also be applied to other intervals in the list of factors.)

Webs of ideas are established through prolonged exposure to the important objects in a mathematical domain—the chance to explore and manipulate these objects, look for patterns and regularities, describe their properties, and reason about their behavior. These webs include key images, generalizations, and definitions that are the foundation of mathematical memory and insight.

Mathematical Memory and Insight

Reasoning leads to an important kind of memory that is different from what we call *memorizing*. Memorizing has had such an ascendancy in school mathematics that we may have come to believe that memorizing is equivalent to memory. Memorizing has its uses. In daily life, we memorize facts we use often—phone numbers, addresses, appointment times, birthdays, names. By "memorizing" here, I refer to facts we remember by sheer effort of short-term memory or through prolonged exposure and practice—facts that are unconnected to a web of reasoning. Although we can memorize and use some facts, we are generally in great trouble when memory fails—for example, when we forget a name or telephone number—if a memorized fact is not connected to related facts in rational ways.

In mathematics, there is also memorizing. It is useful and necessary, but as in daily life, it is sometimes not very reliable. As in daily life, we don't want to entrust too much to memory, but it is convenient to have some remembered facts at our fingertips. However, one of the outcomes of the development and use of mathematical reasoning is a stronger, more reliable kind of memory—the memory of the essence of fundamental mathematical relationships, what I like to call *mathematical memory*.

When the fourth grader asserts that there are no factors of 300 between 100 and 150 because "there's nothing between three and two," she is using reasoning based on a complex view of factors and products. For her, individual factor pairs are connected into a web of factor pairs that have logical relationships. She has a view of how the entire set of factor pairs for a particular number is constructed; she can "see" this set as a mathematical whole. This is what is characteristic of the kind of memory developed through mathematical reasoning—it is a memory of essences and core relationships. It is a memory in which the whole web of ideas has become more than the sum of its parts.

In order to illustrate further what I mean by this *mathematical memory*, I would like to challenge readers to think with me about the angles of polygons. Sometime in my mathematics schooling, one of the many formulas I memorized was the formula for determining the measure of an interior angle of a regular polygon. Figure 1.3 shows a series of regular polygons—*regular* meaning that they have both equal sides and equal angles. The first figure shows an equilateral triangle; its interior angles each equal 60°. Next is a square—an equilateral rectangle—with four equal sides and four equal interior angles, each 90°. If you are like me, you are less likely to remember the measure of the interior angles for the regular pentagon, the regular hexagon, or the regular heptagon. However, there is a formula that can be used to determine the interior angle, given the number of sides of the regular polygon. I was quite successful at memorizing that formula for as long as I needed to know it for the test. However, later, when I encountered this formula again in my mathematics education studies, I found that I had to rememorize the thing every time.

Fig. 1.3. Examples of regular polygons

Through some good mathematical experiences that allowed me to explore polygons in some depth, both on and off the computer, I developed two important, related generalizations through reasoning about polygons. First, I realized that every interior angle could be paired with an angle outside the polygon to make a complete angle of 180°. For example, in figure 1.4, angle *A* plus angle *F* create a 180° angle, as do angles *B* and *G* as well as angles *C* and *H.* That means that if I can find something out about angles *F, G,* and *H,* I will also know something about angles *A,* *B,* and *C.* Second, through further exploration, I eventually came to reason that the sum of all those angles I constructed outside the polygon (angles *F, G, H, I, J* in fig. 1.4) had to be 360°. Those outer angles are the turns I would make if I put the polygon on the floor and walked its perimeter. In order to walk that closed figure, I actually have to turn in a complete circle, making the same number of turns as the number of sides in the polygon. For example, if you walk around the perimeter of a square garden plot,

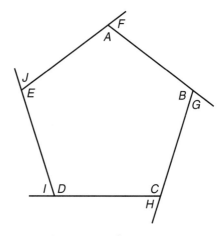

Fig. 1.4. A regular pentagon

starting and ending at the same point and facing in the same direction, you have turned a full 360° since you started.

Now I have all the information I need to find the measure of an interior angle of any regular polygon. Dividing 360° by the number of outer angles gives me the measure of one of the outer angles, so for a pentagon (see fig. 1.4), 360°/5 is 72° for each of angles *F, G, H, I,* and *J.* Then I can find the measure of an interior angle by subtracting 72° from 180°, resulting in 108°. Further, I have now generated the formula to find the interior angle of any regular polygon: divide 360° by the number of sides, and subtract the result from 180°: $180° - (360°/n)$.

So now I have developed a *mathematical memory* for some of the relationships that can be seen in the attributes of regular polygons. It is not that I remember the equation; I still don't. But I can access a deeper mathematical memory for the core relationships involved and generate a method for finding an interior angle any time I want to. Should we ever memorize an equation or a formula or a procedure? Sure. If I were finding the measure of interior angles every day, I would soon memorize the equation for convenience. But if I am trying to understand something new about polygons, it is my mathematical memory that I would depend on—memory that gives me access to that web of related generalizations I have developed. The question for teachers in mathematics classrooms is, What is the nature of the mathematical memory that remains after students do mathematical work—what Davis (1992) calls the "residue" of the mathematical activity? Is it the memory of disconnected bits of information, or is it a deeper mathematical idea, an image, a model that is robust enough to be retained and, eventually, to be connected to other important ideas in the mathematical web?

When I think back to my own tenth-grade course in Euclidean geometry, full of proofs and theorems, I regret that although I memorized eagerly and well, I understood little about the essence of geometric relationships. I did not do much mathematical reasoning; I did not spend time exploring, testing, questioning, proving; I developed, therefore, no mathematical intuition. I might know that the next step should be to "drop a perpendicular" or connect some midpoints, but I never could have thought that up myself. In my later experiences, I came to know those geometric relationships in a deeper way, in a way that I could not easily lose. As Hiebert et al. (1996) put it: "The benefits of reflective inquiry lie not in the solutions to problems but in the new relationships that are uncovered, the new aspects of the situation that are understood more deeply" (p. 15).

Lest I be misunderstood, I am not arguing that each person must reinvent the proof for every mathematical idea we might ever use. However, if we use a theorem or formula in a vacuum—without any experience of doing our own reasoning in that domain—we will be extremely limited in what we can do with the mathematical ideas embodied in that formula. We may be able to solve certain kinds of problems, but we will never be able to pose questions or create our own investigations. We will have developed no "mathematical intuition" in that domain of mathematics. As Kline (1980) points out (p. 313):

> When a mathematician asks himself why some result should hold, the answer he seeks is some intuitive understanding. In fact, a rigorous proof means nothing to him if the result doesn't make sense intuitively. If it doesn't, he will examine the proof very critically. If the proof seems right, he will then try hard to find what is wrong with his intuition.

(It is important to note that Kline also acknowledges that intuition can sometimes be misleading: "Mathematical reasoning not only supplements intuition to confirm or correct it, but even occasionally surpasses it [Kline 1980, p. 317]." The male pronouns used by Kline are of course his choice; I would have wished otherwise, but his thoughts seem worth quoting here. Mathematical intuition—or mathematical insight, if you prefer—which I think is often called mathematical "sense" as well (number sense, operation sense, etc.), is based on mental constructs that are firmly anchored, not on memorizing, but on true mathematical memory.

MAKING MISTAKES: WHY WE MUST HAVE FLAWED REASONING IN CLASS

So far in this essay I have presented examples of students who have used sound reasoning to construct important mathematical generalizations. But, of course, reasoning does not always lead to correct results. Sometimes reasoning is flawed; sometimes very careful reasoning, based on a great deal of good analysis and insight, is flawed. In fact, in order to make mathematical reasoning central in the classroom, as it is in the discipline of mathematics, we must expect to frequently encounter and examine flawed reasoning.

Please notice that I said "flawed reasoning," not "poor reasoning." Poor reasoning might be defined as reasoning that is sloppy, hasty, not thought through, not taking into account important aspects of the problem. We do not want to encourage students to do *poor* reasoning, but in the discipline of mathematics, flawed reasoning occurs often and is one of the reasons that mathematicians frequently turn to colleagues to scrutinize their work. We were privileged to witness an example of this during this decade, when Pierre de Fermat's famous conjecture—often called Fermat's last theorem—was finally proved. Fermat, a seventeenth-century French mathematician, conjectured that the equation $x^n + y^n = z^n$ had no solutions for values of n greater than 2.

To get a sense of what this conjecture entails, let's pause a minute to examine it. If $n = 2$ in this equation, the equation becomes $x^2 + y^2 = z^2$. It is possible to find values for x, y, and z to make this equation true. For example, if $x = 3$, $y = 4$, and $z = 5$, the equation would read

$$3^2 + 4^2 = 5^2, \text{ or } 9 + 16 = 25,$$

which is true. It turns out that there are many—in fact, an infinite number—of solutions to $x^2 + y^2 = z^2$. However, if $n = 3$, giving the equation $x^3 + y^3 = z^3$, or if $n = 4$, resulting in $x^4 + y^4 = z^4$, no solutions can be found. Fermat left notes stating that he had proved that no solutions to this equation existed for any value of n greater than 2. However, he did not leave the proof itself, and the attempt to prove Fermat's assertion had tantalized mathematicians since his time. By this decade, a few partial proofs had been developed; it had been proved, for example, that there is no solution for $n = 3$, for $n = 4$, for $n = 5$, and for $n = 7$. However, no one had been able to prove that it is impossible to find *any* solution. Could there be some strange, large value of n for which this equation might work?

In June of 1993, Andrew Wiles, a professor of mathematics at Princeton, announced his proof. Wiles had worked alone on the problem for seven years but now called on other mathematicians to scrutinize his work for flaws. Unfortunately, a serious flaw that jeopardized the entire proof was found by one of the reviewers. There was no way to know whether this meant that Wiles's attempt would end in failure. It took another year and an extended collaboration with a colleague, but Wiles finally found a new approach that closed the gap in the proof. Wiles recalled, "I was sitting at my desk one Monday morning ... examining the Kolyvagin-Flach method [the part of Wiles's proof that had been shown to be flawed]. It wasn't that I believed I could make it work, but I thought that at least I could explain why it didn't work. I thought I was clutching at straws, but I wanted to reassure myself. Suddenly, totally unexpectedly, I had this incredible revelation" (Singh 1997, p. 297). One of the most fascinating aspects of his revised proof is that it rested on finding a connection between his flawed approach and an earlier method, which he had discarded years before: "It was so indescribably beautiful; it was so simple and so elegant. I couldn't understand how I'd missed it and I just stared at it in disbelief for twenty minutes. Then during the day I walked around the department, and I'd keep coming back to my desk looking to see if it was still there" (p. 297). Only through analyzing and reanalyzing the flaw in his work, only through reexamining the web of generalizations he had built, could Wiles find the new connection that was the key to finalizing his proof.

The occurrence of flawed reasoning in the classroom must happen—and must be expected by all (including the students) to happen—for two important reasons. First, if students are to learn to rely on their own mathematical reasoning, they must continually engage in reasoning mathematically. Here is where we need a great deal of practice in the elementary school classroom. Students must practice looking for relationships, making conjectures, testing their conjectures, and explaining and justifying the generalizations they make. It cannot be expected that anyone working in mathematics—from a mathematician to a fourth grader—will always reason correctly. In forming the habit of reasoning, one must develop the view that it is commonplace to analyze and rethink, to poke at theories, to test them thoroughly, to face one's own and others' questions. Students must get used to this, and they must experience what it is like to try to think through reasoning that did not work.

The second reason why examining flawed reasoning is essential is that flaws often reveal important mathematical issues that many in the classroom, not just the student whose reasoning is being considered, need to think through. In a fifth-grade classroom, students were working on ways of solving multiplication problems. In this classroom, students were used to coming up with approaches to solving computation problems based on what they understood about numbers and operations. For example, they often made use of multiples of 10 and of the distributive property of multiplication to solve problems. Near the beginning of their work on multiplication, Thomas solved the problem 36×17 in the following way:

> What I did was ... I wanted to make 36 times 17 easier, so I added 4 to 36 to make it 40, to make it easier, and I added 3 to 17 to make it 20, so I timesed 40 times 20 ... I knew it wasn't the answer, so I minused 4 because I added 4 to get up to 40 ... and that brought me to 796, and I minused 3 cause I had to add 3 to get to 20, and I got the answer 793. [$40 \times 20 = 800; 800 - 4 - 3 = 793$]

To some of the other students, there seemed to be some logic in this way of reasoning, even though Thomas's result was different from theirs: Isn't it true that if you add an amount and then subtract the same amount, there should be no net change in the result? In this instance, Thomas has run into an essential way in which the operation of multiplication is not like the operation of addition. If the problem had been $36 + 17$, adding 4 onto 36 and then subtracting 4 from the result would work ($40 + 17 - 4$). However, when Thomas added 4 to 36 in the multiplication problem, he was not adding 4 to the result, because the 4 is acted on by the 17 in a different way from the way it is in addition. He was actually increasing the result not by 4 but by 4 *seventeens*.

The teacher decided that even though most other students in the class had obtained the correct answer to the problem, there was still a need to help students articulate carefully how the two operations differ. It was clear that some students were intrigued with Thomas's work—it seemed to have a certain compelling logic. She gave the following assignment for homework that night: copy down Thomas's work and figure out how he is thinking about this problem. The students, including Thomas, already knew that this method led to a result different from the answer most other students had and that there was something to figure out about why what seemed so sensible did not work. In this classroom where mathematical reasoning had been emphasized all year, where students were used to justifying and critiquing their own and others' reasoning, no one, including Thomas, thought that examining his error was unusual or stigmatizing in any way. In both Andrew

Wiles's and Thomas's work, each had to face and understand flaws in his own reasoning in order to go further. As Duckworth (1987) puts it, "The virtues involved in not knowing are the ones that really count in the long run. What you do about what you don't know is, in the final analysis, what determines what you will ultimately know" (p. 68).

A focus on reasoning in the elementary grades requires a continual digging for the general nature of the problem underneath the specific problem itself. What class of problems are we considering? What is the relationship between this problem and others we have done? What conjectures does this work suggest? Students are no longer focused on finding individual solutions to individual problems but on developing a web of generalizations, the foundation of true mathematical memory and insight. Students who leave the elementary grades with a mathematics education that has focused on mathematical reasoning are students who can count on their own thinking and are willing and able to investigate new problem situations for themselves.

REFERENCES

Davis, Robert B. "Understanding 'Understanding.'" *Journal of Mathematical Behavior* 11 (September 1992): 225–41.

Duckworth, Eleanor. *"The Having of Wonderful Ideas" and Other Essays on Teaching and Learning.* New York: Teachers College Press, 1987.

Hiebert, James, Thomas P. Carpenter, Elizabeth Fennema, Karen Fuson, Piet Human, Hanlie Murray, Alwyn Olivier, and Diana Wearne. "Problem Solving as a Basis for Reform in Curriculum and Instruction: The Case of Mathematics." *Educational Researcher* 25 (May 1996): 12–21.

Kline, Morris. *Mathematics: The Loss of Certainty.* Oxford: Oxford University Press, 1980.

National Council of Teachers of Mathematics. *Curriculum and Evaluation Standards for School Mathematics.* Reston, Va.: National Council of Teachers of Mathematics, 1989.

Russell, Susan Jo, David A. Smith, Judy Storeygard, and Megan Murray. Relearning to Teach Arithmetic. A Series of Videotapes. White Plains, N.Y.: Dale Seymour Publications, 1999.

Singh, Simon. *Fermat's Last Theorem.* London: Fourth Estate, 1997.

2

Developing Mathematical Reasoning in the Middle Grades
Recognizing Diversity

Carol E. Malloy

IN THE second half of the twentieth century, we have seen broad and sweeping changes in our national and world culture. Many changes have altered how we think about the teaching and learning of mathematics. Technology, worldwide communication, and the interaction of diverse cultures have helped us to realize that our mathematics classrooms reflect the diversity of our world. Consequently, effective mathematics instruction of students with diverse cultural backgrounds challenges the notion that one culture or one method of reasoning dominates the learning process. In order for all children to become mathematically literate, mathematics educators must be poised to use varied instructional strategies that address the needs of the diverse population of children who will live and become productive in the twenty-first century.

This article on reasoning in the middle grades proposes mathematical questioning (or inquiry) by students and teachers as a strategy to help students use their innate reasoning abilities to sharpen and clarify their understanding of mathematical concepts. Mathematics teachers are providing evidence that when asked to reason about mathematics through inquiry, students fundamentally have a better understanding of mathematics than we might think (Wolf 1997; Sawada 1997). Consider an example of a traditional mathematics problem. The student dialogue that follows the example demonstrates how middle-grades students used different methods of reasoning in the problem-solving process and reflects how the teacher used an atmosphere of inquiry to help students use and understand the mathematical concepts.

Terri's Burger Shack is open 6 days a week and sells an average of 1500 hamburgers a week. Each week, 375 pounds of hamburger and 125 packages of buns are used. The supplier brought 250 pounds of hamburger on Wednesday. How many days would this last?

When the teacher posed this problem to a group of middle school students, the students read the question several times. Jeff was the first to respond: "I think we should look at the number of pounds of hamburger and the packages of buns used each week because I want to be a cook and that's the way cooks would figure out how much hamburger they need."

Teresa said, "But we don't know enough about the size of the hamburgers. Maybe we …"

Sheila interrupted, "All of these numbers are confusing. There are 6 days. How can we find how much they used each day?"

Torian answered, "About 60 because 60 × 6 is just [a little] more than 350! Now I can guess the answer by looking at 250 to figure out how many pounds would be used each day. I think the answer is 4 days!"

Ashley smiled and said, "I got that answer too, but I did it another way. I divided 375 by 6. That's 62.5 pounds of hamburger each day. So I used a number line to subtract 62.5 from 250 until I got to 0. That's 4 times and 4 days!"

At this point the teacher asked the students if they could use Ashley's method to find the answer without the repeated subtraction. It took a few minutes, but one of the students explained that "if Terri's Shack had a 62.5 decrease on the pounds each day, we need to figure out how many times 62.5 will go into 250. Yes, it would last 4 days." The teacher then reviewed each of the methods that the students used by asking the students to explain their methods and the reasoning used in their approach.

In this situation, these students came up with three different methods to find the solution using their own reasoning approaches. Torian used a holistic approach by finding the difference between the average number of pounds used in a week and the number of pounds ordered to estimate and justify 4 as the answer. Ashley mixed analytic and holistic approaches. She found the amount of hamburger used in 1 day and used a number line to repeatedly subtract the daily amount from the 250 pounds. The third student used analytic reasoning by finding the daily amount and dividing it into 250 pounds.

The teacher played an important role in this discussion by allowing students to explore the problem and encouraging them to think about alternative methods. The teacher validated the students' personal reasoning preferences and exposed them to alternative approaches by allowing them to generate questions and answers, explore the problem's context, and most important, use and explain their original solution paths.

REASONING AND DIVERSITY IN THE CLASSROOM

Teachers know that students must progress from using reasoning to develop justifications and sense making in elementary school; through using reasoning to make conjectures and apply both inductive and deductive reasoning in middle grades; to using reasoning to form, validate, and prove assertions in mathematics in high school (National Council of Teachers of Mathematics [NCTM] 1989). In this learning progression, it is important that teachers encourage students to use both culturally based and teacher-taught reasoning skills. Students come to school with culturally based reasoning skills and sense making learned through interactions with their family, friends, and community (Nieto 1996). Often the mathematics instruction that students encounter in schools does not validate their experiences and requires that they adapt their reasoning styles to those that schools value (Banks 1993). As a consequence, students who do not adapt or who do not see formal school mathematics as meaningful become disenfranchised and choose not to participate in mathematics in a meaningful way. Achievement data from national tests seem to indicate that more often than not these disenfranchised, low-achieving students are from cultural and ethnic minorities (National Assessment of Educational Progress 1992; Quality Education for Minorities 1992).

To be inclusive of all students, mathematics instruction must create contexts that allow and encourage all students to be engaged in mathematics in a meaningful manner. This means that mathematics instruction must use contexts and pedagogies that allow students to use their own cultural, ethnic, and gender preferences and approaches. Mathematics instruction must become multicultural in its pedagogy; it must exploit, promote, and value the varied and valid ways that students make sense of mathematics. Reasoning with a multicultural emphasis happens when teachers acknowledge and validate students' approaches to, tools for, and experiences in reasoning that have their foundation in students' homes and communities (Ladson-Billings 1994). Using students' personal reasoning skills as a foundation, teachers can extend their students' mathematical reasoning skills through classroom instruction.

How can middle-grades teachers infuse a multicultural emphasis into their instruction to strengthen students' reasoning? There are two major accommodations to instruction that can support students' and teachers' growth in this area. First, middle-grades teachers must continue to use and extend students' own reasoning approaches even as students are guided to make conjectures based on patterns and observations, to validate and evaluate conjectures, and to apply these mathematical reasoning facts in related situations (NCTM 1989). Traditionally, mathematics has been taught by using an expository method in a linear, rigorous, and analytical manner (Stiff 1990) that addresses the reasoning style of the analytic, field-independent learner (Malloy and Malloy 1998). These students are encouraged to focus on detail, use sequential and structured thinking, recall abstract ideas and irrelevant detail, use inanimate materials, learn from formal lecture, achieve individually without group interaction, and value facts and principles. But using this instructional approach exclusively does not benefit all students. Mathematics pedagogy can and should be modified to give students who have other reasoning styles—the holistic, field-dependent, interdependent learners (Shade 1997)—the opportunity to learn mathematics by seeking solution paths that match their reasoning preferences. Instruction for these students would encourage them to focus on the whole, use improvisational intuitive thinking, recall relevant verbal ideas, use socially oriented materials, learn from informal class discussion, achieve interdependently, and narrate human concepts (Dance 1997; Hale-Benson 1986; Shade 1997; Willis 1992). A mixture of both types of instruction offers new learning opportunities for students who have had learning conflicts with the structure of traditional mathematics classrooms and provides opportunities for continued success to students who have achieved in traditional mathematics classrooms.

The second accommodation to instruction is that middle-grades teachers need to understand the factors that can contribute to students' ability to reason mathematically and how to translate these factors into appropriate pedagogy. Some of the more important factors are prior knowledge of, and experiences in, mathematics; beliefs about knowing and learning mathematics; and cognitive and physical models that represent mathematical ideas (English and Halford 1995; Kloosterman 1996; Sowder 1995). By combining the use of students' personal reasoning styles with an understanding of factors that promote reasoning, mathematics teachers can develop pedagogies for all students that include activities, lectures, and discussions. The approaches used in instruction should be both divergent and convergent, interdependent and independent, structured and flexible, and analytical and holistic. One example of this sort of pedagogy is explained below.

Implementing a Culturally Aware Pedagogy

Student-centered discussions and resulting conclusions that evolve from questions that are posed by either the teacher or other students can propel students with varied learning preferences into active learning in their mathematics classrooms. This inquiry approach can be used effectively to address the factors cited above, namely, personal reasoning approaches, experiences in mathematics, beliefs about learning mathematics, and models that represent mathematics. Posing appropriate questions can enable students to use their own reasoning styles to solve problems. The intent is to have students reason about the problem solution and, at the same time, focus on questions that they can pose to solve other problems in mathematics. (See Brown and Walter [1990] for more on problem posing.)

The two brief discussions presented below summarize dialogues from a classroom in which middle-grades students attempted and successfully solved Problems 1 and 2. One problem is real, the other contrived, and both can be solved in multiple ways.

Problem 1

An ant crawls around the outside of a square whose sides measure 1 inch. At all times the ant remains exactly 1 inch from the boundary of the square. Find, to the nearest integer, the area enclosed by one complete trip around the square.

The teacher asked students to read the problem and plan solutions while taking into consideration the importance of the ant's size, the path of the ant, and what it means to stay one inch away from the boundary of the square. She encouraged the students to talk with one another about the problem and share their questions and solution plans. An account of one group's discussion of the problem follows.

James read the problem and started to ask questions about perimeter and area. He decided that he was supposed to find the area. He asked the other students in the group, "What is the formula?"

Carla explained that she didn't remember the formula and asked, "I wonder if it makes any difference if it is a large or a small ant?"

Avis started to work on the problem by drawing a 1-inch square. She said, "It doesn't matter what size the ant is because it would still have to cover the path. We have to find out how far it walks."

James was still struggling with the correct formula for area versus perimeter and settled on length times width. James drew a small picture of the 1-inch square. Then he thought about the ant walking one inch away from it. He asked, "Why would the ant want to walk on this path?"

Carla explained, "Maybe it was following the path of a honey-jar lid. If it stays one inch away, there has to be a circle in it somewhere. How do we find the real path?"

Avis ventured, "Okay, we know the ant moves one inch from the square. Let's trace its path." She drew four lines parallel to the first square, about one inch away from the horizontal and vertical sides, to indicate the path of the ant. (See fig. 2.1a.) She said, "The length of one side is 3 and the area is 3×3, or 9. This has to be close to the path of the ant."

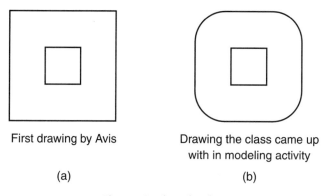

First drawing by Avis

Drawing the class came up with in modeling activity

(a)

(b)

Fig. 2.1. Student sketches

The teacher, who was listening, posed the following questions: "What does it mean to be one inch away from a square?…Why does Carla say the path is circular?" Following a brief discussion, the teacher decided to have the students model the path through a demonstration. The teacher and the students used string and their bodies to stay a fixed distance from a square table. This physical model was pivotal in helping students to reason further about the ant's path. They found that their paths were 3×3 squarelike figures with rounded corners. (See fig. 2.1b.)

Avis said, "Okay, we take the corners off and the area ends up being $9 - 1 = 8$. That's about 8 square units. I know that's an estimate, but it has to be the closest integer!"

The teacher praised Avis for her estimate and had the students summarize what they had learned. Then the teacher used questions about the shape of the area enclosed by the path of the ant to help the students use simple geometric shapes to find the exact area: How many different shapes can you see enclosed by the ant's path? How is the combined area of a figure determined? Can you tell me about the shapes at the corners? Using these questions, the students used their personal reasoning styles to find the area of the modified square with rounded corners. Some worked holistically by subtracting the area outside of the rounded corners, and some worked analytically by adding the area of individual regions. When the students found the exact area was 8.14 square inches, they realized that Avis's estimate was correct. Using what they had learned from the problem, the teacher helped the students to investigate and conjecture about how the area would change if the square had sides of 2 inches and the ant remains exactly 2, 3, 4, or n inches from the boundary.

Problem 2

A baseball team won 48 of its first 80 games. How many games must the team win in its next 50 games in order to maintain the ratio of wins to losses?

With the second problem, the teacher was aware that her students needed some experience in proportional reasoning to find a solution because they were often misled in problems where they were asked to compare ratios. However, she was confident that some students, with intuitive skills in proportional reasoning and some prior knowledge of equivalent ratios or geometric models, could use estimation and guess-and-check to find the answer.

She began the discussion with contextual questions to help the students identify with, and make sense of, the problem. She asked the students to think about the type of team that would play 80 games and whether they, as the team manager, would want to maintain this ratio of wins to losses. The class immediately decided that the problem was referring to a professional team because they played 130 games. They identified the ratio of wins as

48/80 and concluded that because the ratio of wins was more than half, the manager should want to maintain or improve this ratio. The students began to construct different models to solve the problem. They considered wins to losses, wins to total games, and even losses to total games.

Tina estimated that the number of wins would be about 28 games. When the teacher asked her to explain, she said, "Well, it was the first 80 games, then there were 50 more games, and 80 plus 50 is 130. They won 48 out of the first 80. So I think it was about 28 games out of the next 50 to maintain the same ratio."

Jim estimated that the answer must be "fifty something percent. It has to be like 30 something." Maria looked at the ratio of wins to losses as 48 to 32. She simplified the ratio to 6 to 4 but became confused on how to proceed. It was apparent that although the students had an intuitive sense of the problem and its solution, they had difficulty finding a model that would help them solve the problem.

The teacher then tried to have the students think about their experiences both at home and in school with problems similar to this one. She asked, "Could we solve this problem algebraically, using what we know about averages? Or could we solve it with a geometric model using what we know about magnification?" With the teacher's assistance, these students pursued algebraic and geometric paths to develop models based on their initial conclusions.

Jim mentioned baseball averages and explained how the average is found. Using an analytical approach, he showed the class that 48 divided by 80 is 60 percent and that 60 percent of 50 is 30 games. Tina still wanted to look at the total number of games; therefore, she applied Jim's method to find 60 percent of the total games (130). With 78 total wins, she calculated 30 wins in the next 50 games. Maria, remembering the scale factor from previous work in geometry, went back to the wins to losses ratio of 6/4. She simplified the ratio again to 3/2 and saw, looking at the whole, that the 50 games had to be in a ratio of 30/20.

To challenge the students further, the teacher asked them how the solution would change if the team had 30, 75, or 80 more games to play. They also investigated how many of the remaining 50 games the team would have to win if the ratio of wins to losses were changed.

Looking Back at Problems 1 and 2

The questions presented here were used by the teacher to help the students focus on these two problems and are not exhaustive; they are examples of questions that led to multifaceted investigations and reasoning. These two cases demonstrate that questions can be asked either by the students or the teacher. The questions the teacher asked promoted discussions about the context, mathematics content, and connections with other topics in mathematics. She encouraged students to begin with intuition and move to mathematical models, use holistic and analytical approaches, and use inductive and deductive reasoning to reach conclusions.

As these two problems indicate, students with diverse reasoning styles can be engaged in, and learn from, mathematical discussions. Learning occurs when students have a classroom atmosphere that allows them to use inquiry as a tool to explore the context of problems, employ their personal reasoning preferences, experience alternative approaches, and reflect on different solution paths. Teachers should initiate instruction in the areas where students exhibit strengths, and then stretch students into reasoning styles that are both familiar and unfamiliar. For instance, if students are more comfortable with divergent thinking, teachers should use divergence to introduce mathematics concepts. Then they should teach students to use convergence in reaching conclusions.

CONCLUSION

Giving middle-grades students the skills to integrate reasoning, knowledge, and experiences in mathematics depends on the commitment of the teacher, her willingness to accommodate instruction to the learning and reasoning styles of students, and her ability to help students accommodate their reasoning preferences when solutions are not familiar. Using an inquiry approach to promote reasoning in mathematics can help both teachers and students develop an active, nonthreatening environment for mathematics teaching and learning. As the twenty-first century approaches, mathematics teachers must be poised to address many teaching and learning issues in mathematics using multiple learning styles, preferences, and approaches. At the forefront of these issues is helping all students to develop and use their innate reasoning ability in mathematics.

REFERENCES

Banks, James A. "The Canon Debate: Knowledge Construction and Multicultural Education." *Educational Researcher* 22 (1993): 4–14.

Brown, Stephen I., and Marion I. Walter. *The Art of Problem Posing.* 2nd ed. Hillsdale, N.J.: Lawrence Erlbaum Associates, 1990.

Dance, Rosalie. "Modeling: Changing the Mathematics Experience in Post-Secondary Classrooms." Paper presented at The Nature and Role of Algebra in the K–14 Curriculum: A National Symposium, arranged by the National Council of Teachers of Mathematics and the Mathematical Sciences Education Board, Washington, D.C., May 1997.

English, Lyn D., and Graeme S. Halford. *Mathematics Education: Models and Processes.* Mahwah, N.J.: Lawrence Erlbaum Associates, 1995.

Hale-Benson, Janice. *African-American Children: Their Roots, Culture, and Learning Styles.* Baltimore: Johns Hopkins Press, 1986.

Kloosterman, Peter. "Students' Beliefs about Knowing and Learning Mathematics: Implications for Motivation." In *Motivation in Mathematics*, edited by Martha Carr, pp. 131–56. Cresskill, N.J.: Hampton Press, 1996.

Ladson-Billings, Gloria. *The Dreamkeepers: Successful Teachers of African American Children.* San Francisco: Jossey-Bass, 1994.

Malloy, Carol E., and M. Gail Jones. "An Investigation of African American Students' Mathematical Problem Solving." *Journal for Research in Mathematics Education* 29 (March 1998): 143–63.

Malloy, Carol E., and William W. Malloy. "Issues of Culture in Mathematics Teaching and Learning." *Urban Review* 30, no. 3 (1998): 245–57.

National Assessment of Educational Progress. *Mathematics Assessment.* Washington, D.C.: National Assessment of Educational Progress, 1992.

National Council of Teachers of Mathematics. *Curriculum and Evaluation Standards for School Mathematics.* Reston, Va.: National Council of Teachers of Mathematics, 1989.

Nieto, Sonia. *Affirming Diversity.* 2nd ed. White Plains, N.Y.: Longman, 1996.

Quality Education for Minorities. *Together We Can Make It Work: A National Agenda to Provide Quality Education for Minorities in Mathematics, Science, and Engineering.* Washington, D.C.: Quality Education for Minorities, 1992.

Sawada, Daiyo. "Mathematics as Reasoning—Episodes from Japan." *Mathematics Teaching in the Middle School* 2 (May 1997): 416–23.

Shade, Barbara J. R. "Culture and Learning Style within the African-American Community." In *Culture, Style, and the Educative Process*, 2nd ed., edited by Barbara J. R. Shade, pp. 12–28. Springfield, Ill.: Charles C. Thomas, Publisher, 1997.

Sowder, Larry. "Addressing the Story-Problem Problem." In *Providing a Foundation for Teaching in the Middle Grades*, edited by Judith T. Sowder and Bonnie P. Schappelle, pp. 121–42. Albany, N.Y.: State University New York Press, 1995.

Stiff, Lee V. "African-American Students and the Promise of the *Curriculum and Evaluation Standards*." In *Teaching and Learning Mathematics in the 1990s*, 1990 Yearbook of the National Council of Teachers of Mathematics, edited by Thomas J. Cooney, pp. 152–58. Reston: Va.: National Council of Teachers of Mathematics, 1990.

Willis, Marge G. "Learning Styles of African-American Children: Review of the Literature and Interventions." In *African-American Psychology*, edited by A. Kathleen H. Burlew, W. Curtis Banks, Harriette P. McAdoo, and Daudi A. Azibo, pp. 260–78. Newbury Park, Calif.: Sage, 1992.

Wolf, Dennie P. "Learning How to Teach Functions—More than Steps and Techniques." In *Through Mathematical Eyes: Exploring Functional Relationships in Math and Science*, edited by Ron Ritchhart, pp. 1–8. Portsmouth, N.H.: Heinemann, 1997.

3

Reasoning by Analogy
A Fundamental Process in Children's Mathematical Learning

Lyn D. English

And I cherish more than anything the Analogies, my most trustworthy masters. They know all the secrets of Nature, and they ought to be the least neglected in Geometry.

—*Johannes Kepler*

ANALOGIES have stood the test of time. Throughout history, they have played a powerful role in advancing our knowledge of the world. Around the second century B.C., the Greek Stoic Chrysippus first used water waves to suggest the nature of sound. In 1630, Galileo used the known orbit of the moon as the basis for claiming that the earth moves. And in 1865, Friedrich Kekule's well-known dream of a snake biting its own tail was the basis for his hypothesis that the carbon atoms in benzene are arranged in a ring (Holyoak and Thagard 1995).

Young children also reason by analogy in learning about their world. They understand that plants, like people, need appropriate food and water to stay alive. They also understand that animals that resemble people in important ways will have similar internal organs. As adults, we reason by analogy in many walks of life ranging from decision making in law, business, and politics to solving problems in daily living. A common example is the setting of precedents. We usually think carefully about setting a precedent, in whatever context, because precedents serve as powerful analogies for subsequent actions or instances.

Holyoak and Thagard (1995) provide numerous other examples showing how analogy is a basic tool of reasoning. Simply put, analogical reasoning entails understanding something new by comparison with something that is known. Despite the ubiquitous nature of reasoning by analogy in our daily lives, it seems to be underused in the mathematics classroom. Some of the recent results of the Third International Mathematics and Science Study (National Research Council 1996) suggest that students are not reasoning by analogy in that they are not seeing the connections and relationships among mathematical ideas and using these understandings to master new situations. This article examines the processes involved in reasoning by analogy with mathematical ideas and shows how these processes are fundamental to children's learning. Classroom strategies for helping children use these natural reasoning processes are presented.

Reasoning with Mathematical Analogues

Reasoning by analogy requires children to focus on the relational properties of a situation or idea rather than on the surface features. This means it is both a necessary and a powerful tool in children's mathematical learning. For example, whenever we present children with mathematical representations, we are asking them to reason by analogy (English and Halford 1995). This applies to concrete aids, such as multibase blocks, as well as to the array of pictorial representations we use to convey mathematical concepts. These concrete and pictorial aids are analogues of the mathematical ideas. That is, they are designed to mirror the structure of an abstract concept. The analogues serve a tangible source from which the child can construct a mental model of the mathematical concept. A simple example is shown in figure 3.1, where base-ten blocks (the source) are used to convey the meaning of the two-digit numeral 27, which is the target of the child's learning.

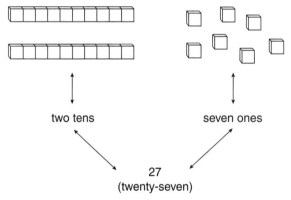

Fig. 3.1. Reasoning by analogy using multibase blocks

To reason with this analogue, the child has to map, or link, the base-ten structure of the two long blocks onto the digit "2" in the tens place of the numeral and likewise the structure of the seven single blocks onto the 7 ones in the ones place of the numeral. For children to make these mappings, they need to clearly understand the structure of the source analogue and must be able to recognize the relational correspondence between the source and the target. It is when children fail to do so that their learning becomes meaningless (English and Halford 1995; Hiebert and Wearne 1992). This simple example highlights the importance of selecting analogues that clearly impart the mathematical concept.

Children need to apply these same reasoning processes when they interpret analogues of fraction concepts. To illustrate, we consider the two examples shown in figure 3.2, involving a set analogue (Example A) and a region analogue (Example B).

FUN FAIR

(A) Kelly is selling bags of candy at the school fair. Each bag has four different kinds of candy: Venus Bars (VB), Magic Chocs (MC), Tim Tams (TT), and Jumping Jacks (JJ). This is what is in each bag.

(i) What fraction of the candies are Venus Bars? Tim Tams?

(ii) Kelly's friend, Henri, and his sister Jacinta, each bought a bag. Henri really liked his bag, but Jacinta didn't like hers. Why might this be? What would you do to make them both happy?

(B)

Come and Explore
SPOOKY CASTLE
If you Dare!

The $5.00 SCARY Tour

| Climb the Mystery Staircases |
| Unlock the Skeleton Rooms |
| Travel the Ghost Tunnels |
| Unlock the Skeleton Rooms |
| Travel the Ghost Tunnels |
| Explore the Dungeons |
| Climb the Mystery Staircases |
| Travel the Ghost Tunnels |

The $5.00 SCARY Tour

(i) What fraction of the tour is spent exploring the ghost tunnels? The skeleton rooms?

(ii) If you were creating this Spooky Castle tour, what fraction of the tour would you give to each scary thing? Explain why.

Fig. 3.2. Reasoning by analogy using fraction representations

The target of Example A is the fraction of candies that are of each different kind, and for Example B, the fraction of the tour spent exploring each of the adventures. Although not discussed here, it is worth noting that the second part of each example is designed to foster children's divergent thinking as well as give us further insights into their understanding of fractions. In completing each example, the child has to map the relational properties of the analogue onto a symbolic representation of the fraction concept. The crux of this mapping process is identifying the relational properties of each source analogue. A common, albeit mistaken, response for the set analogue is "4/6 are Venus Bars and 3/7 are Tim Tams." This is because the part/whole relationship is not as clear in the set analogue as it is in the region analogue. That is, the relationship between the four "VB" parts and the remaining parts is more salient than the relationship between the four VB parts and the whole amount of candies. In contrast, the part/whole relationship in Example B is easier to discern, with the whole amount comprising eight adventures and the ghost tunnels comprising three of these adventures. This relationship can be mapped readily onto the symbolic representation:

$$
\begin{array}{ccc}
\text{3 ghost tunnel adventures} & \longleftrightarrow & \text{3 (parts)} \\
\text{OUT OF} & \longleftrightarrow & \text{———} \\
\text{8 adventures} & \longleftrightarrow & \text{8 (parts)}
\end{array}
$$

The greater relational clarity of the region analogue suggests that it is the more appropriate representation to use when introducing elementary fraction ideas.

We now turn to some different domains, namely, problem solving and problem posing, to further illustrate reasoning by analogy.

REASONING BY ANALOGY IN SOLVING PROBLEMS

More than forty years ago, Polya highlighted the important role of analogies in mathematical problem solving (Polya 1954). Reasoning in this way involves using a known problem structure (referred to as the "source") to help solve a new, related problem (the "target") (Novick 1995). As used here, *structure* refers to the ways in which the mathematical ideas relate to each other in a problem, irrespective of the context in which they are set. In making use of a known source structure to solve a new problem, we might recall a source problem from memory or make use of one that has been supplied for us. Here, what is particularly important in our reasoning is, first, knowing that a source problem could be of assistance; second, being able to identify an appropriate source structure; and third, knowing how to use it in solving the target problem. These processes, however, do not seem to come naturally to children in a formal mathematical context (English 1998, 1997a).

In my research, I was particularly interested in seeing whether middle school children could detect the important relational ideas in addition and subtraction comparison problems and whether they could reason analogically with these ideas in solving more-complex problems. In exploring these issues, I first presented the children with a problem-sorting activity where they were to match problems according to similarity in problem structure (i.e., the children were asked to match problems that would be solved in a similar way). Some of the examples I used appear in table 3.1 (problems 1–4).

TABLE 3.1
Examples of Source and Target Problems

Source Problems

1. Jim has 14 goldfish. Peter has 6 more goldfish than Jim. How many goldfish does Peter have?

2. Penny has collected 11 stickers. Jane has collected 8 more stickers than Penny. How many stickers has Jane collected?

3. Sally has 12 goldfish. She has 5 more goldfish than Samantha. How many goldfish does Samantha have?

4. Suzie has collected 20 stickers. She has collected 5 more than Robyn. How many stickers has Robyn collected?

Target Problems

5. The year 4 and 5 classes at Mayfield School had a street stall. The year 5 class raised $652. The year 4 class raised $155 more than the year 5 class. How much money did the year 4 class raise?

6. James started a new job mowing lawns. In the first week he earned $185. In the second week he earned $55 more than he did in the first week. How much did James earn altogether in the first two weeks?

7. At the Rainforest School's annual sports day, the gold team scored 568 points. This was 49 points more than the green team scored. How many points did the green team score?

8. The Sunshine School had a toad-catching competition. During one week, Sarah and Mary caught 327 toads. This was 52 more toads than James and Dale caught. How many toads were caught by the children altogether?

As other studies have shown, these problems posed considerable difficulty for the children (Hegarty, Mayer, and Monk 1995). Many of the children sorted the problems according to their common surface features (i.e., the similar contexts) instead of looking to find the common structures. Liam's and Rebecca's responses illustrate this kind of reasoning:

Liam: It's obvious! These [Problems 1 and 3] go together because they're asking "how many goldfish" and the others [Problems 2 and 4] because they're asking "how many stickers."

Rebecca: These [Problems 2 and 4] are about collecting more and these [Problems 1 and 3] both have "have" at the end.

Other children, however, could see beyond these surface features and recognized the corresponding relationships, as Linda and Shane did:

Linda: With these two [Problems 1 and 2], the friend has more than the person, and with these two [Problems 3 and 4], the person has more than the friend.

Shane: You work out that if the other person has more, you add it, and if they have less, you take away. So Jim and Penny [Problems 1 and 2] are add and Sally and Suzie are take away.

After the children had sorted the problems, they were asked to solve each one. These examples remained displayed before the child and became the source problems for solving new, target problems. The structure of these target problems corresponded with the structures of the source examples, as can be seen in table 3.1 (i.e., Target Problems 5 and 6 correspond with Source Problems 1 and 2, and Problems 7 and 8 with 3 and 4). Notice, however, that the structures of Target Problems 6 and 8 extend beyond those of the related source problems. That is, there is an additional step to be taken in solving these target problems. In implementing this second activity, I asked the children whether they could find source problems that would help them solve the given target problem. If so, I then directed them to make use of this source example to help them solve the given target problem.

The children's responses to this second activity were rather disappointing. Many of the children could not see how a source problem could help them solve the target problem. Furthermore, they did not understand why reasoning by analogy could be of assistance to them in working the activity. They tended to treat the source and target problems as two unrelated sets of examples, with several children claiming that the target problems were "too different" from the source problems to be of any help. Their reasoning followed these lines:

- *He's mowing lawns, not collecting anything.*
- *It* [the source problem] *has only one person; the rest compare two people.*
- *It* [the source problem] *has a different ending, and it is about earning.*
- *It's not seeing who's got more than someone else.*

A couple of children considered the source problems to be "too easy to help you with that [target problem]" or claimed, "The numbers are too small" (from the source problem).

There were those children, however, who could see how the source problems could help them. This can be seen in the reasoning of James, Sarah, and Kara:

James: This problem [Target Problem 5] is similar to this one [Source Problem 2] because Jane has collected 8 more than Penny and the year 4 class has raised $155 more than the year 5; you've just got to work out what to do for this one [source problem] and you know what to do for that one [target].

Sarah: [After identifying appropriate source problems for a target problem] They all have the first person with a certain amount more than the second, so you know they're all take-away. They [source problems] would help because you could substitute the numbers in this one [target problem] for the numbers in these [the source problems].

Kara: Because these [source] problems have smaller numbers, you could use them to get the basic idea before you do the harder problems [target]. If you understand what to do for this one [source], you'd understand what to do for that one [target]. Using smaller numbers with these problems could help by getting you used to it before going on to the harder ones. They [the source problems] might help if you're just getting used to these types of problems, only if you're just a starter, but I don't need to use it because I've already done this type of problem before.

Like Kara, Timothy explained, "I don't need to use these [source problems] to help me with this problem [target] since I'm pretty familiar with plus." However, very few children gave a comment like this one, reflecting the difficulties many children had in working these problems. This was especially so for the subtraction problems and the more difficult target problems, where many children ignored the additional step.

It is also interesting to note Katrina's explanation for why a source problem would not help her solve one of the more difficult target problems: "You have to add twice, so using these [source problems] would confuse you; they would help for the first part but confuse you for the second part." Katrina seemed to have a basic understanding of reasoning by analogy but lacked an important component. That is, she did not know that the solution procedure of a source problem often has to be adapted or extended to accommodate a new feature in the target problem. This is an important process in analogical problem solving and, not surprisingly, causes considerable difficulty for learners (Novick 1995). Prior to considering some ways of helping children reason by analogy in problem solving, we consider its role in children's problem posing.

REASONING BY ANALOGY IN POSING PROBLEMS

Problem posing involves the creation of a new problem from a given situation or experience and can take place before, during, or after solving a problem (Silver 1994). Problem posing is recognized as a major component of students' mathematical development, with student-generated problems providing a rich and motivating source of problem activities at all grade levels

(Brown and Walter 1993; English 1997b; NCTM 1991; Silver and Cai 1996). Among other benefits, problem posing can improve children's understanding and awareness of problem structures and enable them to distinguish good problems from poor ones (English, Cudmore, and Tilley 1998).

Students can generate their own problems in many ways, as Brown and Walter (1993) have indicated. Reasoning by analogy is a particularly important tool when children model new problems on existing problems. This activity is where they take a given problem structure (the source) and use it to build a new problem (the target). As with our previous examples, this type of reasoning requires children to have a sound understanding of the source structure. That is, they need to identify the "knowns" in the source problem, including the important relational ideas, the "unknowns," and any constraints placed on the goal. Children can create a target problem by modeling it directly on the given source structure or by modifying some of the elements of the source structure. To illustrate these processes, we shall review a couple of responses from children who participated in a recent seventh-grade problem-posing program (English 1997c).

In one activity, the children explored the structures of a range of nonroutine and routine problems and then chose some of these problems as a source for generating their own problems. In modeling their target problem directly on the source, the children mapped the given relational ideas onto a new contextual framework. Nathan's response shows this process, as indicated below. He used the following deductive problem as his source:

> Sarina, Maddie, Ben, and Jacinta each bought a new T-shirt. One T-shirt was blue, one was red, one was green, and one was black. Sarina bought the red T-shirt. Ben did not buy the blue T-shirt. Jacinta does not like green or blue T-shirts. Which T-shirts did Ben, Maddie, and Jacinta buy?

Using his family as the context for his target problem, Nathan created the following problem:

> Mrs. Kelly, Mr. Kelly, Nat, and John all bought some sporting gear. They were soccer balls, a tennis racket, a hockey stick, and a basketball. Nat likes soccer. John does not like hockey. Mr. Kelly does not like basketball. Mrs. Kelly plays hockey. Which bit of sporting gear belongs to each member of the Kelly family?

Nathan explained to his group how he created his problem:

> Well, in this problem [the source], there are four people and four things that they bought. But you don't know what things, exactly which things the person bought. But you are given clues to work this out. So in my problem, I used the four people in my family and I thought about some sporting gear that we have and I made up some clues about what we bought. You have to use them to get the answer.

Notice, however, that Nathan's problem contained two clues with known relations (i.e., Nat belongs with soccer and Mrs. Kelly with hockey), whereas the source problem contained only one (i.e., Sarina belongs with the red T-shirt). Nathan did not take these known relations into account when posing the goal of his problem (i.e., he need only have asked for the sporting gear that Mr. Kelly and John bought). Nevertheless, he was able to create a solvable problem, and he had the opportunity to improve his problem after sharing it with others.

Although the children had relatively few difficulties in modeling a target problem on a given source, they found it more difficult to create a target problem by modifying the source structure. They explored different ways of doing so, one of which entailed adding more "knowns" or more constraints to the source. Creating problems in this way can help children appreciate how a familiar source problem can help with a target problem, even though the two may not correspond exactly (as with Target Problems 6 and 8 in table 3.1). In modifying the source structure, some of the children ended up with a considerably more complex problem. Kate, for example, chose to add more knowns as well as more constraints to the following source problem.

> Carla has an orange sweater, a purple sweater, a yellow sweater, and a black sweater. She also has a white skirt, a brown skirt, and a gray skirt. How many different outfits can she make?

Kate's target problem:

> Tony's Pizza Parlor sells pizzas in 4 different crusts and 5 different toppings. If each pizza must have 2 toppings and 2 crusts and no more, how many different pizzas can you have?

What is particularly important in children's problem-posing activities are opportunities to try one another's problems, give constructive feedback, and refine their original creations. Children's suggestions on how their peers might extend or enrich their problems are important in this process.

Fostering Reasoning by Analogy in Children's Mathematical Learning

The discussion above has highlighted the important role of reasoning by analogy in children's mathematical learning. From the examples given, there appear several ways in which we can promote this reasoning in the classroom. This section addresses some of these.

Consider the Clarity of Mathematical Analogues

Before we use a concrete or a pictorial analogue with our students, it is wise to consider whether it clearly portrays the intended mathematical idea. Commonly used analogues vary greatly in the clarity of their design. Children are more likely to make the link between a source analogue and a target concept if they can readily identify the relational ideas in the analogue. The multibase blocks, for example, have clearly displayed size relationships among the blocks that reflect the magnitude relationships among the quantities being represented. This quality makes multibase blocks an effective analogue for conveying numerical concepts and processes. In other numerical analogues, the relational ideas seem less apparent. Deciphering the analogue itself can be a problem for many children. Some number-line formats fit into this category, as do other analogues with arbitrary structures, such as colored chips and coins when used for place-value activities. Analogues that lack relational clarity often require children to understand the target concept being conveyed—so that they can interpret the analogue! This is the reverse of the process we have been addressing. Some analogues, therefore, are best reserved for more-advanced learning of a concept. However, some abstract analogues can serve as an assessment item for determining the flexibility and transferability of children's existing understandings.

Encourage Children to Detect Problem Structures

From the children's responses to the earlier activities involving reasoning by analogy in problem solving, it is apparent that we need to encourage children to look for the relational ideas in a given problem. Contextual features, although important in defining a problem situation, can prevent children from "looking below the surface" to detect these important relational ideas. Further, children often do not know to look for these important ideas. To help children do so, we can make use of sorting activities of the type addressed previously in the problem-solving section. These activities can be particularly beneficial in group situations where children can discuss and debate their reasons for matching particular problems. Children can learn from one another when they explain and justify their reasoning. They are more likely to modify or reject earlier views in favor of new ones that they can later see as more appropriate (Maher and Martino 1996).

This happened in a group discussion where Adam and Lauren explained to Josephine why they disagreed with her matching of the following problems:

(i) Carla has a blue T-shirt, a red T-shirt, and a green T-shirt. She also has a black skirt, a brown skirt, and a gray skirt. How many different outfits can she make?

(ii) Sarina, Maddie, Ben, and Jacinta each bought a new T-shirt. One T-shirt was blue, one was red, one was green, and one was black. Sarina bought the red T-shirt. Ben did not buy the blue T-shirt. Jacinta does not like green or blue T-shirts. Which T-shirts did Ben, Maddie, and Jacinta buy?

Josephine explained why she matched these problems: "I put these two together because they are both talking about T-shirts." Adam and Lauren, who had also made inappropriate matchings in their initial sorting, responded:

> We did that too, Josephine, but then we realized that they are only similar because they are both talking about T-shirts. Look, you wouldn't solve those two in the same way, because they're asking different things—like this one asks which T-shirt did Ben, Maddie, and Jacinta buy, and they want you to work out which one—which color T-shirt, and in this one, with Carla, there's only one person and they want to know how many different outfits Carla can make out of her three shirts and her three skirts.

Their explanation greatly assisted Josephine, who subsequently reviewed and modified her problem groupings.

Emphasize the Processes of Reasoning by Analogy in Children's Problem Activities

It is also evident from the children's responses that many did not know how to reason by analogy within a formal learning context. The reasoning processes they seemed to lack include (a) knowing that a previously solved problem could help in solving or posing a related target problem; (b) being able to identify an appropriate familiar problem, that is, a source problem, to help solve a new problem; (c) being aware that a source problem can still be of assistance even if the target problem contains additional ideas; and (d) knowing how to make use of an identified source problem in solving or posing a target problem. It is also important to know when and where to reason by analogy in solving and posing problems. Such reasoning is, of course, one of many important mathematical reasoning forms and may not always be needed, or always be appropriate, for a particular learner in a particular activity. Kara and Timothy, for example, indicated that they did not need to reason by analogy in solving the target problems because they already knew how to solve them.

We can help children make appropriate and effective use of analogical reasoning by modeling the processes ourselves and encouraging children to do likewise in their problem experiences. Discussions along the lines shown in tables 3.2 and 3.3 could help alert children to these processes in their problem-solving and problem-posing activities.

Table 3.2

Discussion Points for Fostering Reasoning by Analogy in Problem Solving

- Can you think of a recent everyday problem you have tried to solve outside of school? What was this problem? Did you solve it? How did you go about solving it?
- When you were trying to solve your problem, did you think back to a similar problem that you had solved previously? Why or why not? Did it help you? How did it help?

- Let's think about some of the problems you have been solving in class. When you're given a new problem to solve, do you ever make use of a "helping problem," that is, a similar one you've solved before? Why or why not?
- How might a problem you've solved before help you? When might it *not* help you?
- Choose one of the problems from our Problem Bank,[1] one that you have not solved before. As you study your problem, try to find all the important ideas, those that you need to think about in solving the problem.
- Now consider whether you could make use of a "helping problem." If so, can you think of one? Perhaps you might find one in our Problem Bank.
- How will you use this helping problem to solve your new one?
- Do you think you made a good choice of a helping problem? Why or why not? Might you have made a better choice?

1. Children's own problem creations should form a major component of the Problem Bank. Some examples that could be included are shown in table 3.4. These problems were posed by children during the seventh-grade program and illustrate another way in which children can generate their own problems, that is, from open-ended statements (English 1997d).

TABLE 3.3
Discussion Points for Fostering Reasoning by Analogy in Problem Posing

- Let's look back over these problems you have solved. Which one's did you enjoy the most? Why? Which one's did you like the least? Why? We'll start with the ones you enjoyed.[1]
- You can have fun making up your own problems for your friends to try! Take the problems you enjoyed and let these be your helping problems. They can help you *create* new problems, just like they helped you *solve* new problems. Your new problems will be solved in a similar way to your helping problems.
- Which parts of your helping problem will you use to make your new problem? Why will you use these parts? How are they important in designing your problem?
- What if I made up a problem like this one, which we all know (Carla's outfits), but I used sweaters and jeans in my problem … what feedback might you give me if you tried my problem?
- How might you make your new problem an exciting and interesting one for your class friends? Would that also make it interesting for your friends in, for example, Texas and Australia?
- Are you going to make your new problem an easy one to solve or a challenging one? Why?
- How might you make your new problem a challenging one for your friends? Is there another way in which you could make it challenging? Will your new problem still be similar to your helping problem? Why? Will it be different in any way?
- Before you share your new problem, you need to critique it. Why is it important to do this? What will you need to consider in critiquing your own problem and in

critiquing your friends' problems? Is there anything else you might need to consider, especially if you exchange your problems with your friends in Texas and Australia? (This problem sharing would be through the Internet.)

1. Related discussion could take place on the problems that the children liked the least. Children could explain what they would do to each of their disliked problems so that they would want to solve it. They could then use their ideas to create a new problem and indicate how it is different from, or similar to, the original problem.

TABLE 3.4
Samples of Students' Problems Created from Open-Ended Statements
(for Inclusion in the Problem Bank)

Problems Posed for This Statement: "Sally has saved $354 and Mary has saved $476."

Jayne's problem
Sally and Mary are saving to go to Africa. If the round-trip flight costs $500, how much more will Sally and Mary have to pay altogether if Sally has saved $354 and Mary has saved $476?

Nathan's problem
Sally has saved $354 and Mary has saved $476. If Mary owed Sally $149 and also Mary had to pay her son's school fees which were 1/3 of the money left over, how much money has Sally and how much has Mary now?

Problems Posed for This Statement: "The answer is 234. What is the question?"

Ethan's problem
Jane, Mary, and Tom had a test. Jane got 234 correct. Mary got 233 correct and Tom got 235 correct. What was the average score?

Julian's problem
There were 200 motor bikes in the bike shop. At the end of 7 days, 134 bikes were sold. In the next 3 days, there was a ship load of 100 bikes. How many bikes in the bike shop now?

Problems Posed for This Statement: "Mr. Graeme has 5 different ties and 9 different shirts."

Kara's problem
Mr. Graeme has 5 different ties and 9 different shirts and 8 pants. Tie colors are purple, pink, black, green, and blue. Shirts are paisley, check, black, blue, green, spots, red leather, light blue, and purple. Pants are green, red, blue, black, purple, pink, spots, and yellow. If he never matches colors and never wears spots and checks together, and if he wears two outfits each day, how many days would it take to wear them all?

Mohan's problem
Mr. Graeme has 5 different ties. One costs $10.95 on special. Normally they cost $17.00. He bought 4 ties for $17.00 and 1 for $10.95. One shirt costs $32.00. He bought 9 of the same shirts. How much money did he spend?

Tessa's problem

Mr. Graeme has 5 different ties and 9 different shirts. That week he holds his birthday party and receives 10 times the amount of ties and 5 times the amount of shirts. He then donates half of his clothes, only to find when he comes home he has been robbed and lost a fifth of each item. He claims insurance and then doubles the amount of each item. How many different combinations of shirts and ties can he make?

CONCLUDING COMMENTS

This article has highlighted the important role of reasoning by analogy in children's mathematical development. We ask children to reason by analogy whenever we use mathematical representations, be they elementary concrete aids, illustrations and diagrams, or more-abstract analogues. Included in this last category are familiar algebraic relations that serve as analogues (i.e., mental models) for more-advanced relations (English and Halford 1995). All these representations will fail dismally, however, if children are unable to identify the relational ideas being conveyed and if they cannot make the link between the analogue and the target concept. It is imperative that we analyze the analogues critically that we use in our classrooms to ensure that they readily portray the intended mathematical concepts and processes.

Reasoning by analogy is an important tool in problem solving and problem posing. In contrast to children's frequent use of analogies in daily living, reasoning by analogy in dealing with formal mathematical problems does not seem to come naturally to them. We need to encourage and guide children in applying the reasoning processes addressed in this article. In particular, children require many opportunities to explore problem structures, identify related structures, and build a knowledge and appreciation of when, why, and how to reason by analogy in solving and posing problems.

As students enter the new millenium, their ability to use many different forms of mathematical reasoning will become increasingly important. Although we cannot predict just which forms will require special attention, we can safely say that reasoning by analogy and reasoning in a critical manner will remain essential to students' mathematical growth, both in and out of the classroom. The wisdom of Kepler and Polya will remain with us as we venture into the new era.

REFERENCES

Brown, Stephen I., and Marion I. Walter, eds. *Problem Posing: Reflections and Applications*. Hillsdale, N.J.: Lawrence Erlbaum Associates, 1993.

English, Lyn D. "Children's Reasoning Processes in Classifying and Solving Computational Word Problems." In *Mathematical Reasoning: Analogies, Metaphors, and Images*, edited by Lyn D. English, pp. 191–220. Mahwah, N.J.: Lawrence Erlbaum Associates, 1997a.

———— . "Development of Seventh-Grade Students' Problem Posing." In *Proceedings of the Twenty-first Conference of the International Group for the Psychology of Mathematics Education*, vol. 2, edited by Erkki Pehkonen, pp. 241–48. Helsinki: University of Helsinki, 1997c.

———— . "Development of Seventh-Grade Students' Problem Posing from Open-Ended Situations." In *People in Mathematics Educatiomn*, edited by Fred Biddulph and Ken Carr, pp. 39–49. Hamilton, New Zealand: University of Waikato Press, 1997d.

———— . "Promoting a Problem-Posing Classroom." *Teaching Children Mathematics* 4 (November 1997b): 172–79.

———— . "Reasoning by Analogy in Solving Comparison Problems." *Mathematical Cognition*, 4, no. 2 (1998): 125–49.

English, Lyn D., and Graeme S. Halford. *Mathematics Education: Models and Processes.* Mahwah, N.J.: Lawrence Erlbaum Associates, 1995.

English, Lyn D., Donald D. Cudmore, and Dominic Tilley. "Problem Posing and Critiquing: How It Can Happen in Your Classroom." *Teaching Mathematics in the Middle School* 4 (October 1998): 124–29.

Hegarty, Michael, Richard E. Mayer, and Christopher A. Monk. "Comprehension of Arithmetic Word Problems: A Comparison of Successful and Unsuccessful Problem Solvers." *Journal of Educational Psychology* 87 (March 1995): 18–32.

Hiebert, James, and Diana Wearne. "Links between Teaching and Learning Place Value with Understanding in First Grade." *Journal for Research in Mathematics Education* 23 (March 1992): 98–122.

Holyoak, Keith J., and Paul Thagard. *Mental Leaps: Analogy in Creative Thought.* Cambridge, Mass.: MIT Press, 1995.

Maher, Carolyn, and Amy M. Martino. "The Development of the Idea of Mathematical Proof: A Five-Year Case Study." *Journal for Research in Mathematics Education* 27 (March 1996): 194–214.

National Council of Teachers of Mathematics. *Professional Standards for Teaching Mathematics.* Reston, Va.: National Council of Teachers of Mathematics, 1991.

National Research Council. *Mathematics and Science Education around the World: What Can We Learn from the Survey of Mathematics and Science Opportunities (SMSO) and the Third International Mathematics and Science Study (TIMSS)?* Washington, D.C.: National Academy Press, 1996.

Novick, Laura R. "Some Determinants of Successful Analogical Transfer in the Solution of Algebra Word Problems." *Thinking and Reasoning* 1(April 1995): 5–30.

Polya, George. *Mathematics and Plausible Reasoning.* Vol.1, *Induction and Analogy in Mathematics.* Princeton, N.J.: Princeton University Press, 1954.

Silver, Edward A. "On Mathematical Problem Posing." *For the Learning of Mathematics* 14 (February 1994): 19–28.

Silver, Edward A., and Jinfa Cai. "An Analysis of Arithmetic Problem Posing by Middle School Students." *Journal for Research in Mathematics Education* 27 (November 1996): 521–39.

4

The Nature of
Mathematical Reasoning

Robert J. Sternberg

Eₐʀₗy in my career, I gave an assignment in a statistics course that yielded results that were so depressing that I never gave the assignment again. I asked my students to predict their midterm examination grade from a variety of variables. Two of the predictor variables were the score on a conventional standardized test of mathematical aptitude and the number of hours a week spent studying for my course. The depressing results were that the aptitude test correlated about .8 with midterm grades and the hours a week spent studying correlated about −.8 (on a scale where −1 indicates a perfect inverse relationship, 0 indicates no relationship, and 1 indicates a perfect positive relationship). In other words, those with high measured mathematical aptitudes tended to be those who scored high on the exam, and they did not even have to work hard to achieve their high grades.

One conclusion that could have been drawn from this experience is that mathematical abilities, and in particular, mathematical reasoning abilities, are adequately measured by conventional tests of concepts, word problems, and computation problems. I was not prepared to draw this conclusion, however, for several reasons.

First, a number of students with whom I had worked had received grades of A in their statistics (and other mathematics) courses, yet seemed totally unable to apply what they had learned to their work. They seemed to have well-developed *analytical* mathematical-reasoning skills, but they did not seem to know how to apply these skills in a *practical* way.

The preparation of this article was supported in part under the Javits Act Program (grant number R206R50001), as administered by the Office of Educational Research and Improvement, U.S. Department of Education. Grantees undertaking such projects are encouraged to express their professional judgment freely. This article, therefore, does not necessarily represent the positions or policies of the government, and no official endorsement should be inferred.

Second, my conversations with Greg Zuckerman, a mathematics professor at Yale, had revealed his frustration that students could receive grades of A in difficult mathematics courses and be ineffective mathematicians, never seeming to have a creative idea or to recognize what constitutes important mathematical problems. An engineering professor once made a similar comment to me: Students could receive a grade of A in their courses and yet be unable to solve engineering problems that required innovative solutions. Again, these students seemed to have the analytical mathematical-reasoning skills but did not seem to know how to apply these skills in a *creative* manner.

These comments led me to reassess the way I was teaching my mathematical (and primarily statistical) courses at all levels. I reached the conclusion that the reason for the high correlation between the mathematical-aptitude test and the grades in my course was not that there is some intrinsic, necessary correlation but rather that the tests are designed to predict grades in the way we typically teach. The same principle actually applies not only to mathematical aptitudes and achievement but to aptitudes and achievement in all areas of endeavor in school (see Sternberg [1997]).

In effect, we have created a closed system that consistently rewards students who are skilled in memory and analytical abilities, whether in mathematics or other domains, but fails to reward students who are skilled in creative and practical abilities (Sternberg 1997). This system would not be troubling were it not for the fact that the system breaks down once students leave school. The result is that we may fail to recognize mathematical abilities in students who could be quite successful or recognize such abilities in students who actually have lower abilities than expected.

Mathematics will continue to matter in the lives of most of our students, not in test scores or course grades, but in their ability to apply the mathematics they learn to practical, everyday problems. Such problems involve individuals as consumers, such as when they calculate which of two items is a better buy, and as vendors, such as when they operate businesses of one kind or another.

The available data support the informal observations given above that the ability to apply mathematics practically is different from the abilities valued both in conventional mathematical-aptitude tests and in courses. For example, Lave (1988) studied the consumer end of mathematical reasoning. She found that individuals who had no difficulty determining which of two products was a better buy in the supermarket were often unable to apply exactly the same operations in the context of a paper-and-pencil mathematical-ability test. Abilities revealed by a practical test were not revealed by an abstract-analytical test.

Nuñes (1994) studied the vendor end of mathematical reasoning (see also Carraher, Carraher, and Schliemann [1985, 1987]). She investigated the performance of Brazilian street children who were successfully doing the mathematics they needed to operate a successful street business. She found that many children who were successfully doing mathematics on the street were failing mathematics in school. Once again, abstract-analytical abililties seemed to be very different from practical ones.

Creative mathematical abilities also appear to be distinct from abstract-analytical ones. Although conventional tests of mathematical aptitudes may measure analytical mathematical reasoning, they do not measure, nor do their inventors claim they measure, creative mathematical thinking—the kind that is required not only in mathematicians but in any pursuit that uses mathematics, such as in the world of finance. Our own research suggests such a separation.

In one study (Sternberg and Williams 1997), we investigated the predictive validity of a test widely used for admission to graduate schools (the Graduate Record Examination, or GRE). This test measures at a higher level the same abilities that the Scholastic Assessment Test or American College Test measures at a lower level. We found that performance on the GRE did predict school grades and, in particular, that the mathematical section significantly predicted grades in a required first-year quantitative (statistics) course. We also found, however, that the mathematical section failed to predict professors' ratings of students' analytical, creative, practical, research, or teaching abilities or the rated quality of the students' doctoral dissertation. In other words, test scores predict grades, but beyond grades, the prediction decays.

One does not have to turn to formal experimental studies in order to see the difference between the more academic and analytical kinds of processing and the more creative and practical kinds of processing. In teaching mathematically oriented courses, I have started requiring not only homework and examinations but also independent projects. The project requires each student to explore some mathematical topic on his or her own with some guidance from me, but only as requested and when truly needed. I have found over the years that the correlation between examination and project grades is usually positive, but only weak to moderate. Hence, the students who do the best on the one kind of task are not necessarily those who do the best on the other. In other words, allowing students to exercise their creative and practical mathematical abilities in a project has enabled some of them to capitalize on strengths that would not be revealed if the students had been assessed only for their examination performance.

One might argue that if tests predict grades as they are usually given, then that is enough. However, there is reason to be skeptical: The tests were designed to predict grades, so regardless of what students are graded on, the tests are designed to succeed in that predictive job. Is it possible that if we taught in a different way, the predictive value of conventional tests of mathematical abilities might go down, or that the predictive value of alternative tests of mathematical abilities might go up?

In order to investigate this possibility, we designed an ability test that measured analytical, creative, and practical thinking in the verbal, mathematical, and figural domains through multiple-choice items and that also included essays (Sternberg et al. 1996). Of most interest here are the parts of the test that evaluate mathematical reasoning.

The first part, the analytical part, involved the solution of number-series problems, such as 2, 5, 9, 14, 20, ___ . The second part, which required students to think more creatively, or at least counterfactually, involved learning about new mathematical operations. For example, one could define a new mathematical operator "flix" whereby a flix $b = a + b$ if $a < b$ and $a - b$ if $a \geq b$. Students would then have to solve problems in which they used the new operation. The third part, which required students to think more practically, involved reading a chart or a diagram, such as a train schedule, a recipe, or a diagram of an athletic stadium. The students then had to solve practical mathematics problems using the visual aid. In general, we found relatively modest correlations among the three ways of thinking (whether in the mathematical or other domains). In other words, the individuals who are strong in analytical, creative, and practical thinking are not necessarily the same people.

The test we designed was used to identify high school students' patterns of abilities. We invited students to take a summer course at Yale if they were high in any of the three kinds of abilities (analytical, creative, practical) or high or low in all three. We then taught them a course that emphasized either the conventional approach relying on memory or approaches that concentrated on analytical, creative, or practical thinking (see Sternberg [1997]; Sternberg et al. [1996]). The course happened to be in introductory psychology, but it might have been in anything. Students were taught in a way that either largely matched or mismatched their own pattern of abilities. For example, in analytical-instruction groups, students had to analyze, explain, and evaluate facts and ideas. In the creative-instructional groups, students had to create, invent, and discover concepts and ideas. In the practical-instruction group, students had to apply, use, and implement what they had learned in everyday situations. Thus, activities were either good or not-so-good fits to students' ability patterns. We found that students who were at least partially matched outperformed students who were mismatched.

In a further study (Sternberg, Torff, and Grigorenko 1998), elementary and high school students were taught (a) in a conventional way that emphasized memory skills, (b) in a way that emphasized analytical (critical) thinking, or (c) in a way that emphasized analytical, creative, and practical thinking. Students taught to think in all three ways performed better in the course, whether assessed by performance assessments or by conventional assessments stressing factual recall.

Our data have suggested that analytical, creative, and practical thinking are somewhat different in kind and that the people who excel in them are different. When students are taught in a way that matches their pattern of abilities, they perform better. Moreover, all students benefit when they are taught in all three ways, so that (1) they can learn new information in a variety of ways, and (2) they can capitalize on their strengths and find ways to correct or compensate for their weaknesses.

How, exactly, does one translate these different ways of learning into different ways of teaching? Of course, the translation will depend, to some extent, on what is being taught.

For example, consider percentages. An *analytic* way of teaching about percentages is to have students learn a formula and analyze when to apply it to abstract mathematical problems. A *creative* way is to have students invent their own problems requiring percentages, or to have them imagine situations where percentages apply. A *practical* way is to describe an everyday problem involving percentages (such as selling products) and have students do problems from the everyday situation.

METACOMPONENTS OF MATHEMATICAL REASONING

Underlying the analytical, creative, and practical aspects of mathematical reasoning is a common set of higher-order processes, or metacomponents (Sternberg 1985), that are needed to solve mathematical and other kinds of problems. In order to understand fully the nature of mathematical-reasoning ability, one has to understand the nature of these metacomponential (or metacognitive) processes.

The Identification of a Problem

One cannot solve a problem until one identifies the nature of the problem to be solved. In mathematics classes, we often make this step easy by presenting a problem on a chalkboard or in a textbook and then describing it as a problem of a certain kind (a mixture problem, a time-rate-distance problem, a percentage problem, or whatever). But if we always make this step easy, students lose out.

Many teachers find that students do well on quizzes in the mathematical subject matter they are studying but then do much less well on end-of-unit or end-of-year tests. There can be any number of reasons for the difference in performance, but one reason is often that the students know how to use the techniques they have learned but do not know which techniques to use when. Thus, when faced with a quiz on a particular mathematical technique, they have no problem; but when having to choose which technique to use on a broader-ranging test, they run into trouble. They cannot define the problems with which they are presented, because they have learned how to use the techniques but not the circumstances under which the techniques may be applied.

Formulating a Strategy for Solving the Problem

Having figured out what the problem is, the student needs to figure out a strategy that will effectively solve it. Sometimes, students may need to construct the strategy for themselves; other times, they may simply need to choose from among available strategies that have been previously learned.

In a series of studies, Janet Davidson and I studied upper elementary school students' abilities to solve problems involving mathematical insight (Davidson and Sternberg 1984; Sternberg and Davidson 1983), such as this one: "You have black and brown socks in a drawer all mixed together in a ratio of 4 to 5. How many socks do you have to remove from the drawer in order to be sure of having a pair of the same color?" These problems are more difficult than conventional problems in large part because it is not obvious what strategy to apply to them: students have to formulate a strategy without the benefit of having had explicit instruction in solving problems of the given kind. The problem thus requires a kind of flexible, or even creative, thinking that is not typical of more stereotypical mathematics problems.

Mentally Representing Information about a Problem

Students need not only to set up a strategy but also to figure out a kind of mental representation upon which the strategy will act. Mental representations in problem solving are important. For example, we have found that in solving transitive inference problems (such as "John is taller than Pete. Pete is taller than Bill. Who is tallest?") some students use a verbal representation to solve the problems but others use a spatial representation, imagining a linear array with John at the top, Pete in the middle, and Bill at the bottom.

Differences in mental representation can spell the difference between success and failure in mathematics because often, in our teaching, we teach students to represent problems in only one way. In my own teaching, I had taught a particular advanced statistical technique—factor analysis—using an algebraic representation of information. (My own thinking tends to be algebraic, and this form of representation seemed to work not only for me but also for many of the students.) One year, I decided to experiment and teach in a geometric manner the same technique I had taught algebraically. In this way, I could reinforce the lesson and also show students that the two representations of information ultimately led to the same result.

The classroom outcome was very interesting: Many of the students who had had difficulty understanding the lesson when it was presented algebraically now understood it when it was presented geometrically; others who had understood it algebraically did not understand it geometrically. By teaching alternative representations, more students were able to benefit from the lesson.

Allocating Resources

Students need to learn how much time, energy, and outside help as well as what kinds of aids (such as calculators) they will require in order to solve a given problem. Given that their time is limited, they need to figure out how best to allocate that limited time.

In one study, students were given complex reasoning problems that required them to make various kinds of extrapolations (Sternberg 1981). The problems were presented in a way that enabled us to determine how students allocated their time. We found that the students who were better problem solvers expended more time up front before they started the problems, deciding what they were going to do. The poorer problem solvers put in less time up front but then spent more time on each individual problem. Their emphasis on local rather than global planning cost them time wasted through repeated operations and trips down garden paths and resulted in higher error rates when solving the problems.

Monitoring and Evaluating Solutions

While students are solving problems—and after they have finished—they need to evaluate their work. Often students make mistakes because they have not thought through whether their answers even make sense. In our work on the development of inductive reasoning processes (Sternberg and Nigro 1980; Sternberg and Rifkin 1979), we have found that older children tend to be more exhaustive in their information processing than younger children are. In other words, they check more carefully to see that their solutions use all the relevant information in the problems.

CONCLUSION

Mathematical reasoning requires analytical thinking, of course, but it also requires creative and practical thinking. Some of the metacognitive processes involved include identifying the nature of the problem, formulating a strategy to solve the problem, mentally representing the problem, allocating resources to the solution of the problem, and monitoring and evaluating the solution. A good assessment of mathematical reasoning will evaluate all these aspects of mathematical reasoning. Good instruction will take all of them under consideration.

Of course, the account of mathematical reasoning furnished here is not the only one that can be given (see Sternberg and Ben Zeev [1996]). There are alternative accounts, and although the account here is by no means complete, it does point out some of the major aspects of mathematical reasoning, and how we can use a theory of reasoning to improve our instruction and assessment in mathematics.

REFERENCES

Carraher, Terezinha N., David W. Carraher, and Ana D. Schliemann. "Mathematics in the Streets and in Schools." *British Journal of Developmental Psychology* 3 (1985): 21–29.

————— . "Written and Oral Mathematics." *Journal for Research in Mathematics Education* 18 (March 1987): 83–97.

Davidson, Janet E., and Robert J. Sternberg. "The Role of Insight in Intellectual Giftedness." *Gifted Child Quarterly* 28 (1984): 58–64.

Lave, Jean. *Cognition in Practice: Mind, Mathematics, and Culture in Everyday Life.* New York: Cambridge University Press, 1988.

Nuñes, Terezinha. "Street Intelligence." In *Encyclopedia of Human Intelligence*, Vol. 2, edited by Robert J. Sternberg, pp. 1045–49. New York: Macmillan, 1994.

Sternberg, Robert J. *Beyond IQ: A Triarchic Theory of Human Intelligence.* New York: Cambridge University Press, 1985.

————— . "Intelligence and Nonentrenchment." *Journal of Educational Psychology* 73 (1981): 1–16.

————— . *Successful Intelligence.* New York: Penguin, Plume, 1997.

Sternberg, Robert J., and Talia Ben Zeev, eds. *The Nature of Mathematical Thinking.* Mahwah, N.J.: Lawrence Erlbaum Associates, 1996.

Sternberg, Robert J., and Janet E. Davidson. "Insight in the Gifted." *Educational Psychologist* 18 (1983): 51–57.

Sternberg, Robert J., Michel Ferrari, Pamela C. Clinkenbeard, and Elena L. Grigorenko. "Identification, Instruction, and Assessment of Gifted Children: A Construct Validation of a Triarchic Model." *Gifted Child Quarterly* 40 (1996): 129–37.

Sternberg, Robert J., and Georgia Nigro. "Developmental Patterns in the Solution of Verbal Analogies." *Child Development* 51 (1980): 27–38.

Sternberg, Robert J., and Bathsheva Rifkin. "The Development of Analogical Reasoning Processes." *Journal of Experimental Child Psychology* 27 (1979): 195–232.

Sternberg, Robert J., Bruce Torff, and Elena L. Grigorenko. "Teaching Triarchically Improves School Achievement." *Journal of Educational Psychology* 90 (1998): 374–84.

Sternberg, Robert J., and Wendy M. Williams. "Does the Graduate Record Examination Predict Meaningful Success in the Graduate Training of Psychologists? A Case Study." *American Psychologist* 52 (1997): 630–41.

5

Young Children's
Mathematical Reasoning
A Psychological View

Eileen P. Tang

Herbert P. Ginsburg

MATHEMATICS education and psychology, both about 100 years old, have been intertwined throughout their history. The chief aim of mathematics educators is, of course, to teach mathematics effectively. But in attempting to do this, they have found it necessary to draw upon psychology or to invent their own. From the earliest days of the field, mathematics educators have made psychological assumptions and observations about children's learning and thinking. More than 100 years ago, McLellan and Dewey (1895) went so far as to propose that psychology should serve as a foundational science for education: "Knowing the nature and origin of number and numerical properties as psychological facts, the teacher knows how the mind works in the construction of number, and is prepared to help the child to think number.... [R]ational method in arithmetic must be based on the psychology of number" (p. 22).

Psychologists, too, have been fascinated with the study of mathematical thinking. For them, it provides the opportunity to examine important issues of cognitive development, such as innate ideas (e.g., do babies have concepts of number?), practical intelligence (e.g., how do people use mathematics in everyday job situations?), cultural differences (e.g., does mathematical thinking develop differently in literate and illiterate societies?), and abstract thought (e.g., how do people understand a notion like infinity?). Indeed, the study of number or of mathematical thinking more generally has provided some of the most distinguished psychological theorists and researchers,

The writing of this article and the research described in it were made possible by a grant from the Spencer Foundation. The data presented, the statements made, and the views expressed are solely the responsibility of the authors.

including figures as diverse as Thorndike (1922) and Piaget (1952), with a set of windows into the developing mind.

Through the combined efforts of mathematics educators and psychologists, a rich psychology of mathematical thinking has evolved over the years. We make no attempt here to present the fascinating history of the field (see Kilpatrick [1992] for an excellent review). Instead, this article describes fundamental aspects of the emerging "modern" view of the psychology of mathematical reasoning (for a review, see Ginsburg, Klein, and Starkey [1998]), which is derived from research conducted in a wide range of settings, from the American elementary school to the African village, and employing a wide range of methods, from standard tests to clinical interviews.

To illustrate basic characteristics of young children's mathematical reasoning, we rely on the words and actions of the children themselves. We present excerpts from clinical interviews with several five-year-old children to illustrate the following aspects of reasoning that have been stressed by contemporary psychologists and mathematics educators:

- The individual interpretation of problems
- The use and deployment of "everyday" strategies
- Multiple representations
- The fluidity of thinking
- The "zone of proximal development"
- The embeddedness of cognition in personality
- Metacognition (the awareness of one's own thinking)

After describing each of these aspects of reasoning, we discuss implications of each for mathematics education. We conclude with reflections on the complexity of mathematical reasoning and the possible universality of early mathematical competence.

Individual Interpretation

Piaget believed that the child's way of seeing the world may differ from an adult's (e.g., Piaget [1951]). As a result, the child may interpret a problem in an idiosyncratic manner differing from what the adult intended. The answer that the child then produces may be incorrect from the adult's point of view but correct from the child's. In other words, the child's "wrong" answer may actually be the correct answer to a question different from what the adult posed.

Consider the following exchange between Joon, the interviewer, and five-year-old Robert. Earlier, the interviewer had given Robert addition word problems involving a trip to the supermarket, and Robert had answered them correctly with little difficulty. However, the next question appeared to pose a problem:

Joon: So, you put four apples in your shopping cart. Then, you get four more. How many do you have altogether?

Robert: Zero!

Robert answered confidently and without hesitation, but his answer was clearly wrong. Moreover, it did not seem to make any sense! Since this behavior was inconsistent with his previous success, the interviewer decided to probe further.

Joon: Zero?

Robert: Yeah. You said … you said *take* … you take four from … [*holds up four fingers*] … take away … have four.

Robert appears to interpret the interviewer's question in a completely different manner from what she intended. The interviewer used the key word *more* to indicate to Robert that addition was required to solve the problem. However, as his answer indicates, Robert believes the interviewer said "take four more" rather than "get four more," and he chose to focus on the key word *take,* which usually indicates subtraction, rather than the interviewer's key word *more.* The interviewer realized Robert did not understand that the question required addition, not subtraction, and tried to alleviate the confusion.

Joon: Oh, no, you get four more. [*Emphasis on "more"*]

Robert: Four more. [*Also emphasizes "more."*] That's zero. Look, take four … take … take away four more. We got four more. I ate them, then zero. [*Holds out his arms, palms up, in a shrug.*]

Joon: You ate them!

Robert: Yeah! [*Mimes popping an apple into his mouth. He then shrugs again, and smiles.*]

Despite the interviewer's attempts at clarification, Robert stayed with, and defended, his subtraction interpretation. Thus, his explanation revealed that he believed the interviewer presented him with a problem of 4 − 4, in which case his answer of "zero" is entirely correct.

This excerpt demonstrates that children are active interpreters of what adults say and that their interpretations may not correspond with the adult's. The interviewer used the words *four more* in her question; in her mind, this was a clear cue that addition was required to obtain a solution. However, in Robert's view, the problem required subtraction. Perhaps this was due to his belief that the interviewer initially used the word *take,* a key word generally associated with subtraction. However, his subsequent emphasis on the word *more* when the interviewer tried to clarify the problem seems to indicate that to him such a key word does not necessarily mean the same thing as it does to the interviewer, that is, that addition should be used. Rather, he incorporated her words into his own story, justifying his answer of zero apples with a perfectly sensible explanation of why he got such a result: while he was at the supermarket, he ate them.

This principle of individual interpretation—a central tenet of constructivism—is essential for mathematics educators. Children come to the classroom with a background of individual experiences that influence how they view the world. They actively use these experiences to construct meaning for a given task and often do not consider, or even understand, that the adult may have a different point of view. We must always keep in mind that the child's perspective may differ from the adult's. In evaluating the adequacy of the child's reasoning, we must understand "where the child is coming from." If the child's response does not at first seem to make adult sense, we must make every effort to go behind our adult "egocentrism" in order to discover the child sense that may underlie the answer. We cannot appreciate the child's reasoning unless we know what the child is reasoning about.

The Use and Deployment of "Everyday" Strategies

Before children enter formal schooling, they develop "everyday" strategies for doing mathematics. They can compare magnitudes, distinguish between more and less, count, and add and subtract. These "informal" strategies originate in everyday experience with objects and events in the child's environment (Ginsburg 1989). The child sees one group of objects being combined with or added to another set; the child wants more of this or that. As Vygotsky (1978) put it: " ... children's learning begins long before they enter school ... children begin to study arithmetic in school, but long beforehand they have had some experience with quantity—they have had to deal with operations of division, addition, subtraction, and the determination of size. Consequently, children have their own preschool arithmetic, which only myopic psychologists could ignore" (p. 84).

One major component of successful reasoning is the effective choice and use of strategies (Siegler 1996). Presented with a problem, the child needs first to solve it by using the most effective strategy from those available. As we shall see in the next episode involving Eileen, the interviewer, and five-year-old Pedro, children are often able to deploy their "everyday," or "informal," strategies efficiently in response to varying problem demands.

The interviewer began the session with the goal of investigating how Pedro would go about enumerating collections of coins varying in number. In the first problem, she had intended to place on the table six coins in a random order, but by chance the coins were arranged in a regular way, with four pennies in one line and two pennies in another line parallel to the first.

Eileen: How many pennies are there?

Pedro: [*He looks at the pennies closely, then looks away for several seconds.*] Six.

Eileen: Six. How did you know that?

Pedro: I don't know.

Eileen: Why don't you show me how you figured out that there were six?

Pedro: Because there were four right here and two right here.

Eileen: And how many is that altogether?

Pedro: Six.

Asked to enumerate a small set of objects, Pedro seemed to use a combined perceptual and mental strategy. Because the coins were conveniently (but accidentally) arranged in lines of four and two, he was able to interpret the problem as involving the combination of two smaller sets and not (as the interviewer had intended) as the enumeration of a single, larger set. (Again, the principle of individual interpretation!). Then Pedro was able to determine the number of each of the two smaller sets merely by looking at them. This strategy, called *subitizing*, is more sophisticated than touching each object and counting one by one. Finally, Pedro combined the two cardinal values using some form of mental addition, arriving at the correct total. In brief, taking advantage of the accidental arrangement of the objects, Pedro interpreted the problem as addition, not enumeration, "saw" the number of each subset, and added them mentally.

The interviewer then continued her questioning, looking to see if he would alter his strategy when faced with larger sets. She placed fifteen pennies in front of Pedro; this time, they were in a random configuration.

Eileen: Can you tell me how many pennies there are here?

Pedro: [*He starts counting regularly from left to right, then top to bottom, but ends with rather haphazard pointing.*] Eighteen.

Given a larger set, Pedro clearly changed his strategy. He physically pointed to the objects, touching them as he said the counting words. However, his answer was incorrect because he did not employ a systematic method for counting each object once and only once. Particularly at the end, he lost track of which objects he had counted and which remained to be counted, skipping some objects and double-counting others. His informal strategy failed because of an overreliance on memory. Noticing his problem, the interviewer offered a suggestion:

Eileen: Eighteen there, OK. Do you want to try it again? Make sure you touch each one only one time.

Pedro: [*He counts each one right to left, top to bottom. He skips one but goes back to count it.*] Fifteen.

Given one simple hint, Pedro attempted to employ a more careful strategy. He tried a more systematic counting method to help him *remember* which objects had been counted and which had not. This is hard to do when a rather large number of objects in a haphazard arrangement is to be counted. Yet Pedro was able to execute the strategy reasonably well, making only one mistake, which he corrected.

The interviewer then chose to increase the difficulty even further, testing the limits of his memory-dependent strategy by asking him to count a set of thirty pennies, again placed in no specific configuration. This time Pedro seemed to *discover* a better strategy. He first noticed two pennies slightly apart from the rest of the pile. He touched these two as he said, "One, two," and moved them slightly to the side as he did so. Then, as he counted the third penny, he pulled it away from the pile of coins and placed it with the two pennies he had already counted. He continued on in this fashion, counting each "new" penny and pushing it aside as he transferred it from the original pile of coins into the new collection. Pedro's "pushing aside" strategy has the advantage of reducing reliance on memory. Removing the object from the original pile signifies that the object has been counted and need not be counted again. In effect, the child lets the pile remember for him. The strategy insures that each object will be counted once and only once. Using the pushing-aside strategy, Pedro correctly counted the thirty pennies and smiled at the interviewer when he finished.

Eileen: How many are there?

Pedro: Thirty.

Eileen: Why did you move them to the side like that when you counted?

Pedro: Because … I don't want to count them again.

Note that Pedro was not only able to recognize the merits of the pushing-aside technique after he discovered it but could also articulate why the strategy was useful. He understood that double-counting causes him difficulty and that the new strategy could help prevent the problem ("I don't want to count them again"). His smile at the end shows how confident he was in his answer.

This episode demonstrates how strategy usage is not simply governed by a "one method for all problems" rule. Pedro had several informal strategies available—subitizing, mental addition, counting one by one, and relying on memory to determine what had been counted—and applied them selectively depending on the numerical size of the set. Furthermore, he was open to developing and using a new strategy, especially when it served to help him overcome a difficulty.

Mathematics educators can put children's everyday strategies to good use. They are familiar and comfortable, and children can use them profitably in the classroom. Indeed, a sensitive teacher may use the everyday strategies to provide a solid foundation for future academic learning (Baroody 1987). Moreover, the teacher needs to be aware of the child's flexibility in strategy use. Children are accustomed to using different methods for different purposes under different conditions. This tendency—especially valuable for applied mathematics—should be actively encouraged in the mathematics classroom.

MULTIPLE REPRESENTATIONS

Reasoning may involve different types of representation (Bruner 1966). During an interview with four-year-old Kenneth, the interviewer wanted to discover what strategies he would use when given an addition problem involving imaginary objects. She first drew two houses on a piece of paper, one next to the other, and proceeded to tell a story.

Eileen: Now, in this house, there are three kids, and in this house there are two kids. How many kids are in all these houses?

Kenneth: 1 ... 2 is in here...[He taps the house with two children.] ... and a lot is in here. [He taps the house with three children.]

Eileen: There're three in there. So, there are three in here and two in there. How many kids are there altogether?

Kenneth: 1, 2, 3 ... 4? [He taps the house with two children twice as he says "1, 2," then taps the house with three children twice as he says "3, 4," then pauses after he says "4." He stops and looks up at Eileen questioningly.]

Kenneth attempted to use an unusual method, namely, taps, to represent the imaginary children. He hoped that these auditory cues would help him keep track of the number of children in each house. To use auditory representations accurately to add two sets, Kenneth would have to remember the number of taps representing the number of children in the first house, remember the number of taps representing the children in the second house, and then somehow combine the two remembered sets of taps to get the sum. However, the strategy broke down because it was cumbersome, placing great demands on memory. Kenneth was able to represent the two children in the first house correctly, but once he tried to count the children in the second house, he got into trouble. His questioning tone of voice indicated that he was not sure of his answer.

Does Kenneth's difficulty with auditory representation indicate that he cannot employ any effective type of representation? Not necessarily. The interviewer therefore decided to explore Kenneth's use of alternative forms of representation. She brought his attention to the pile of pennies and the pencil on the table, and offered him the opportunity to change his mode of representation.

Eileen: Can you use the pennies—or can you use the pencil—to help you? Remember, there are three in this house and two in this house. So, how many kids are there altogether?

Kenneth: [*He takes three pennies, one by one, and places them in a straight line on the house with three children. Then he takes two more pennies, one by one, and places them in a straight line on the house with two children. He looks at what he did, and then he pushes the pennies together in one group. Then, he deliberately moves them one by one, arranging them in the form of the number 5 on a die. He then sits back and looks at the pennies.*] Five.

By choosing to represent the imaginary children with pennies, Kenneth converted the problem into simpler form. Now he merely had to combine two sets of concrete objects to get their total. This situation lends itself to a simple counting strategy. However, Kenneth surprisingly chose a more efficient method. He deliberately arranged the five pennies into a figure that he recognized, namely, the "quincunx" arrangement of five objects, as on the face of a die, which allowed him to "see" the number directly—that is, to determine the set's number by subitizing.

The episode demonstrates that children's reasoning can employ different forms of representation, some more effective than others for certain types of problems. Like the strategies demonstrated by Pedro, representational knowledge also arises from everyday experiences, but the child requires exploration and practice to apply it effectively to different mathematical problems. Tapping may be a good way to represent rhythms in music, but it is not usually an *efficient* way to count sets. Pennies can stand for numbers, but they are not ideal for representing music. Children need to sort out how different forms of representation can be used as effective tools for different forms of reasoning.

What is the lesson for the mathematics educator? Do not assume that the standard methods and symbols for representing mathematical ideas are transparent to the child. Explore with the child several different methods for representing even the simplest of mathematical ideas.

FLUIDITY OF THOUGHT

In Piaget's view, thinking is based on a set of more or less stable logical structures like the child's concrete operations or the adolescent's propositional logic (Inhelder and Piaget 1958). At a given stage of development, the child tends to use one or another set of logical operations.

By contrast, contemporary writers stress the fluidity of thinking (Siegler 1996). For example, Flavell, Miller, and Miller (1993) point out that in studying children's thinking, we usually find "all sorts of in-between patterns of performance: children who succeed on some versions of the task but not on others, and who thus seem sometimes to 'have' the concept and at other times to 'not have' it" (p. 321). The child's thinking is "more like a developmental succession of different things than like a unitary, present or absent cognitive entity" (p. 322).

We illustrate this phenomenon through an episode in which Pedro deals with the classical conservation problem. In this situation, the child is first presented with two sets of objects characterized by the same number and the same physical arrangement—for example, a line of seven red checkers and a line of seven blue checkers, one below the other. At first, the child generally agrees that the amounts are the same. Then, as the child watches, one of the lines is made longer than the other, and the child is asked whether the amounts are still the same in number. The goal is to determine whether the child recognizes that the equivalence relation is conserved across the physical transformation. Influenced by the change in length, the young child— approximately five or six years of age and below—usually responds that the spread-out line has more because "it's bigger."

During her interview with Pedro, the interviewer set up a conservation task involving parallel lines of seven pennies. One line was directly under the other, and both lines were of the same length.

Eileen: How many are in this line?
Pedro: 1, 2, 3, 4, 5, 6, 7.
Eileen: How many pennies in that line?
Pedro: 1, 2, 3, 4, 5, 6, 7.
Eileen: Which line has more?
Pedro: Both of them.

Pedro offered a very curious response. Instead of saying, "They are the same," or something similar, he replied, "Both of them." However, children often have idiosyncratic ways of using words to refer to objects and situations. To Pedro, both lines have "more," which was his way of saying they are equal. It is important to interpret children's language carefully because they may use words in unconventional ways. Their "incorrect" language may not indicate a lack of reasoning ability.

The interviewer then spread out one line, as Pedro watched.

Eileen: Which line has more?
Pedro: This one. [*He points to the spread-out line.*]
Eileen: How come?
Pedro: Because this one's bigger. [*He points again to the spread-out line.*]

This last response is a textbook example of a failure to conserve, in which the child bases his judgment on the appearance of the sets, not on their number. Remembering that Pedro frequently used counting to solve problems, the interviewer prompted him to do the same here.

Eileen: Well, how many pennies in this line? [*She points to the shorter line.*]

Pedro: 1, 2, 3, 4, 5, 6, 7.

Eileen: How many pennies are in this line? [*She points to the longer line.*]

Pedro: 1, 2, 3, 4, 5, 6, 7.

Eileen: Which one has more?

Pedro: Both of them.

Eileen: Both of them have more? How do you know that?

Pedro: Because there's seven here and seven there.

This episode underscores the fluid nature of thinking. Pedro began by exhibiting a lack of conservation ability. By Piaget's classical criteria, he might be categorized as a "preoperational" thinker. But this characterization of reasoning is too static. At the adult's suggestion, Pedro was able to overcome his failure to conserve by employing his familiar strategy of counting. Within the context of the interview, he was both a nonconserver and a conserver. Pedro reorganized his thinking by applying a familiar strategy to support his emerging understanding of a new concept; his thinking was fluid.

Mathematics educators should expect considerable variety in the individual child's thinking. Because the child's methods shift and change, we should not classify children prematurely either by means of test scores or stage designations. We need to employ sensitive methods of assessment to capture the child's fluidity of thought.

THE ZONE OF PROXIMAL DEVELOPMENT

Vygotsky (1978) has stressed the need to consider not only the child's current level of cognitive functioning but also the child's level of "potential development as determined through problem solving under adult guidance or in collaboration with more capable peers" (p. 86). Vygotsky believed that it is important to examine the child's "dynamic mental state, allowing not only for what has been achieved developmentally but also for what is in the course of maturing" (p. 87). His concern was in the "buds" of development (or even more accurately in the process of budding) than in its fruits. Thus, Vygotsky was interested in one particular aspect of the fluidity of thought, specifically the ways in which adult guidance could tap into the child's potential competence.

The next episode illustrates some of Vygotsky's notions. The interviewer, Marlene, had presented five-year-old Omar with several addition problems involving sums less than 10, and he answered them all correctly. Noticing that Omar used finger counting as a solution strategy, she then challenged him with a problem involving a sum greater than 10—that is, more than the number of fingers available.

Marlene: OK, you have five pennies. Then you get six.

   Omar: [*He holds out his right hand with all five fingers spread out, then looks at his left hand.*] Six. OK, that makes ten. [*Looks at Marlene.*]

The results confirmed the interviewer's suspicion that Omar's finger-counting strategy did not appear to work when the sum is greater than 10—the maximum number of fingers. However, since he had shown good addition ability earlier, she decided to probe further. Why did he get ten as the answer?

Marlene: OK, how did you figure that out?

   Omar: I had to guess in my mind. [*He leans his head on his hands, and taps his forehead dramatically with his right forefinger.*]

Marlene: You had to guess? Hmmm...

   Omar: I was using my fingers but I didn't have no more.

Marlene: You ran out of fingers, huh?

   Omar: [*Nods.*] And I had to guess.

Omar did not believe that six plus five equals ten. Instead, it was his best "guess." Use of this word is revealing. It indicates an ability to monitor his own work, as well as awareness that his answer could be wrong. In other words, Omar indicated that in the process of trying to achieve a solution, he had run out of fingers to count, and therefore gave the best possible answer under the circumstances.

To examine Omar's budding reasoning—his reasoning in the "zone of proximal development" (Vygotsky 1978)—the interviewer continued by suggesting an alternative strategy.

Marlene: What if we have your fingers and my fingers together? [*She places both her hands on the table palms down with her fingers spread out.*] Now can you do it? Let's try it. You have five pennies...

   Omar: [*He holds up five fingers on his right hand.*]

Marlene: ... and you get six more.

   Omar: [*He holds up the thumb of his left hand and places it next to Marlene's left hand.*]

Marlene: OK, let's try.

   Omar: 1, 2, 3, 4, 5, 6, 7, 8, 9, 10, 11. [*He first closes his right hand into a fist, then puts out fingers one at a time up until he reaches "five." He then uses his right hand to point to the remaining six fingers. He smiles as he finishes.*]

By hinting at an alternative method ("What if we have your fingers and my fingers together?"), the interviewer was able to discover a good deal about

Omar's *potential* level of reasoning, "what is in the course of maturing." When his original strategy broke down, he guessed, knowing that his answer may not be correct. However, when given minimal help from an adult, he was able to adapt his strategy to the more difficult problem and find the correct answer. It would have been misleading to judge Omar's reasoning ability from his unassisted problem solving—that is, from his current level of cognitive function. Examining Omar's behavior in the context of adult assistance affords a more accurate view of his potential development, as well as a window into the processes underlying his thinking.

For mathematics educators, the central issue, of course, is what children are capable of learning, not what they now know or fail to know. Education is about the future of children, not their present conditions of learning, which are often regrettable.

REASONING AND PERSONALITY

Reasoning is not an isolated phenomenon. Cognitive activity is a social construction (Newman, Griffin, and Cole 1984), embedded within the individual's personality, goals, and interpretation of the task at hand (Ginsburg and Asmussen 1988). This idea can be found in psychological theory as far back as Freud as well as in more modern theories of performance (e.g., Davidson and Sternberg [1985]; Schröder and Edelstein 1991) that stress the dynamic nature of thought and such personal factors as cognitive style, goal selection, motivation, and cultural influence. To fully understand reasoning ability, it is necessary to situate it within the child as a whole person.

Two contrasting excerpts illustrate this point. The first episode comes from the interview with Robert. The interviewer had put a large group of different coins on the table and asked Robert to sort them. From the interviewer's point of view, this is a very straightforward task, requiring only the grouping of similar coins. However, Robert decided to take the task one step further.

Joon: Do you want to put all the quarters together?

Robert: Uh-huh. [*Places the four quarters in a line. Crosses his arms as he finishes the task and looks at Joon and the table.*]

Joon: OK, how about all the dimes together?

Robert: [*Arranges all the dimes in a line. As he finishes the task, he spontaneously counts the coins that he arranged.*] It's four of these and six of these!

Joon: Yeah! [*Smiles.*] And can you see anything else?

Robert: Now three of these. [*Takes out the three nickels from the pile and puts them together.*] And four of these and six of these. [*He indicates the quarters first, then the dimes.*]

Joon: [*Looks at the pile, then spreads out the remaining coins.*] Great! Do you see something else here, too?

Robert: [*While Joon is talking, he starts counting the lines he established earlier (mouthing the numbers silently), touching each coin with a finger.*] That makes thirteen! [*He looks up at Joon and smiles.*]

Robert was not content with only sorting the coins. He interpreted the clinical interview as an assessment situation. Since he believed he was being judged on how much he knows, he decided to demonstrate *all* he knows. If Robert sees a counting opportunity, he is going to take it, even though he is not asked to do so. Robert is a child who takes the initiative and is comfortable making his own decisions *even* in the presence of an adult with a different agenda.

Robert: I see something else. And three of these. [*He takes out the three tokens from the pile, but then looks at Joon.*] Can I stack up these with these? [*He indicates the nickels.*]

Joon: OK. [*Smiles back.*]

Robert: [*He moves the tokens into the same line as the nickels.*] So, that's six and that's six. [*He indicates the line of nickels/tokens and the line of dimes, not counting them as he enumerates.*]

Joon: Oh, great!

Robert: [*He starts counting the lines, again mouthing the numbers silently and tagging each coin with a finger. He counts each row in order, first quarters, then dimes, then nickels/tokens.*] That makes sixteen!

Robert knew that the task required adherence to a particular sorting rule. However, here he asked permission to break that rule, since he wanted to have two sets of six. Again, his goals were more important to him than following the instructions of the interviewer, but they were always constrained by his primary desire to demonstrate how much he knew. This desire leads him to solve problems he is not asked to solve, so that from a simple sorting task we learn that he can sort, count, and add as well as perceive, plan, and create new patterns.

The interview with Kenneth reveals another way in which personality affects cognitive activity. During the middle of the interview, the interviewer introduced representation questions, placing a paper and pencil in front of Kenneth. However, he decided at this point to do his own thing, and after saying "I know what I can do!" he started drawing faces on the paper. Unlike Robert, who takes the initiative but remains within the general confines of the mathematical tasks presented to him, Kenneth takes the initiative but moves in his own, new direction. It appeared as if Kenneth was unconcerned, or perhaps unaware, of the fact that his ability was being assessed. If he wants to draw, he is going to draw, regardless of what the interviewer wants him to do.

The interviewer indulged Kenneth for a while, but then tried to bring him back on task by taking one of the faces that he drew and using it as a representation task.

Eileen: Let's pretend this face is a monster, and the monster can have anything on his face that he wants. Now, there are four pennies over here. [*She points to four pennies in a line on a second sheet of paper.*] That means the monster is going to have the same number of ears. Can you give the monster the same number of ears?

Kenneth: [*He looks at the face, and then takes the pencil and draws two horizontal lines at either end of the line of four pennies.*]

Eileen: How many ears is that?

Kenneth: Those aren't ears—those are eyebrows.

Again, Kenneth did what he wanted to do. He drew on the paper with the pennies instead of on the "monster's face." He also drew eyebrows instead of ears, and he made sure the interviewer knew that in no uncertain terms. It appears as if Kenneth believed that his role was equal to that of the interviewer and therefore that he should be able to introduce and modify tasks if he so chooses.

The interviewer realized that in order to keep Kenneth interested, she had to follow his lead. However, she still wanted to know if he could represent the pennies in his drawing.

Eileen: OK. So how many eyebrows are there?

Kenneth: Two.

Eileen: How many pennies are there?

Kenneth: Four.

Eileen: Can you give him the same number of eyebrows as pennies?

Kenneth: [*He stares at the paper for several seconds. Then he removes the two center pennies, leaving two pennies next to the "eyebrows" he had made.*]

This episode clearly shows how creative Kenneth can be—he always seems to look for the unconventional solution. Instead of making more eyebrows, as the interviewer had intended, he decided to remove the appropriate number of pennies. The interview shows that he can in fact represent equal groups with different objects, but not in the way the interviewer has in mind.

Although Kenneth and Robert both displayed initiative, the way in which it was manifested depended both on their personality and their goals. On the one hand, Robert is personable and very engaged in the interview; his remarks to the interviewer are punctuated with excitement and smiles. His primary goal is to demonstrate his knowledge, and he does so by volunteering new information about what he can do. However, it is always related to mathematics because that is the constraint that the interviewer established.

On the other hand, Kenneth has as his goal playing a part in running the interview. He introduces new tasks that do not relate to the mathematical questions the interviewer is asking, and he looks for new and creative solutions. He has a more matter-of-fact demeanor than Robert's and is comfortable being in charge. In fact, it is the interviewer who has to adapt her goals to his—quite the opposite of the traditional adult-child relationship that normally occurs during assessment situations.

In brief, these excerpts reveal how important it is for the mathematics educator to take the child's personality and goals into account when assessing reasoning ability and when teaching. The child's way of dealing with mathematics problems and modes of learning is in part an expression of the individual personality. An understanding of this "personality of cognition" can help organize the educator's attempts to interpret the child's behavior, to motivate the child, and to teach the child more effectively.

METACOGNITION

One theme that runs across many of these excerpts is children's metacognitive ability. Such "thinking about one's own thinking" is a complex ability, requiring a child both to reflect on her or his own thought processes and to describe these processes to another person. Although the children in the foregoing interviews do not display complete mastery of such activities, it is important to recognize their early manifestations. Often self-awareness was displayed by a tone of voice, such as Kenneth's use of a questioning tone when he answered "four" to indicate that he was not quite sure of his answer. Smiles, however, often permeated answers the children believed to be correct. Pedro and Omar further demonstrated a growing ability to talk about their thinking. Pedro was able to describe to the interviewer why his "pushing aside" strategy was effective and how it helped him overcome counting difficulties. Omar even used the word *guess* to describe uncertainty about his answer; the word reveals Omar's ability to monitor his own work as well as an awareness that his answer could be wrong.

Mathematics educators need to be attentive to indications of metacognition, a fundamental component of children's reasoning processes. We need both to appreciate the value of metacognitive activity and to develop ways to foster it. Indeed, helping children to understand their own thinking and to express it clearly to others should be a basic aspect of the mathematics curriculum (Ginsburg, Jacobs, and Lopez 1993).

CONCLUSIONS

The examples presented in this paper were taken from our interviews with low-income African American and Latino children attending a publicly supported day-care center in New York City. We chose to describe these children's reasoning for several reasons. One is that we wanted to show that even very young children at the preschool and kindergarten levels have an interest and some competence in complex and dynamic forms of mathematical reasoning. Imagine how much more complex and sophisticated older children's reasoning can be!

Our second reason for describing these children is to show that, despite some opinion to the contrary, low-income minority children are capable of complex mathematical reasoning. They arrive in school with considerable capability for abstract thought and potential for learning mathematics. Indeed, early potential for learning mathematics may well be universal. Virtually all young children may well be capable of the kinds of reasoning we have described. Yet educators often fail to recognize, nourish, and promote mathematical abilities, particularly those of the disadvantaged. As a result, poor children's subsequent inferior performance in later school mathematics should be attributed more to our failures in educating them than to their initial lack of ability.

REFERENCES

Baroody, Arthur J. *Children's Mathematical Thinking.* New York: Teachers College Press, 1987.

Bruner, Jerome S. *Toward a Theory of Instruction.* Cambridge, Mass.: Harvard University Press, Belknap Press, 1966.

Davidson, Janet E., and Robert J. Sternberg. "Competence and Performance in Intellectual Development." In *Moderators of Competence*, edited by Edith D. Neimark, Richard DeLisi, and Judith L. Newman, pp. 43–76. Hillsdale, N.J.: Lawrence Erlbaum Associates, 1985.

Flavell, John H., Patricia H. Miller, and Scott A. Miller. *Cognitive Development.* 3rd ed. Englewood Cliffs, N.J.: Prentice Hall, 1993.

Ginsburg, Herbert P. *Children's Arithmetic: How They Learn It and How You Teach It.* 2nd ed. Austin, Tex.: Pro-Ed, 1989.

Ginsburg, Herbert P., and Kirsten A. Asmussen. "Hot Mathematics." In *Children's Mathematics: New Directions for Child Development*, edited by Geoffrey B. Saxe and Maryl Gearhart, pp. 89–111. Jossey-Bass Social and Behavioral Science Series, no. 41. San Francisco: Jossey-Bass, 1988.

Ginsburg, Herbert P., Alice Klein, and Prentice Starkey. "The Development of Children's Mathematical Thinking: Connecting Research with Practice." In *Handbook of Child Psychology Vol. 4, Child Psychology and Practice,* 5th ed. edited by Irving E. Sigel and K. Ann Renninger, pp. 401–76. New York: John Wiley & Sons, 1998.

Ginsburg, Herbert P., Susan F. Jacobs, and Luz S. Lopez. "Assessing Mathematical Thinking and Learning Potential." In *Schools, Mathematics, and the World of Reality*, edited by Robert B. Davis and Carolyn S. Maher, pp. 237–62. Boston: Allyn & Bacon, 1993.

Inhelder, Bärbel, and Jean Piaget. *The Growth of Logical Thinking from Childhood to Adolescence.* New York: Basic Books, 1958.

Kilpatrick, Jeremy. "A History of Research in Mathematics Education." In *Handbook of Research on Mathematics Teaching and Learning,* edited by Douglas A. Grouws, pp. 3–38. New York: Macmillan Publishing; Reston, Va.: National Council of Teachers of Mathematics, 1992.

McLellan, James A., and John Dewey. *The Psychology of Number and Its Applications to Methods of Teaching Arithmetic.* New York: D. Appleton, 1895.

Newman, Denis, Peg Griffin, and Michael Cole. "Social Constraints in Laboratory and Classroom Tasks." In *Everyday Cognition: Its Development in Social Context,* edited by Barbara Rogoff and Jean Lave, pp. 172–93. Cambridge, Mass.: Harvard University Press, 1984.

Piaget, Jean. *The Child's Conception of Number.* Translated by Caleb Gattegno and Frances M. Hodgson. London: Routledge & Kegan Paul, 1952.

———. *The Child's Conception of the World.* Translated by Joan Tomlinson and Andrew Tomlinson. Savage, Md.: Littlefield Adams Quality Paperbacks, 1951.

Schröder, Eberhard, and Wolfgang Edelstein. "Intrinsic and External Constraints on the Development of Cognitive Competence." In *Criteria for Competence: Controversies in the Conceptualization and Assessment of Children's Abilities,* edited by Michael Chandler and Michael Chapman, pp. 131–50. Hillsdale, N.J.: Lawrence Erlbaum Associates, 1991.

Siegler, Robert S. *Emerging Minds: The Process of Change in Children's Thinking.* New York: Oxford University Press, 1996.

Thorndike, E. L. *The Psychology of Arithmetic.* New York: Macmillan, 1922.

Vygotsky, Lev S. *Mind in Society: The Development of Higher Psychological Processes.* Edited by Michael Cole, Vera John-Steiner, Sylvia Scribner, and Ellen Souberman. Cambridge, Mass.: Harvard University Press, 1978.

6

Reasoning about Operations
Early Algebraic Thinking in Grades K–6

Deborah Schifter

IN RECENT years, dissatisfaction with the teaching of algebra has been growing. This dissatisfaction is paralleled by increasing recognition that to address the problems of algebra teaching faced at middle and high school levels, elementary school mathematics education must be reconceived. Now, both sets of concerns are converging in discussions of early algebraic thinking and the kinds of activities that might be introduced at the elementary school level to prepare children for the algebra content they will be expected to master later on (Kaput in press a, in press b; National Council of Teachers of Mathematics 1997).

These discussions are taking place in the midst of the larger effort to reform the teaching and learning of mathematics. In response to research findings of the last two decades on children's mathematical reasoning and the construction of conceptual understanding, the reforms propose a pedagogy that puts students' thinking at the center of instruction. Teachers' primary responsibility is no longer to demonstrate the next algorithm their students are expected to commit to memory. Instead, classrooms are organized as communities of inquiry in which significant and challenging mathematical problems are set, and students learn to pose their own questions, formulate conjectures, and assess the validity of various solutions.

The cases presented in this paper were created with support from the National Science Foundation under Grant No. ESI-9254393. Any opinions, findings, conclusions, or recommendations expressed here are those of the author and do not necessarily reflect the views of the funders. Acknowledgments are owed to the staff and teachers of the Teaching to the Big Ideas (TBI) project whose discussions contributed to the ideas presented here. Especially helpful were the essays written by Lisa Yaffee and Sophia Cohen about how the TBI episodes reflect findings in the research literature. Al Cuoco, Virginia Bastable, and the staff of the Center of Development of Teaching offered helpful comments on early drafts. And, as always, Alan Schiffmann contributed his skills and insight throughout the development of this paper.

In this paper, I argue that as the field turns its attention to elementary school mathematics as preparation for algebra, it is important to begin with an examination of the kind of mathematical reasoning that is already happening in grades K–6 classrooms aligned with the reforms. Specifically, I argue for a close look at students' development of *operation* sense: How far can children's engagement with the four basic operations take them in preparation for their studies of algebra? And what would be appropriate next steps?

WHY SHOULD PRACTICE BE REFORMED?

Research has demonstrated that students are capable of powerful mathematical reasoning (cf. Grouws [1992]) but that conventional instruction, rather than building on children's natural ways of thinking about mathematics, centers instead on the memorization of facts and computational procedures (Cohen, McLaughlin, and Talbert 1993; Goodlad 1984). As a result, in the process of schooling, students tend to lose contact with their own mathematical ideas and, unable to keep hold of the growing number of procedures needing to be remembered, come to rely on faulty "rules of thumb" (Carpenter et al. 1981; Kouba et al. 1988).

For example, young children learning the conventional U.S. algorithms for multidigit subtraction recall that in order to perform the calculation, one must operate on the digits of each column separately. They also learn that "you can't subtract a larger number from a smaller." Thus, a common error in solving problems like 53 – 17 is to subtract the smaller digit from the larger in each column, producing, in this case, the answer 44. For an example from older grades: students asked to calculate 12/13 + 7/8 are likely to arrive at 19/21 by adding the two numerators and the two denominators, respectively. Thus, in the NAEP of 1980, when asked to approximate this sum and given the choices 1, 2, 19, and 21, students were more likely to choose 19 or 21 than either 1 or 2 (Carpenter et al. 1981). These cases reveal students who lack a sense of the numbers they are operating on or an understanding of the action of the operation in question. In the first problem above, they have lost touch with the idea that 17 from 53 must result in a number less than 43 (10 taken from 53); in the second, that both 12/13 and 7/8 are numbers slightly less than 1, and so their sum must be between 1 and 2.

Numerous studies have also shown that when working on word problems, many students do not analyze the situation modeled in the problem when determining which operation to apply. Instead, they select that operation by guessing, by trying all operations and choosing one that gives what seems to them a reasonable answer, or by studying such properties as the size of the numbers involved (Graeber and Tanenhaus 1993).

The weight of these and similar findings, replicable many thousands of times each school day, provides evidence of the need to transform mathematics pedagogy, to create classrooms in which making sense of mathematics is both the means and the goal of instruction.

PREPARING GRADES K–6 STUDENTS FOR ALGEBRA

If, in earlier grades, students lose their ability to make sense of mathematics and now, as a consequence, can no longer model situations appropriately or even attach meaning to arithmetic expressions, on what can their algebra be built? For example, what can students who think that 12/13 + 7/8 is closer to 19 than to 2 make of the identity $a/b + c/d = (ad + cb)/bd$? Even the simpler $a(b + c) = ac + ab$ may have little or no meaning to students who have never thought about the distributive property in the context of arithmetic. Or, how can students write an algebraic equation to solve a word problem when they have no understanding of the kinds of situations modeled by the operations? And when learning techniques for solving equations (e.g., $7 + 5x = 17 \rightarrow 5x = 17 - 7$), what meaning can these steps have to those who have never considered how the operations of addition and subtraction are related?

Now, in the context of the current effort to reform the teaching of mathematics, it is both possible and necessary to pose another, more fundamental, set of questions: *What happens if pedagogy is specifically designed to keep students in touch with their ways of making sense of mathematics? When instruction places students' thinking at the center, gives students opportunities to articulate their own reasoning, and encourages them to build on their ideas, how does their work in arithmetic prepare them for algebra? What experiences do students have with such notions as equivalent equations or the commutative, associative, and distributive properties of the operations they use?* (See also article 7, by Kamii and Warrington, in this volume.)

This paper examines a set of elementary school classrooms in which teachers are working to transform their instruction, and students, to articulate their own mathematical ideas. The particular lens employed focuses on examples that illustrate the principles of pedagogical reform, offer information about students' development of operation sense, and provide clues about young children's preparation for algebra. Although the children from these classrooms have not been followed into their first year of algebra instruction, their work allows us to formulate hypotheses that should be pursued in other settings.

WHERE DO THESE EXAMPLES COME FROM?

Over the last decade, many programs have been designed to help in-service teachers reconstruct their practice around students' thinking (Fennema and Nelson 1997). This paper draws its examples from Teaching to the Big

Ideas (TBI), a four-year teacher-enhancement project sponsored by the National Science Foundation and jointly conducted from 1993 to 1997 by the Education Development Center (EDC), TERC, and SummerMath for Teachers at Mount Holyoke College (Schifter, Russell, and Bastable in press). As a major emphasis of the project, teachers and staff closely monitored students' discussion, recording dialogue in order to identify central mathematical ideas as they arose naturally in classroom contexts. Those ideas were then analyzed to see how they shift, change, and grow as they are embedded in the mathematics as it evolves through the grade levels. With their developing expertise, the teachers emerged as research collaborators with the staff.

One mechanism developed for such investigations is *episode writing*. Using transcriptions of classroom dialogue or samples of students' written work, teachers regularly wrote two- to five-page narratives capturing some aspect of the mathematical thinking of one or more students. The six scenarios presented in this paper are taken from episodes written by TBI teachers. (The first five episodes appear in the professional development curriculum, *Developing Mathematical Ideas* [Schifter, Bastable, and Russell 1997]. In all six episodes, pseudonyms are used for teachers and students. Where references are made to publications in which teachers are identified by name, teachers' names are used here as well.)

A Glimpse into a Grades 1–2 Classroom: Illustrating the Principles of Reform

In the following episode, Jody Sorensen, who teaches a combined first- and second-grade class, describes her students' work on an arithmetic problem.

> When the children arrive in the morning each day, right away they work on the problem of the day, which I have written on a chart or on the chalkboard. One day last week I had this word problem written on a chart: *Sabrina and Yvonne have 14 stickers when they put their stickers together. Yvonne has 6 stickers. How many stickers does Sabrina have?*
>
> Solving the problem of the day has become a routine in my class in that after they settle in, children just go and get any materials they need (cubes, links, counters) to solve the problem. They know that they have to keep a record of their strategies for solving the problem by using models, pictures, words, or number sentences so that they would be able to explain their thinking process to someone else.
>
> Liza is a first grader, and this is how she solved the problem. First she drew 14 hearts on her paper. Then she put numbers 1 to 6 inside the heart shapes for the first 6 hearts. Then she started again from 1 to 8 on the remaining hearts. She marked off the first 6 hearts. Below her picture of hearts she wrote, "6 + 8 = 14." [See fig. 6.1.]
>
> Most adults would think of this as a subtraction problem, but Liza represented it with an addition sentence. When I saw what she was doing, I wanted to make

$$6 + 8 = 14$$

Fig. 6.1. Liza's representation of the valentine problem

sure that she was clear on her process and that she understood the problem. I asked Liza what the 14 was. She said that this was the number of stickers Sabrina and Yvonne had together. When I asked her how many stickers Sabrina had, she quickly pointed to the hearts labeled 1 to 8 that she had not put a [box] around and said, "Sabrina has 8 stickers." Her responses assured me that she understood what the problem was, and that her strategy was clear to her.... .

Maya is [also] a first grader. She took 14 cubes and made a tower. Then she took 6 cubes and made another tower. Then she put her 14-cube tower and her 6-cube tower next to each other [as shown in fig. 6.2]. Then she counted how many cubes there were beyond her 6-cube tower and found that there were 8 cubes.

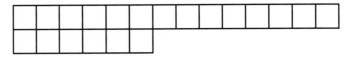

Fig. 6.2. Maya's representation of the valentine problem

When I saw what Maya had done, I was struck by the fact that her model consisted of more than 14 cubes. I asked her what the 8 cubes represent, and she said it was Sabrina's stickers. She said that the 6-cube tower below the 14-cube tower was only a way for her to remember how many stickers Yvonne had. She was using the extra 6 cubes as a marker so that she could easily see how many stickers Sabrina had. I then asked her what the 14 cubes represented, and she said that these were the stickers that Yvonne and Sabrina had together. Maya could explain her process clearly, using objects, but when I asked her if she could tell me a math sentence that shows what she had just done, she could not.

Children enter school with informal mathematical knowledge derived from experience. Even before receiving formal instruction about addition or subtraction, they can join, compare, or take away quantities by counting. Thus, when teachers give word problems, children can solve them by acting out the events described (Carpenter, Fennema, and Franke 1996). Building on these perceptions, teachers working to transform their practice are learning to give their students opportunities to solve mathematics problems using the knowledge they bring to the classroom.

In Sorensen's lesson, Liza drew 14 hearts to represent the 14 valentines shared between Sabrina and Yvonne; Maya set out cubes. The representations they preferred allowed the children to count out all components of the problem. By keeping track of which valentines belong to which girl, they were able to conclude, in answer to the word problem, that Sabrina has 8. Although Liza could model the situation with a mathematics sentence, "6 + 8 = 14," Maya could not.

Their teacher asked questions of each of the children, giving them opportunities to explain their solution processes, at times probing to explore the extent of their understanding. Although it was important that Maya learn to represent word problems with number sentences, Sorensen did not insist that she use symbols that did not yet have meaning for her.

When her students were given repeated opportunities to use methods that made sense to them and when they were encouraged to solve problems using different strategies and share their solution methods with one another, they developed an increasingly sophisticated repertoire of strategies. Sorensen found evidence of this as she monitored the children's work on the valentine problem. For example, some of her students used number strips and counted on from 6; others counted on using cubes; and still others, able to keep track of the numbers without counting, reasoned numerically to a solution.

> Cecile, a second grader, did not use pictures or objects. … She explained her way like this: "I know that 7 + 7 = 14, so I took 1 from one of the 7s and put it on the other 7, so now it is 6 + 8 and it's 14." I asked Cecile what she was thinking when she started with 7 + 7 = 14. She said, "7 + 7 is easier for me to think about and that makes 14, so if I move 1 from one of the sevens to the other, I have 6 + 8 and that is 14."

> … This is what Joe said about his process: "I took two 6s and added them. That is 12. But this is not the correct number, so I added 2 to the 12 and it is 14. So now it is 6 + 6 + 2 = 14. 6 + 8 = 14." Joe's way is similar to Cecile's. They both relied on their knowledge of doubles to get to the right number.

Two second graders, Cecile and Joe, exhibited especially sophisticated methods for solving the valentine problem: Starting from remembered facts (7 + 7 = 14; 6 + 6 = 12), they reasoned their way to the solution.

Jessie, still another of Sorensen's second graders, represented her solution with two arithmetic sentences:

> If Yvonne has 6 stickers and they have 14 altogether, I figured it out by minusing 6 from 14.

$$14 - 6 = 8$$

> I also figured it out like this:

$$6 + \underline{\hspace{1cm}} = 14$$

As Sorensen reflected on this lesson, she felt satisfied with how her students were thinking about the mathematics.

> All the children had appropriate ways of solving the problem. They used methods that were familiar to them; some used number combinations that were easy for

them to think about. They understood the problem and were able to explain their strategies and represent the problem in different ways. My goal for all my students is for them to feel comfortable in communicating their thinking process as well as to expand their repertoire of strategies for problem solving. I try to encourage them to solve a problem in more than one way and to share their strategies with someone else.

Although students' reasoning is at the center of Sorensen's teaching, her role is far from passive. In addition to selecting their task of the day, she listens actively for her students' thinking, and though not explicit in this episode, her classroom interactions are designed to move that thinking forward.

I feel that I need to be … asking some questions to elicit their ideas and helping them to begin to ask their own questions that will move them from their confusion.

Word Problems as a Context for Learning about Operations

A central activity in conventional mathematics teaching is, first, to present rules for computation, which students are expected to diligently memorize, and then to give word problems as an exercise in application. In general, it is quite easy for students to find the numbers in the problem; the challenge is to identify what to do with them. The "correct" operation is the one that, when applied to those numbers, produces the answer to the word problem. To help students meet this challenge, teachers frequently assign for memorization lists of key words or phrases associated with one of the four operations. So, for example, if students see the word *left* in a problem, they will subtract; if they see the words *times more than,* they will multiply. Students also frequently develop such strategies as selecting the operation according to the size of the numbers involved or testing out operations until they produce an answer that seems reasonable. When working on word problems, the goal for both teachers and students is to select as straightforwardly as possible the operation that will provide the answer (Graeber and Tanenhaus 1993).

If this is the criterion by which to judge the success of an exercise involving word problems, Jody Sorensen's lesson would have to be assessed a failure. Indeed, of those students mentioned in the episode, only one, Jessie, responded with the number sentence that in a conventional classroom would be deemed *correct:* 14 − 6 = 8. However, Sorensen's goal for the lesson was quite different, and in the end she felt satisfied that "all the children had appropriate ways of solving the problem."

In fact, Sorensen did not prepare her students for the valentine problem by first showing them how to add and subtract. On the contrary, she set that problem in order to provide them with a context for constructing for themselves understandings of those operations. Similarly, many of the children worked at the problem without knowing the relevant number fact beforehand. Instead, that problem posited a situation that they could act out. In so doing, they could make discoveries about the quantities involved.

Since children work with different word problems over time and since teaching is structured to encourage children to share their strategies and to experiment with new ones, children experience the wide range of problems that can be modeled by each operation. They also come to see how a single situation can be modeled by different operations.

In Sorensen's second-grade classroom, Jessie observed that both "14 – 6 = 8" and "6 + __ = 14" represent the valentine problem. The episode does not indicate whether Jessie regularly explored the different operations that can model a particular situation. Nor do we know whether, or how, this idea developed in class in later lessons. However, when we look across classrooms and across grades, we frequently see children making observations like Jessie's.

Having learned mathematics in the traditional way, many TBI participants were initially unsure of how to proceed when their students' solution methods relied on operations other than the ones teachers intended. For example, Georgia Wilson was working on division with her combined third- and fourth-grade class.

Each week, I wrote story problems that I considered to be division problems, problems I would solve using division. Here are some examples of the problems and their responses to them.

Problem 1: Jesse has 24 shirts. If he puts eight of them in each drawer, how many drawers does he use?

Vanessa wrote, "24 – 8 = 16, 16 – 8 = 8, 8 – 8 = 0," and then circled "3" for the answer.

Problem 2: If Jeremy needs to buy 36 cans of seltzer water for his family and they come in packs of six, how many packs should he buy?

This time Vanessa added: "6 + 6 = 12, 12 + 12 = 24, 24 + 6 = 30, 30 + 6 = 36… ."

Other students use these same methods. Is it significant that sometimes they add and sometimes they subtract? What are their choices based on? I thought problems 1 and 2 were the same kind of problem, and yet they were treated differently… .

Matthew worked on the following problem: *You go into a pet store that sells mice. There are 48 mouse legs. How many mice are there?* Matthew organized his work beautifully. [See fig. 6.3.] And then in a neat box he wrote 12 m × 4 l = 48 l. And above the box is the number 12. What does this say about Matthew's understanding of division? He knows that 12 is the answer but he feels satisfied with a multiplication number sentence where the answer is not the answer to the problem; rather it is part of the problem. He knows how to find the answer; he knows how division and multiplication relate to one another, but instead of the answer I had expected, 48 ÷ 4 = 12, he wrote a multiplication number sentence.

During a conversation with three kids about a similar problem, Matthew said, "This is another division problem. It's 63 divided by 9. What number times 9 is

```
 1 m   4 ℓ
 2 m   8 ℓ
 3 m  12 ℓ
 4 m  16 ℓ
 5 m  20 ℓ
 6 m  24 ℓ
 7 m  28 ℓ
 8 m  32 ℓ
 9 m  36 ℓ
10 m  40 ℓ
11 m  44 ℓ
12 m  48 ℓ
```

Fig. 6.3. Matthew's work to solve the mouse problem

63? 7." When I asked him to explain what about the problem made it a division problem, he said, "I don't know, but it is—but my thinking is multiplication."

What does this say about kids' understanding of division, if they use all the other operations except division?

Wilson's observations about her students' different solution methods are significant. Vanessa had internalized the operations of addition and subtraction and used them to model the (imagined) actions of Wilson's division problems: putting shirts into drawers or loading up a grocery cart with 6-packs of seltzer. Matthew, it seems, could recognize a problem as requiring division but used multiplication, finding a missing factor, to solve it. These children's understandings of division will build from here, deeply connected and in relation to other operations.

Sarita Worsley made a similar discovery when she presented the following word problem to start a unit on division of fractions with her sixth graders. *You are giving a party for your birthday. From the Ice Cream Factory, you order 6 pints of ice cream that they make. If you serve 3/4 of a pint of ice cream to each guest, how many guests can be served?* Worsley reported that first her students drew diagrams—6 squares each divided into 4 sections—to solve the problem.

[The students] explained that every three sections was what one person would receive and that was equal to 3/4. There was enough to do that eight times, so each variety would serve eight people.

However, when they expressed this problem in a number sentence or equation, the range of answers was interesting.... I was trying to get the students to see that this was a division problem: $6 \div 3/4 = 8$. Instead they came up with the following equations and had very impressive reasoning to justify their thinking. [See fig. 6.4.]

When Worsley wrote this episode, she was taken aback by her students' approaches—she had expected them to recognize this as a division of fractions problem, "$6 \div 3/4 = 8$," and now wasn't sure how to respond. She has

EQUATIONS	JUSTIFICATION
$24 \div 3 = 8$	There are 24 pieces, 3 pieces to a serving, 8 people can be served.
$8 \times 3/4 = 6$	8 servings of 3/4 of a pint each gives you 6 whole pints.
$3/4 + 3/4 + 3/4 + 3/4 + 3/4 + 3/4 + 3/4 + 3/4 = 6$	3/4 each gives you 6 whole pints.
$6 - 3/4 - 3/4 - 3/4 - 3/4 - 3/4 - 3/4 - 3/4 - 3/4 = 0$	Take 3/4 pint for each serving. You do this 8 times.

Fig. 6.4. Worsely's students' work on the ice-cream problem

since come to appreciate the validity and power of their observations, realizing that, in fact, these four equations *do* match what is going on in the problem. Once her students solved her birthday–ice-cream problem by multiplying, adding, or subtracting fractions as well as by dividing whole numbers, they could explore how all these strategies are related to one another *and* to the division of fractions.

As one examines these episodes, one recognizes, *implicit in the children's work*, observations and strategies that could be called algebraic. When challenged to find multiple paths to the solution of word problems, children see that the same situation can be modeled by different operations. Although not yet ready for algebraic notation, they operate with an implicit understanding of the following equivalencies:

$$14 - 6 = x \leftrightarrow 6 + x = 14$$
$$63 \div 9 = x \leftrightarrow 9 \times x = 63$$
$$x \times 3/4 = 6 \leftrightarrow 6 \div 3/4 = x \leftrightarrow 24 \div 3 = x$$

Calculation as a Context for Learning about Operations

In conventional elementary mathematics teaching, a major goal—perhaps *the* major goal—is to have children remember their basic mathematics facts and the standard computational algorithms. Children are commonly given sets of computation problems and asked to produce pages of correct answers as quickly as possible (Cohen, McLaughlin, and Talbert 1993; Goodlad 1984). Implicit in the conventional computational algorithms is the use of the base-ten structure of the number system and the application of the commutative, associative, and distributive properties. However, as calculation is typically taught, the emphasis is on remembering the sequence of steps that will produce an answer as quickly as possible. Lessons on calculation are not seen as opportunities to develop deeper understandings of place value or the properties of operations.

Yet, as the previous episodes demonstrate, if operations have meaning for children, they can themselves devise a variety of appropriate computational procedures. When Cecile and Joe didn't know what number added to 6 yields 14, they recalled 7 + 7 = 14 or 6 + 6 = 12 and figured out how those facts could be used to answer the question. Eventually, Cecile and Joe—and, one hopes, all children who move through second grade—will have number facts like 6 + 8 = 14 firmly in place. In the meantime, as these children worked to solve the problem, they already displayed an important mathematical "habit of mind": When faced with a problem that you cannot solve immediately, begin with a problem that resembles it that you *do* know how to solve, and see if there's a way to transform it into the more difficult one.

In the case of these second graders, 7 + 7 = 14 and 6 + 6 = 12 were facts they already knew. The transformation Cecile applied was to decompose a 7 to 6 + 1 and then group the 1 with the other 7 to produce 6 + 8 = 14. Joe saw that, from 12, he needed 2 to get to 14, so he added 2 to one of his addends, 6 + (6 + 2) = 12 + 2 = 14.

Soon, the fact that 6 + 8 = 14 will be remembered. And, as these children are challenged to compute with larger numbers, they will exercise the same habit of mind, employing a variety of solution strategies—as did, for example, the second graders in Lynn Norman's class as they explored two-digit subtraction.

> Fiona worked on a … word problem that involved regrouping (of 37 pigeons, 19 flew away). She dropped the 7 from the 37 for the time being. She then subtracted 10 from 30. Then she subtracted 9 more. She puzzled for a while about what to do with the 7, now that she had to put it back somewhere. Should she subtract it or add it? I asked her one question: Did those seven pigeons leave or stay? She said they stayed, and added the 7.
>
> $$37 - 19$$
> $$30 - 10 = 20$$
> $$20 - 9 = 11$$
> $$11 + 7 = 18$$
>
> … As Fiona goes through the steps in her algorithm she is able to keep track of when to add and when to subtract. The 7 is being subtracted (from 37) and then added again (at the end, to 11). The 9 from the 19 is in a way added to the 10 in 19, but it gets subtracted, because Fiona needs to subtract all of the 19. The 7 is part of what is being subtracted from. The 9 is part of what is being subtracted. It is a complicated process and it is amazing to me that a second grader can make sense of it for herself.

In Norman's example, Fiona began with a two-digit subtraction problem and decomposed it into parts she could more readily manipulate. Her strategy aimed toward working with tens, which made handling large numbers easier, but she had to understand how the operations work in order to put the numbers back together correctly.

Continuing her episode, Norman compared the thinking of students like Fiona—and others who devise their own strategies—to that of children who used the conventional algorithm.

> If a child memorizes the procedure, there is no real "keeping track." They must learn the steps, but they do not need to keep track of what the 3 in 37 means or how much of the 19 they have subtracted so far. All they do is use the recipe. If they get confused or forget a step or go out of order, children using this procedure don't tend to go back and make sense of the numbers or the problem, or try to keep track of what is going on.

Norman's concern was not about the conventional algorithm per se, but how her students tended to use it. She found that when they mechanically apply an algorithm to which they can attach no meaning, they stop thinking about the size of the numbers and the nature of the operation. For that reason, and in contrast to her past practice, she now commits more class time to giving her students opportunities to devise their own procedures.

> Finally, an almost unrelated observation: This year, for the first time, I have never seen a single child "subtract up" in the ones column if the bottom number is greater than the top one. I have always had many children do this other years. ... I am not sure what to make of this, but I hope it is because the children this year carry more of the meaning of the problem with them, because they are allowed to construct their own ways of solving it.

Susannah Farmer wrote about her third graders' first attempts to think through the multiplication of multidigit numbers. She had given them the following problem—*There were 64 teams at the beginning of the NCAA basketball tournament. With 5 players starting on each team, how many starting players were in the tournament?*—and students offered a variety of solution methods, breaking up the 64 and applying the distributive property. For example:

$$20 \times 5 = 100$$
$$20 \times 5 = 100$$
$$20 \times 5 = 100$$

Then the last part, 4×5, is 20. All together, 320.

and:

$$60 \times 5 = 300$$
$$4 \times 5 = 20$$
$$320$$

After sharing their methods, Farmer presented another problem: *We have 18 kids here today and each needs 12 tiles for the next activity. How can we figure out the number of tiles to give out?*

I was surprised that no one suggested using a calculator, their usual response to big numbers. But who needs a calculator when you have Josh!

That would be 18×12, and I know 10×10 is 100 and 8×2 is 16, so if you add them together it would be $100 + 16 = 116$.

Everyone seemed satisfied with the answer, whether out of agreement or lack of interest, I wasn't sure. After all, the process mimicked what they'd just been doing. I was thinking what to say that would help them see the error of their ways, when David's voice broke the quiet: "That's wrong."

"What do you mean, David?" I asked.

He explained, "I did 18×10 and got 180, but I thought at first I was wrong, so I double-checked. I noticed that Josh didn't do 8×10, so my answer was right." David is very knowledgeable about the workings of our number system, but leaves gaps in his verbal explanations. His mind races, and neither his mouth nor our brains can keep up. "I didn't do the 2 yet, so I do 18×2. Then you add it up—$180 + 36$."

"Wow," I thought, amazed at his understanding, but realizing that the rest of the class looked dazed. Luckily, there will be more chances for [these children] to show what they know about multiplication.

When challenged to solve computational problems with large numbers, Farmer's students, like Norman's, broke given problems apart to work with smaller, more manageable bits. In this case, they had to hold onto what multiplication *does* in order to keep track of what to do with the parts. To solve the problem, 64×5, Farmer's third graders suggested various ways of decomposing 64, multiplying each part by 5, and totaling the partial products.

A problem with two 2-digit factors, 18×12, produced some confusion. Josh applied a strategy used effectively with addition—decompose the two numbers into tens and ones, operate on the tens and operate on the ones, and then add the results together—but which does not work for multiplication. His classmate, David, recognized the error ("I noticed that he didn't do 8×10") and offered a strategy that works: Decompose the 12 into $10 + 2$, multiply 18 by each of those parts, and then add the results.

As the children depicted in these episodes worked on computations with numbers beyond familiar facts, they found equivalent expressions containing numbers with which they *did* know how to work. Implicit in their strategies is the application of commutative, associative, and distributive properties of the operations. (The claim is that the commutative, associative, and distributive properties are implicit in the children's work. This is not the same as the children using the notation presented in the following lines. In particular, there is no evidence in the episodes that the children have a sense of "=" as it is used in these equations.)

$$7 + 7 = (6 + 1) + 7 = 6 + (1 + 7) = 6 + 8 = 14$$
$$37 - 19 = (30 + 7) - (10 + 9) = 30 - 10 - 9 + 7$$
$$64 \times 5 = (60 + 4) \times 5 = (60 \times 5) + (4 \times 5)$$
$$18 \times 12 = (10 + 8) \times (10 + 2), \text{ which does } not \text{ equal } (10 \times 10) + (8 \times 2)$$

Given opportunities to articulate their own ways of solving problems and challenged to make sense of their classmates' solutions, we see these children learning to navigate the number system with considerable fluency.

Algebraic Notions, Implicit and Explicit

If the major goal of traditional elementary school mathematics teaching is to have students learn to compute, the classroom episodes presented above demonstrate that for reform-based mathematics instruction, the goal of teaching computation is not replaced but surpassed. In a practice designed to build on children's ways of solving mathematical problems, the children begin by enacting those problems, counting out all the quantities involved. Challenged and given opportunities, students develop more sophisticated strategies—strategies they employ with understanding. Indeed, we have seen how word problems and computational exercises can provide contexts for constructing meanings for the operations and for the structure of the number system.

Algebraic methods are clearly implicit in the children's work described above. As they apply different operations to solve a single word problem, they evidence a sense of how the operations are related. For example, as the children come to see that any missing-addend problem can be solved by subtraction, or that any division problem can be solved by finding the missing factor, they acquire experience with the inverse relationships of addition and subtraction, multiplication and division, and thus with equivalent equations. And as they develop fluency in a variety of computational strategies, they implicitly apply the laws of commutativity, associativity, and distributivity.

When students have learned arithmetic as a set of memorized procedures and have lost contact with their own abilities to make sense of calculations and operations, it is no wonder they have to rely on remembered rules and procedures to pass an algebra course. For example, what if Josh, Susannah Farmer's third grader, had never had the opportunity to confront his error, solving 18×12 by calculating $10 \times 10 + 8 \times 2$? What if his elementary school mathematics education had never given him occasion to think through what multiplication does, why 18×12 is, instead, equivalent to $18 \times 10 + 18 \times 2$? But when, one day, Josh finally enters an algebra class, having had such opportunity, having been given such occasion, he will understand why, rather than simply hope to remember that, $(a + b)(c + d)$ does not equal $ac + bd$.

In the classroom episodes presented above, we have seen children developing a sense of arithmetic that extends beyond finding answers to given calculation or word problems. Where instruction is designed to help children reason about operations and devise procedures for navigating the number system, there is greater emphasis on examining the variety of problem-solving strategies the children employ and assessing their validity than on the answer to any given problem those strategies produce. Their approaches frequently involve solving problems with different, equivalent equations, or performing calculations by working with equivalent arithmetic expressions. Thus, when Josh and his class-mates eventually confront "$a(b + c) = ab + ac$," they will bring to it their discussions of why 18×12 is equal to $18 \times 10 + 18 \times 2$ rather than $10 \times 10 + 8 \times 2$.

However, in algebra these notions are no longer implicit. Students must come to articulate an understanding of distributivity and of the inverse relationship of addition and subtraction. When asked to factor $ab + ac$, they cannot take cues from the numbers because a, b, and c represent any number. Instead, they must rely on their understanding of multiplication and addition, of what those operations do. Although children in the episodes freely employ what adults recognize as distributivity, can they abstract multiplication from its application to particular situations or particular numbers to make a claim about a general property of the operation? When children have rich and meaningful experiences in arithmetic, what is involved in learning how to recognize, articulate, and justify their observations of the properties of the operations themselves?

These are the questions that half the TBI teachers and staff chose to explore in the spring of 1996. In their monthly episodes, those teachers investigated their students' generalizations in the context of arithmetic. (The other half of the project investigated students' thinking in the context of geometry.) To what extent does children's natural curiosity draw them to observe and examine patterns in the number system? How do they articulate their observations, and what is the extent of their generalization? How do the children justify their claims of generality?

When Katherine Kline began to think about arithmetic generalizations in her second-grade classroom, she wrote,

> I thought of an idea that quite a few children in my class have been quite vocal about and seemingly quite certain of—something they call *turn-arounds*. Turn-arounds came up first when we were generating ways to "make" ten early in the year. The children made a list like 5 + 5, 4 + 6, 3 + 7—and then would suggest 6 + 4, 7 + 3, etc., and referred to them as turn-arounds. Soon everyone was calling 4 + 6 and 6 + 4 turn-arounds, and it became almost a vocabulary term without ever really discussing its implications. So [since our TBI group has been thinking about generalizations] I decided to ask them to think about turn-arounds and see if they might define it, describe it, or illuminate something about it for me.

It seems that, in coining the expression *turn-arounds*, Kline's second graders had themselves identified the commutative property of addition. Sticking with their term, she decided to set up a lesson in which her students would explore the idea of turn-arounds while she, in turn, would probe their thinking.

The children in Kline's class were ready to take on this investigation of the commutative property of addition. Although for months they had been talking about turn-arounds as a fact, they now engaged in this exploration with energy and curiosity. Among Kline's discoveries was that although her students' earlier observations about turn-arounds seemed to imply the recognition of a generalized property, not all her students were convinced that it always works. Natalie, though, was fairly sure: "Turn-arounds always work. I just know they do."

Teacher: How do you know?

Natalie: Well, look, 27 + 4 = 31 and 4 + 27 = 31.

Teacher: But does this always work, for any number, no matter how big it gets?

Natalie: Well, let me try it.

> So Natalie tried numbers in the hundreds and added them together both ways and felt convinced that it always worked. Her reasoning seemed to be based on her having done many of them and having had them always work out to be the same answer.

Other children, less confident than Natalie, tested out numbers larger than those they usually encountered. For example, Ingrid used her calculator to verify and later recorded, "22 + 100 = 122, 100 + 22 = 122; 8 + 99 = 107, 99 + 8 = 107; 100 + 3 = 103, 3 + 100 = 103."

Emily was less confident. In order to explore the conjecture, she turned to a representation of addition frequently used in Kline's classroom—joining two sets of cubes. Kline's colleague, Lynn Norman, who was visiting Kline's classroom that day, described how Emily thought about 70 + 35.

> At the end of class, when the children shared what they worked on, Emily showed how she worked with adding 70 and 35. She had 70 cubes in stacks of 10, and this was separated by a wooden block from 35 cubes in stacks of ten and one five. [See fig. 6.5.]

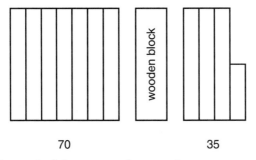

70   35

Fig. 6.5. Emily's representation to explore turn-arounds

She said she added 35 to 70 by counting on: 80, 90, 100, 105. Then she moved the two groups of cubes so that the 35 was to the left of the block and the 70 was to the right. She counted on again: 45, 55, 65, 75, 85, 95, 105. This pair worked because they added up to 105 in either order. Kline asked if Emily thought it would still work for different numbers. Emily said she didn't know because she only did these.

To think about the question, Emily decided to work with different representations of quantity and of addition than Natalie or Ingrid had. Initially, she felt that her method demonstrated that 70 + 35 yields the same answer as 35 + 70, but she didn't know if it would also work for other numbers. And though the class discussion moved on to other topics, Emily continued to think through just what she could learn from her representation.

A few more children shared and then Emily raised her hand again. She said that she could use the same cubes but divide them up differently and it would still work. When asked to demonstrate, she moved the block to another spot and said that the two new parts would also add up to 105, no matter what order she added them. She said it would work no matter how she divided the cubes because there would always be 105.

Relying on her representation, Emily was convinced that regardless of how she decomposed 105 cubes into two parts, the sum of the parts would always be 105. Thus (one might think of her conclusion as a corollary), any two parts of 105 can be added in either order. Norman wrote:

It seems Emily has reached a general rule, at least for the number 105. For any [partitions] of 105, she seems to be sure that you can add them in any order and still get 105. Having the 105 cubes in front of her seems to help her be sure. As her classmate, Nathan, said, she will always get the same answer because she is always starting with the same number of cubes. Her apparently firm grasp of the conservation of number is providing a base for her to make more generalizations about how numbers behave, and her work with 105 will probably help her to generalize further. When will she be sure that "it works for all numbers"?

Emily's initial conclusions had been limited to specific configurations of her blocks. However, as she continued to reflect, and as Nathan and others commented on her representation, she cautiously extended her claim to any paired addends of 105. However, Nathan was prepared to go further: "She will always get the same answer because she is always starting with the same number of cubes." That is, Nathan's generalization does not rest on the specific number, 105, but is valid for collections of any number of cubes.

In this class, the justifications these second graders used are at different levels of abstraction. Students like Natalie and Ingrid tested commutativity by checking particular number facts, choosing numbers outside the range of familiarity. They treated addition as "something you do to two numbers to get a result," and their test of commutativity rested on repeatedly coming up with the same answer for pairs of number facts. Others, like Emily and Nathan, began to explain commutativity by how quantities are related under addition. Emily relied on a representation of addition—joining two quantities of blocks. At first, she failed to see how her representation extended beyond particular numbers she had chosen: 70 + 35 and 35 + 70. However, after some thought, she saw that when 105 is broken into any two quantities, that sum is conserved no matter the order in which you rejoin the two quantities. For Emily, the next step would have been to realize, as Nathan already had, that this relationship extended beyond those 105 cubes she had laid out to any number whatsoever.

In our work with teachers, we have seen children's curiosity about regularity in the number system piqued by many different topics: Kline's students will later extend their explorations to consider turn-arounds for subtraction; Virginia Brown's (1996) third graders discuss why the "backwards" of a multiplication fact gives the same answer; Jeannie Wall's third graders investigate patterns among factors of multiples of 100 (Russell 1997); and children throughout the elementary grades make discoveries about the properties of square number, or odds and evens (Bastable and Schifter in press).

CONCLUSION

When students begin their study of algebra, they learn a new language, an efficient way of representing properties of operations and relationships among them. To those already familiar with those properties and relationships, the challenge is to learn the conventional system of notation. But what about those students who have never had the opportunity to develop operation sense, who have no idea about *what* this new notation is supposed to communicate?

When students see an equation like $a + b = b + a$ for the first time, their attention is drawn to the unfamiliar symbols, a and b. Do they realize that exactly the same idea is expressed by $x + y = y + x$? Do they realize, in fact, that it is not "a, b, x, or y that represent any number, that play the central role in that equation, but "+"? That is, that $a + b = b + a$ is a statement about the operation of addition?

By the time Katherine Kline's students enter middle school, they will likely have dropped the term *turn-arounds*. However, their second-grade explorations, and the experiences that build on them, will provide grounding for their understanding of what they will come to call *commutativity*. They will know that addition is commutative, and they will learn that this idea can be expressed as "$a + b = b + a$." They will even know, from their investigation of turn-arounds for subtraction, that that operation, although not commutative, exhibits another type of regularity when terms are reversed, thus, "$a - b = -(b - a)$."

Concern about the extent and quality of mathematics education in middle and high school courses has led researchers, curriculum developers, and policymakers to begin thinking about the kinds of elementary school experiences needed to prepare students for algebra. In this paper, I have attempted to make the case for an emphasis on the development of *operation sense* as crucial to this preparation. Furthermore, I hypothesize that once the teaching of elementary school arithmetic is aligned with reform principles—when classrooms are organized to build on students' mathematical ideas and keep students connected to their own sense-making abilities—then children so taught will be ready for algebra.

References

Bastable, Virginia, and Deborah Schifter. "Classroom Stories: Examples of Elementary Students Engaged in Early Algebra." In *Employing Children's Natural Powers to Build Algebraic Reasoning in the Content of Elementary Mathematics*, edited by James Kaput. Hillsdale, N.J.: Lawrence Erlbaum Associates, in press.

Brown, Virginia. "Third Graders Explore Multiplication." In *What's Happening in Math Class? Volume 1: Envisioning New Practices through Teacher Narratives*, edited by Deborah Schifter, pp. 18–23. New York: Teachers College Press, 1996.

Carpenter, Thomas P., Mary K. Corbitt, Henry S. Kepner, Mary M. Lindquist, and Robert E. Reys. *Results from the Second Mathematics Assessment of the National Assessment of Educational Progress*. Reston, Va.: National Council of Teachers of Mathematics, 1981.

Carpenter, Thomas P., Elizabeth Fennema, and Megan L. Franke. "Cognitively Guided Instruction: A Knowledge Base for Reform in Primary Mathematics Instruction." *Elementary School Journal* 1 (January 1996): 3–20.

Cohen, David K., Milbrey W. McLaughlin, and Joan E. Talbert, eds. *Teaching for Understanding: Challenges for Policy and Practice*. San Francisco: Jossey-Bass Publishers, 1993.

Fennema, Elizabeth, and Barbara S. Nelson, eds. *Mathematics Teachers in Transition*. Hillsdale, N.J.: Lawrence Erlbaum Associates, 1997.

Goodlad, John. *A Place Called School: Prospects for the Future*. New York: McGraw-Hill, 1984.

Graeber, Anna O., and Elaine Tanenhaus. "Multiplication and Division: From Whole Numbers to Rational Numbers." In *Research Ideas for the Classroom: Middle Grades Mathematics*, edited by Douglas T. Owens, pp. 99–117. New York: Macmillan Publishing Co., 1993.

Grouws, Douglas A. ed. *Handbook of Research on Mathematics Teaching and Learning*. New York: Macmillan Publishing Co., 1992.

Kaput, James. "Teaching and Learning a New K–12 Algebra with Understanding." In *Teaching and Learning Mathematics with Understanding*, edited by Elizabeth Fennema, Thomas P. Carpenter, and Thomas Romberg. Hillsdale, N.J.: Lawrence Erlbaum Associates, in press a.

————— ed. *Employing Children's Natural Powers to Build Algebraic Reasoning in the Content of Elementary Mathematics.* Hillsdale, N.J.: Lawrence Erlbaum Associates, in press b.

Kouba, Vicky L., Catherine A. Brown, Thomas P. Carpenter, Mary M. Lindquist, Edward A. Silver, and Jane O. Swafford. "Results of the Fourth NAEP Assessment of Mathematics: Number, Operations, and Word Problems." *Arithmetic Teacher* 35 (October 1988): 14–19.

National Council of Teachers of Mathematics. "Algebraic Thinking" focus issue. *Teaching Children Mathematics,* vol. 6, February 1997.

Russell, Susan Jo. "Learning about Whole Numbers: Multiplication and Division." Videotape. Cambridge, Mass.: TERC, 1997.

Schifter, Deborah, Virginia Bastable, and Susan Jo Russell, eds. *Developing Mathematical Ideas.* White Plains, N.Y.: Dale Seymour Publications, 1999.

Schifter, Deborah, Susan Jo Russell, and Virginia Bastable. "Teaching to the Big Ideas." In *The Diagnostic Teacher,* edited by Mildred Solomon. New York: Teachers College Press, in press.

7

Teaching Fractions
Fostering Children's Own Reasoning

Constance Kamii

Mary Ann Warrington

CHILDREN'S difficulty with simple computations such as 1/3 + 1/2 has been documented repeatedly by the National Assessment of Educational Progress (Post 1981; Kouba, Carpenter, and Swafford 1989). Since the 1970s, only about a third of the nation's 13-year-olds have been giving correct answers to such problems.

The instruction in the early grades that produced these results has typically focused on teaching algorithms. Students have been memorizing rules for finding equivalent fractions and common denominators and for multiplying and dividing fractions. The remedy recently being recommended is manipulatives such as fraction pies. Although these materials are often marketed as tools to enhance conceptual learning, the use of these manipulatives is often directed by teachers giving rules on how to use them to produce correct answers.

However, a constructivist approach has been developing since the 1980s. In constructivist teaching, children are not taught algorithms but instead are given word problems and asked to do their own reasoning to solve them. Confrey (1995), Empson (1985), Mack (1990), Olive (1996), and Streefland (1991) have all shown that children *can* invent their own procedures for dealing with fractions.

The approach described in this paper is constructivist and is based on Piaget's constructivism (1937/1954, 1967/1971, 1977). We first discuss the most important parts of Piaget's theory, with evidence from research, and then we show how we encourage children to do their own reasoning in the classroom. To limit the length of this paper, this discussion will focus on part-whole relationships with continuous quantities.

PIAGET'S CONSTRUCTIVISM

Piaget made a fundamental distinction among three kinds of knowledge on the basis of their ultimate sources and modes of structuring. The three kinds are physical knowledge, social (or conventional) knowledge, and logicomathematical knowledge.

THREE KINDS OF KNOWLEDGE

Physical knowledge is empirical knowledge of objects in external reality. The color and shape of counters, fraction pies, and every other object in the environment are examples of properties that are *in* objects and can be known empirically by observation. Our knowing that counters do not roll away like marbles is also an example of empirical, physical knowledge.

By contrast, our knowledge of languages, holidays, and standard units like centimeters is *social knowledge*. The knowledge of spoken words such as *one-fourth* and written symbols like *1/4* thus belongs to social knowledge. Whereas the ultimate source of physical knowledge is partly in objects, the source of social knowledge is partly in conventions made by people.

Logicomathematical knowledge consists of relationships. As can be seen in Piaget, Inhelder, and Szeminska (1948/1960), the ultimate source of logicomathematical knowledge (relationships) is each individual's mental actions. Below is an example illustrating how MEY, a four-year-old, has difficulty in making part-whole relationships while trying to give fair shares of a clay "cake" to two dolls.

> MEY (4; 8) has no difficulty in cutting the round cake in two (unequal) parts, but when asked to do the same with the rectangle he cuts a narrow slice off either end which leaves him with the central portion: "What about the bit that's left?—*That's nothing what's left.*" (P. 306)

MEY's difficulty is due to the problem of making a part-whole relationship mentally. By the age of six or seven, when children become able to make hierarchical relationships, they become able to cut the cake into two, three, or four equal parts that constitute the whole.

Perhaps the most surprising finding of this study is four-year-olds' answers to a conservation question. After the "cake" had been cut, the pieces were reassembled, and an uncut "cake" of the same dimensions was brought out. The children were then asked whether the two cakes had the same amount to eat. Some four-year-olds said that the uncut whole was more to eat, but others replied that the parts put together was more. By age five or six, however, they became sure that the two were the same amount to eat.

This task shows that relationships are constructed, or made, by each individual. Four-year-olds can think about the whole and the parts *at two different times*. However, they cannot think about the whole and the parts *simultaneously* because their thought is not yet reversible. Reversibility refers to the ability to perform two opposite mental actions simultaneously. Logicomathematical knowledge is thus not empirical knowledge, and its ultimate source is each individual's mental actions.

Piaget's constructivism is a scientific theory based on more than fifty years of research replicated all over the world. The details about ages have been found to vary, especially when tasks are made easier. However, the fact that children universally construct their own logicomathematical knowledge has not been disproved.

TEACHING FRACTIONS IN LIGHT OF PIAGET'S CONSTRUCTIVISM

Using Manipulatives (Physical Knowledge)

Fraction pies and strips are often recommended to show, for example, that 2/8 = 1/4. Students are also given paper strips to fold to see that 3/4 > 2/3. However, when we understand that this empirical knowledge is physical knowledge, it becomes clear that this empiricist approach cannot help children to learn about equivalent fractions.

Kamii and Clark (1995) showed with older children that equivalent fractions are not empirical knowledge. Presenting fifth and sixth graders with two identical sheets of paper (8.5 × 5.5 inches), the interviewer first ascertained the child's belief that the two sheets were the same size. The interviewer then folded one of the sheets horizontally into fourths (see fig. 7.1a) and cut 1/4 off. She then folded the other sheet vertically (see fig. 7.1b) and cut it into eight equal strips. After asking the child to count the strips, the interviewer asked, "If these pieces of paper were chocolate, and I gave myself this big piece (3/4) but not this one (pushing 1/4 away), how many of your strips would you use to give yourself exactly the same amount to eat (see fig. 7.1c)?"

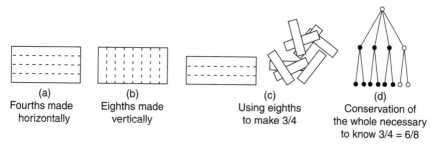

| (a)
Fourths made
horizontally | (b)
Eighths made
vertically | (c)
Using eighths
to make 3/4 | (d)
Conservation of
the whole necessary
to know 3/4 = 6/8 |

Fig. 7.1. The materials and hierarchical thinking involved in the "chocolate" task

All the students had worked with fraction pies and fraction strips, and all of them could write "6/8" when asked for "another name for 3/4." However, only 13 percent of the fifth graders ($n = 61$) and 32 percent of the sixth graders ($n = 59$) said "six" by using their knowledge of fractions. All the other students took an empirical, spatial approach and tried unsuccessfully to cover the 3/4 piece with the strips.

When a student was unsuccessful, the following countersuggestion was offered by the interviewer: "Another student said that 1/4 = 2/8 (demonstrating the correspondence between each fourth and two strips). So she said the answer was six strips because 2/8 + 2/8 + 2/8 = 6/8 = 3/4 (demonstrating). What do you think of this idea?" Forty-nine percent of the fifth graders and 24 percent of the sixth graders rejected the correct answer in favor of a spatial approach.

These fifth and sixth graders had been taught algorithms (social knowledge) with manipulatives (physical knowledge). The equivalent fractions of 3/4 = 6/8 could not be observed empirically in the "chocolate" task and required the conservation of the whole (see fig. 7.1d). This hierarchical thinking requires reversibility of thought, and children have to construct equivalent fractions through their own reasoning. In other words, equivalent fractions cannot be learned empirically from fraction pies and paper folding.

Teaching Algorithms (Social Knowledge)

Algorithms are conventions (social knowledge) resulting from centuries of construction by adult mathematicians. For example, the algorithm of "invert and multiply" is efficient, but even most adults do not understand the why of this convention. With respect to whole-number computation, Kamii (1994) presented many data proving that algorithms are harmful to the development of children's numerical reasoning. Mack (1990) came to the same conclusion about fractions after finding that algorithms often keep students from even trying to do their own reasoning. She also found that students often remember erroneous algorithms and have more faith in these rules than in their own thinking.

FOSTERING CHILDREN'S OWN REASONING (LOGICOMATHEMATICAL KNOWLEDGE)

The principles of teaching we keep in mind in light of Piaget's constructivism are the same as those involved in whole-number computations (Kamii 1985, 1989, 1994). The important thing is to focus on reasoning (logicomathematical knowledge) and not to teach fractions through physical and social knowledge. Some of the basic principles for teaching fractions can be summarized in the following way:

1. Do not tell children how to compute by using algorithms. Instead, present them with problems and ask them to use what they know to figure out what they do not know. The reason for not showing how to solve problems is that logicomathematical knowledge develops out of children's own mental

actions. We want them to struggle to invent a solution because it is this struggle that stimulates the construction of new relationships.

2. Do not tell children that an answer is right or wrong. Instead, encourage them to agree or disagree among themselves and to debate what makes sense and what does not. As can be seen in Piaget (1980), the exchange of points of view is essential for the construction of logic and objectivity.

3. Encourage children to use their own tools for reasoning instead of providing them with ready-made representations, or "embodiments." Children reason best with their own drawings because these drawings come out of their own thinking and therefore facilitate their reasoning.

4. Ask children to estimate solutions to problems first because estimation is an effective way to build strong number sense. Estimation also makes problems approachable to all students.

We now address the question of how to encourage children to do their own reasoning in the classroom. This discussion is divided into four parts: making fractions, addition and subtraction, division, and multiplication.

Making Fractions

Burns (1987) asked third graders, "How can four people share six cookies equally?" She followed up with similar questions about five cookies, and then three, two, and one cookie. More recently, Empson (1995) reported that these kinds of problems can be solved by first graders. Burns and Empson encouraged children to invent fractions (see fig. 7.2). We use the same approach to making fractions and have also observed that repeated halving (halves, fourths, and eighths) is easier for children than thirds, sixths, and ninths.

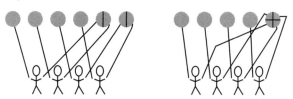

Fig. 7.2. Dividing six cookies, then five cookies, among four children

Addition and Subtraction

Adding and subtracting fractions tend to be quite difficult for children when unlike denominators are involved. Streefland's (1991, p. 68) pizza problem is excellent because it encourages children to draw and to invent like denominators (as well as equivalent fractions) using doubling and halving. His problem, paraphrased, is the following:

A family consisting of Father, Mother, Peter, and Ann had pizzas for lunch. The first one was shared equally. Mother then cut the second pizza into four parts, too, but said, "Oh, how silly of me! I've had enough. You three can share this one." But Ann said, "No, one of these pieces (of the second pizza) is enough for me." She then turned to Peter and her father and said, "You two can divide the rest." How much pizza did each person eat?

Peter and Father each got 1/4 + 1/4 + 1/8 (see fig. 7.3a), and children can see in their drawings (see fig. 7.3b) that the answer cannot be 3/16. They struggle, but having reasoned that Ann got 1/4 + 1/4 = 2/4 = 1/2, some children think of cutting all the fourths into eighths. This reasoning leads to the kind of hierarchical thinking illustrated in figure 7.1d.

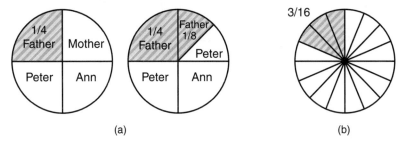

Fig. 7.3. Drawings made to figure out 1/4 + 1/4 + 1/8

An example of a harder problem involving thirds and sixths is the following:

Suzy, her father, and her mother divided a chocolate bar equally among themselves. Suzy then gave half of her share to a friend who came over. Suzy's mother decided to give her share (the mother's 1/3) to Suzy. How much chocolate did each person get?

Children make drawings such as figure 7.4a, and many fourth graders invent a common denominator by cutting the thirds into sixths (see fig. 7.4b).

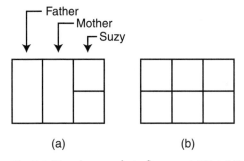

Fig. 7.4. Drawings made to figure out 1/3 + 1/6

Next come such problems as 1/2 + 1/3 in the following form:

Pat saved half a chocolate bar yesterday and a third of the same kind of chocolate bar that she got today. How much chocolate has she saved?

This problem is difficult because one of the denominators is not simply half or the double of the other. However, children make drawings such as figure 7.5a and struggle to make a unit fraction that will work with both rectangles. Some soon mentally "transport" the halves onto the thirds as shown in figure 7.5b and realize that the middle of the rectangle coincides with the middle of the other rectangle showing thirds. They then think of changing all the thirds into sixths.

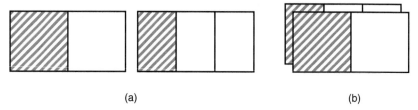

(a)   (b)

Fig. 7.5. Drawings made to figure out 1/2 + 1/3

As stated earlier, the teacher refrains from saying that this reasoning is correct or incorrect. Instead, he or she encourages the exchange of points of view. The teacher's job is not to explain mathematics but to facilitate critical thinking and the honest, respectful exchange of ideas among the students. When students explain their reasoning to others, they clarify their own thinking and learn to communicate clearly.

Division

To teach division with fractions, we begin with the simplest of problems. It is important to clarify the students' conceptual understanding of division with whole numbers before asking them to apply it to fractions. The teacher might write "4 ÷ 2" on the board and ask, "What does this mean?" When the class has concluded that one of the meanings of 4 ÷ 2 is "how many times 2 goes into 4," the teacher has a grasp of how the students view division. The teacher can then introduce fraction problems such as 1 ÷ 1/2, 1 ÷ 1/3, and 1 ÷ 2/3.

Children are encouraged to figure out the answers using drawings and their own reasoning. We have found that children are likely to figure out the answer for 1 ÷ 2/3 from their knowledge of 1 ÷ 1/3 = 3. This reasoning tends to be that the answer to 1 ÷ 2/3 must be half of 3 because 2/3 is twice as much as 1/3. The thinking involved to reason through such a problem without ready-made rules allows children to make mathematical relationships that empower them to solve more complex problems.

Next, the teacher might introduce the division of a unit fraction by a whole number, and the division of a nonunit fraction by a whole number. Examples:

$$1/3 \div 3$$

$$2/3 \div 3$$

To solve 1/3 ÷ 3, children usually make drawings such as those in figure 7.6 and determine that the answer is 1/9. When they come to 2/3÷ 3, they reason that if the dividend is 2 × 1/3, the answer has to be 2 × 1/9, or 2/9.

 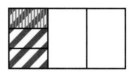

Fig. 7.6. Drawings made to figure out 1/3 ÷ 3

The sequencing of problems is important when we want children to use what they know to invent new relationships. The division of a fraction by a fraction comes next, with easy fractions such as halves and fourths. For example:

I bought 5 3/4 pounds of chocolate-covered peanuts. I want to freeze the candy in half-pound bags and eat it later. How many half-pound bags will I have?

After agreeing on the estimate of "between 10 and 12 bags because 5 pounds would make 10 bags, and 6 pounds would make 12 bags," most of the students make drawings to figure out the answer to 3/4 ÷ 1/2. Seeing that 1/2 goes into 3/4 once, with a remainder of 1/4, they conclude that the answer is 11 bags, with a remainder of 1/4 pound.

The most impressive solution came from the child who said, "I just doubled it (5 3/4) and divided by 1," meaning "I changed the problem to 11 1/2 ÷ 1 (= 11 1/2). When her peers asked, "Can you do that?" she explained that doubling the numbers did not change the problem. By arguing that 10 ÷ 5 = 20 ÷ 10 because both gave the answer of 2, she proved that doubling both the dividend and the divisor did not change the answer. As illustrated here, when children are encouraged to do their own reasoning, they develop not only a deep understanding of mathematics but also the confidence to defend their answers.

The next problem might be as follows: I have 4 2/5 cups of candy and want to put 1/3 cup in each small bag for Halloween. How many bags can I make? The estimate of "a little more than 12 bags" is easy by now. The solution to 2/5 ÷ 1/3 that students then invent is usually by thinking of a common denominator. They change the problem to 6/15 ÷ 5/15 and get the answer of "1, with a remainder of 1/15."

Multiplication

When teaching multiplication, we do not say "multiply" or use the symbol × until well into our instruction. We believe that saying "*of* means to multiply" imposes words on children that do not make sense to them. We begin with easy problems such as the following:

If you had half of an apple pie and ate half of that, how much pie did you eat? If you then ate half of what was left? If you then ate half of what was left?

The next problem might be this one:

If you had 3/4 of a pie and ate half of it, how much pie did you eat? If you then ate half of what was left? If you then ate half of what was left?

Thirds are easy by this time because multiplying a number by a third is the same thing as dividing it by 3. Problems such as those shown below are easy to do:

$$
\begin{array}{lcl}
1/3 & \text{of} & 3 \\
2/3 & \text{of} & 3 \\
1/3 & \text{of} & 9 \\
1/3 & \text{of} & 1 \\
1/3 & \text{of} & 1/3 \\
2/3 & \text{of} & 1/3 \\
2/3 & \text{of} & 2/3 \\
\end{array}
$$

To solve 2/3 of 2/3, children make drawings such as those in figure 7.7. Knowing that 1/3 of 1/3 is 1/9 (fig. 7.7a), students figure out that 2/3 of 1/3 is the double of 1/9 (fig. 7.7b). Knowing that 2/3 of 1/3 is 2/9, they figure out that 2/3 of 2/3 is the double of 2/9 (fig. 7.7c).

Children can then be given word problems such as the following:

There was half a pound of jelly beans in a container. Kim and Ann ate 2/3 of the jelly beans in the container. How much did they eat?

A more difficult problem appears below.

Michael walked 6 5/8 miles to help raise money for sickle cell anemia. Ariel walked 1/3 the distance Michael walked. Shanon walked twice as far as Ariel. How far did Shanon walk?

Finally, the written form involving "×," such as "1/2 × 4/5," is social knowledge that should be introduced when children's logicomathematical knowledge is solid. The teacher writes the problems shown below, one by one, asking, "What do you think this means?"

Problem	What Children Say	What the Teacher Writes
1/2 × 1	"One, half a time is 1/2."	1/2
3 × 1/2	"One-half, three times is 1 1/2."	1 1/2
1/2 × 1/2	"One half, half a time is 1/4."	1/4

1/2	of	1/2	"Half of a half is 1/4."	1/4
1/2	×	4/5	"Four-fifths, half a time is 2/5."	2/5
1/2	of	4/5	"Half of four-fifths is 2/5."	2/5

Students reason that "1/2 × 4/5" must mean the same thing as "1/2 of 4/5" because "half of" does mean "half a time."

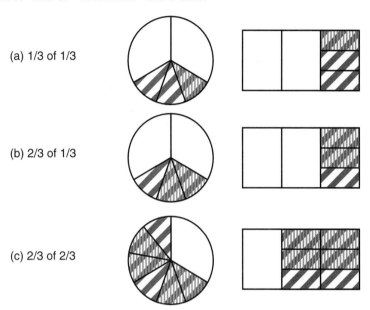

(a) 1/3 of 1/3

(b) 2/3 of 1/3

(c) 2/3 of 2/3

Fig. 7.7. Steps in figuring out 2/3 of 2/3

Conclusion

Our way of teaching may seem inefficient to people who believe in teaching algorithms. However, when constructing logicomathematical knowledge, there cannot be any shortcut. When we try to take shortcuts and teach mathematics as if it were social knowledge, students often write answers such as "1/2 + 1/3 = 2/5" and "2 × 2/5 = 4/10." Children who have done their own reasoning can simply look at "2/5" and know that 2 × 2/5 = 4/5. Those who have made sense of mathematics every step of the way are also certain about the mathematics that is truly their own and are confident about their ability to solve new problems. In teaching mathematics, we need to encourage children to rely on their own thinking so that they will become able to go on to create ever higher levels of reasoning.

References

Burns, Marilyn. *A Collection of Math Lessons from Grades 3 through 6*. New Rochelle, N.Y.: Cuisenaire Company of America, 1987.

Confrey, Jere. "Splitting Reexamined: Results from a Three-Year Longitudinal Study of Children in Grades Three to Five." In *Proceedings of the 17th Annual Meeting, International Group for the Psychology of Mathematics Education, NA,* Vol. 1, edited by Douglas T. Owens, Michelle K. Reed, and Gayle M. Millsaps, pp. 421–26. Columbus, Ohio: ERIC Clearinghouse for Science, Mathematics, and Environmental Education, 1995.

Empson, Susan B. "Using Sharing Situations to Help Children Learn Fractions." *Teaching Children Mathematics* 2 (October 1995):110–14.

Kamii, Constance. *Young Children Continue to Reinvent Arithmetic, 2nd Grade.* New York: Teachers College Press, 1989.

———. *Young Children Continue to Reinvent Arithmetic, 3rd Grade.* New York: Teachers College Press, 1994.

———. *Young Children Reinvent Arithmetic.* New York: Teachers College Press, 1985.

Kamii, Constance, and Faye B. Clark. "Equivalent Fractions: Their Difficulty and Educational Implications." *Journal of Mathematical Behavior* 14 (December 1995): 365–78.

Kouba, Vicky, Thomas P. Carpenter, and Jane O. Swafford. "Number and Operations." In *Results from the Fourth Mathematics Assessment of the National Assessment of Educational Progress,* edited by Mary M. Lindquist, pp. 64–93. Reston, Va.: National Council of Teachers of Mathematics, 1989.

Mack, Nancy K. "Learning Fractions with Understanding: Building on Informal Knowledge." *Journal for Research in Mathematics Education* 21 (January 1990):16–32.

Olive, John. "Modifications of Children's Multiplicative Operations with Whole Numbers and Fractions That May Generate Rational Numbers of Arithmetic." In *Proceedings of the 18th Annual Meeting, International Group for the Psychology of Mathematics Education, NA,* Vol. 1, edited by Elizabeth Jakubowski, Dierdre Watkins, and Harry Biske, pp. 317–23. Columbus, Ohio: ERIC Clearinghouse for Science, Mathematics, and Environmental Education, 1996.

Piaget, Jean. *Biology and Knowledge.* Chicago: University of Chicago Press, 1971. (Original work published 1967)

———. *The Construction of Reality in the Child.* New York: Basic Books, 1954. (Original work published 1937)

———. *Recherches sur l'Abstraction Réfléchissante,* Vol. 1. Paris: Presses Universitaires de France, 1977.

Piaget, Jean. Preface. Kamii, Constance, and Rheta DeVries, *Group Games in Early Education.* Washington, D.C.: National Association for the Education of Young Children, 1980.

Piaget, Jean, Bärbel Inhelder, and Alina Szeminska. *The Child's Conception of Geometry.* London: Routledge and Kegan Paul, 1960. (Original work published 1948)

Post, Thomas R. "Fractions: Results and Implications from National Assessment." *Arithmetic Teacher* 28 (May 1981), 26–31.

Streefland, Leen. *Fractions in Realistic Mathematics Education.* Dordrecht: Kluwer Academic Publishers, 1993.

8

Developing Mathematical Reasoning within the Context of Measurement

Kay McClain

Paul Cobb

Koeno Gravemeijer

Beth Estes

OUR purpose in this paper is to describe how one group of students developed personally meaningful ways to reason mathematically within the context of measurement. To clarify our viewpoint, we present episodes taken from a first-grade classroom in which we conducted a four-month teaching experiment. (The authors of this paper were all involved in the teaching experiment. The fourth author was also the classroom teacher.) One of the goals of the teaching experiment was to develop instructional sequences designed to support first graders' construction of meaningful understandings for (1) measurement and (2) mental computation and estimation strategies for numbers up to 100. A primary focus when developing the instructional sequences was to support students' multiple interpretations of problem situations. These interpretations would then serve as the basis for classroom discussions in which students explained their mathematical reasoning. Our intent in presenting the episodes is not to offer examples of exemplary teaching. It is, instead, to provide a setting in which we can examine measurement as a context for supporting students' construction of sophisticated ways to think and reason mathematically. (See also article 10, by Artzt and Yaloz, in this volume.)

In the following sections of this paper, we first outline the intent of the instructional sequences developed in the course of the teaching experiment.

Against that background, we then describe episodes from the classroom that highlight students' ability to reason mathematically while investigating issues related to measurement.

THE INSTRUCTIONAL SEQUENCES

The first sequence of the teaching experiment dealt with measurement. The second one built on the measuring activities to support students' construction of mental computation and estimation strategies for reasoning with numbers to 100. In the instructional sequence that dealt with measurement, our initial goal was that students might come to reason mathematically about measurement and not merely measure accurately. This approach differs significantly from many that are frequently used in American schools in that the focus was on the development of understanding rather than the correct use of tools. In particular, we hoped that the students would come to interpret the activity of measuring as the accumulation of distance (cf. Thompson and Thompson 1996). For instance, as the students were measuring by pacing heel-to-toe, we hoped that the number words they said as they paced would each come to signify the measure of the *distance* paced rather than the *single pace* that they made as they said a particular number word (e.g., saying "twelve" as students paced the twelfth step would indicate a distance that was twelve paces long instead of just the twelfth step). Further, our intent was that the results of measuring would be structured quantities of known measure. If this were so, students would be able to think of a distance of, say, 20 steps that they had paced as a quantity itself composed of two distances of ten paces, or of distances of five paces and fifteen paces. In doing so, it would be self-evident that whereas distances are invariant quantities, their measures vary according to the size of the measurement unit used.

As we shall see, measuring with composite units became an established mathematics practice in the course of the teaching experiment. Initially, the students drew around their shoes and taped five shoe prints together to create a unit they named a *footstrip*. Later, in the setting of an ongoing narrative about a community of Smurfs, the students used a bar of ten Unifix cubes to measure. These instructional activities evolved into measuring with a strip that was the length of 100 Unifix cubes. This in turn made it possible for the students' activity of measuring to serve as the starting point for the second instructional sequence that addressed mental computation and estimation with two-digit numbers. Our immediate concern was not merely that students would acquire particular calculational methods. Instead, we also focused on students' construction of numerical relationships that are implicit in these methods. This view shifts the importance from calculational strategies per se to the mathematical interpretations and understandings that make the use of flexible strategies possible.

CLASSROOM EPISODES

In the classroom in which we worked, the teacher often attempted to initiate shifts in the level of classroom discourse so that what was done mathematically subsequently might become an explicit topic of conversation. As part of this process, the teacher encouraged students to explain their reasoning by grounding their explanations in the use of tools or by drawing pictures on the white board (cf. McClain and Cobb in press). For example, in discussing solutions to a simple task such as *There are 11 cats and 3 dogs. How many more cats than dogs are there?*, the students drew tallies on the white board to represent the cats and the dogs and then explained their reasoning with reference to the tallies. This helped the students communicate their thinking and often resulted in their solution methods becoming topics of conversation and investigation.

The instructional activities used in the teaching experiment were typically posed in the context of an ongoing narrative. To accomplish this, the teacher engaged the students in a story in which the characters encountered various problems that the students were asked to solve. The narratives both served to ground the students' activity in imagery and provided a point of reference as they explained their reasoning. In addition, the problems were sequenced within the narratives so that the students developed increasingly effective measurement tools with the teacher's support. Further, the narrative supported the emergence of tools out of students' problem-solving activity.

The first narrative involved a kingdom in which the king's foot was used as the unit of measure. The initial instructional activities involved measuring by pacing. The first tool the students developed to resolve a problem was called a *footstrip* and consisted of five shoe prints taped together heel-to-toe. A number of mathematically significant issues emerged during the first part of the sequence, including that of describing distances measured with footstrips (e.g., 5 footstrips versus 25 paces).

The second narrative developed during the measurement sequence involved a community of Smurfs who often encountered problems that involved finding the length or height of certain objects. The teacher explained that the Smurfs' food came in cans and that they decided to measure objects by stacking cans to the height of the object to be measured. In the classroom, the students used Unifix cubes as substitutes for cans and measured numerous objects for the Smurfs such as the height of the wall around the Smurf village, the length of the animal pens, and the depth of the water in the river. After several measuring activities, the teacher explained to the students that the Smurfs were getting tired of carrying around the large number of cans needed for measuring. The students agreed that this was cumbersome and discussed alternative approaches. Several suggested iterating a bar of cubes (cans), presumably influenced by the prior activity of measuring with the footstrip. This discussion seemed to influence their decision to measure with a bar of ten cubes that they called a *Smurf bar.*

When measuring with the Smurf bar, all the students measured objects by iterating the bar along the length of the item to be measured and counting by tens. However, some students counted the last cubes of the measure within in the last iterated decade (see fig. 8.1).

Fig. 8.1. Counting 21, 22, and 23 within the second decade

Solutions of this type became the focus of discussions as can be seen in an incident that occurred two weeks after the measurement sequence began. The teacher had posed the following task: *The Smurfs are building a shed. They need to cut some planks out of a long piece of board. Each plank must be 23 cans long. Show on the board where they would cut to get a plank 23 cans long.* Students had been given long pieces of adding machine tape as the board and were asked to use a single Smurf bar to measure a plank the length of 23 cans. Angie was the first student to share her solution process with the class. She showed how she had measured a length of 23 cans by iterating the bar twice and then counting 21, 22, and 23 beyond the second iteration. When she finished, Evan disagreed.

> *Evan:* I think it's 33 because 10 (*place bar down as in figure 8.2a*), 20 (*moves bar as in figure 8.2b*), 21, 22, 23 (*points to the cubes within the second iteration, thus measuring a length that was actually 13 cubes*).
>
> *Angie:* Um, well, see, look, if we had 10 (*moves bar as shown in figure 8.2a*) that would be 11, 12, 13.
>
> *Evan:* But it's 23.

(a)

(b)

Fig. 8.2. (*a*) Showing the first iteration in measuring 23 cans; (*b*) showing the second iteration in measuring 23 cans

At this point, Evan and Angie appeared to be miscommunicating. Although Angie appeared to understand how Evan found a length that differed from hers, she was unable to explain her reasoning to him. This miscommunication continued as Andy explained why he agreed with Evan. The teacher then asked both Evan and Angie to share their solution methods again.

Teacher: Let's be sure all the Smurfs can understand 'cause we have what Angie had measured and what Evan had measured. We need to be sure everybody understands what each of them did, so Evan, why don't you go ahead and show what it is to measure 23 cans.

Evan: Ten (places bar as shown in figure 8.2a), 20 (moves bar as shown figure 8.2b). (*Pause*) I changed by mind. She's right.

Teacher: What do you mean?

Evan: This would be 20 (*points to end of second iteration*).

Teacher: What would be 20?

Evan: This is 20 right here (*places one hand at the beginning of the "plank" and the other at the end of the second iteration*). This is the 20.

Teacher: So that where your fingers are shows a plank that would be 20 cans long? Is that what you mean? Any questions for Evan so far?

Evan: Then if I move it up just 3 more. There. (*Breaks the bar to show 3 cans and places the 3 cans beyond 20.*) That's 23.

It appeared that in the course of reexplaining his solution, Evan reflected on Angie's method and reconceptualized what he was doing when he iterated the bar. Initially, for Evan, placing the Smurf bar down the second time as he said "20" meant the twenties decade. Therefore, for him, 21, 22, and 23 lay within the second iteration. However, he subsequently reconceptualized "20" as referring to the distance measured by iterating the bar twice and realized that 21, 22, and 23 must lie beyond the distance whose measure was 20. This type of reasoning was supported both by the teacher's asking Evan to explain his method so that everyone would understand and by Evan's counting the cans that he iterated when moving the bar (i.e. , the measure of the first two iterations was 20 because he would count 20 cans). As a consequence, for Evan, the activity of measuring with a Smurf bar now appeared to be about structuring space. He broke off three cubes from the Smurf bar to show 23 instead of working within the third iteration to find 21, 22, and 23.

As the episode continued, Angie continued to explain her thinking:

Angie: I have a way to help Andy because he thinks like Evan before he changed his mind. You see like this is 10, but you know that, right? (*Andy nods in agreement as Angie places down the first iteration.*)11, 12, 13,..., 19, 20 (*moves bar to second iteration and counts each cube individually, pointing to the cubes as she counts. She then moves the bar to the third iteration as she continues counting.)* 21, 22, 23. So it goes two tens and three more.

Here, in grounding her explanation in the counting of the individual cans that composed the Smurf bar, Angie attempted to clarify her reasoning to Andy. As her explanation indicates, measuring involved the accumulation of distance in that iterating the bar while counting by tens was a curtailment of counting individual cans. As a consequence, it was self-evident to her that she needed to measure beyond the second iteration to specify a length of 23 cans.

It is important to note that the teacher's overriding concern in this episode was not to ensure that all the students measured correctly. In fact, the teacher frequently called on students who had reasoned differently about problems in order to make it possible for the class to reflect on and discuss the quantities being established by measuring. Her goal was that measuring with the Smurf bar would come to signify the measure of the distance iterated thus far rather than the single iteration that they made as they said a particular number word. Her focus was therefore on the development of mathematical reasoning that would make it possible for the students to measure correctly with understanding.

After the students had measured several planks and other items with the Smurf bar, the teacher explained that the Smurfs decided they needed a new measurement tool so they would not have to carry any cans around with them each time they wanted to measure. In the ensuing discussion, several students proposed creating a paper strip that would be the same length as a Smurf bar and marked with the increments for the cans. Students then made their own *ten-strips* and used them to solve a range of problems grounded in the Smurf narrative. During a discussion about the meaning of measuring by iterating a ten-strip, the teacher taped several of the students' strips end-to-end on the white board to show successive placements of the strip. In doing so, she created a *measurement strip* 100 cans long. Crucially, this new tool emerged from, and was consistent with, the students' current ways of measuring. As a consequence, they could all immediately use prepared measurement strips with little difficulty. They simply placed the strip along the dimensions of the object to be measured and counted along the strip by ten or sometimes by five.

All the instructional activities we have discussed thus far involved measuring the lengths or heights of physical objects. The transition from the measurement sequence to the mental computation and estimation sequence occurred when the students began to use the measurement strip to reason about the relationship between the lengths or heights of objects that were not physically present. One of the first instructional activities in the mental computation and estimation sequence involved an experiment the Smurfs were conducting with sunflower seeds. The teacher explained that the

Smurfs typically grew sunflowers that were 51 cans tall. However, in one of the experiments the sunflowers grew only 45 cans tall. Students were then asked to find the difference in heights and were given only a measurement strip. As a consequence, they could not create objects 45 cans and 51 cans long to represent the sunflowers, but instead had to reason with the strip.

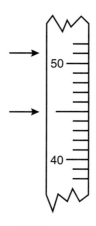

Fig. 8.3. Measurement strip marked to show 51 and 45 cans

Students first worked in pairs to solve the task and then discussed their solution in the whole-class setting. The teacher began by placing a vertical measurement strip on the wall and asking students to mark both 51 cans and 45 cans (see fig. 8.3).

An issue that emerged almost immediately in the discussion was that of whether to count the lines or the spaces on the strip.

Teacher: Think about how you would show us how much shorter that seed (*points to the 45*) grew than the regular seed. Preston, how would you show that?

Preston: Here (*points to 51*) all the way down to here (*points to 45*) would be seven.

Teacher: Can you show me the seven?

Preston: Here is 51 and here is 45 and here is 1, 2, 3, 4, 5, 6, 7 (*points to lines as he counts*).

Pat: I have a question. You are supposed to count the spaces, not the lines.

At this point, the teacher asked Pat to explain why he thought you use the spaces and not the lines.

Pat: The cans of food are bigger than the lines, and you are trying to figure out how many cans, not lines.

Teacher: So when you say *space,* you think of this space as a can of food (*points*)?

Pat: And that's how much, and you're trying to figure out how much that is.

For Pat, reasoning with the measurement strip was related to the prior activity of measuring with a Smurf bar. As a consequence, the spaces signified Unifix cubes or cans for him. In contrast, reasoning with the strip did not appear to be grounded in prior activity for Preston, and he was simply trying to figure out a way to use it to solve the task at hand. However, Pat's explanation led Preston to modify how he reasoned with the strip. This is evidenced by the fact that Preston asked if he could use a can or cube to help him solve the task. He placed a single cube on the measurement strip and iterated the spaces between 45 and 51 to arrive at the answer of six rather than seven.

> *Preston:* I changed my mind. I changed my mind because the lines are smaller than the squares [cubes].

Immediately after the exchange between Pat and Preston, Andy gave an explanation that involved reasoning about the quantities in a different way.

> *Andy:* If you went from 50 down five, you'd get to 45 cans. Think 5 less than 50. But you are really one more, so it's six, since it's 1 more than 50.

Andy's explanation indicates that for him, as for Pat, 45 and 51 signified distances from the bottom of the strip measured in cans. The task for him was to find the difference between these two quantities, and he did so by reasoning with the strip. We would, in fact, argue that the strip supported the shift he made from a counting to a thinking strategy solution in which he reasoned that 50 to 45 was five, so 51 to 45 is six.

It is important to note that the solution method offered by Andy fit with the teacher's pedagogical agenda of supporting students' development of increasingly sophisticated strategies. However, the teacher was also aware of differences in her students' reasoning and did not want to create a situation where students simply imitated strategies that they did not understand. As a result, she continued to acknowledge the differing ways that students reasoned about tasks while highlighting solution methods that fit with her agenda. This served to support proactively the development of the students' mathematical reasoning. The diversity in students' reasoning as they used the measurement strip can be seen in an episode that occurred one week later. The students were first asked to work in pairs to find their height and their partner's height. Once the results had been recorded on the white board, the teacher asked the students to find the difference in heights for each of the pairs. Students were not instructed *how* to solve this task, and several ways of reasoning emerged.

When students returned to whole-class discussion, the teacher asked them to share ways that they found the difference between Luis's and Andy's heights, which were 67 cans and 72 cans respectively. She then marked both 67 and 72 on the measurement strip. Mari first explained that she and her partner had found a difference of six cans. Mae appeared to anticipate how they had reasoned and asked:

> *Mae:* Did you count the 67 or did you go on to 68?
> *Mari:* We counted the 67.

At this point, Mari went to the measurement strip that was posted on the wall and took a Smurf bar to try to determine exactly how many cans would fit between 67 and 72. For her, it seemed essential that she actually measure with cans or cubes. As she did so, Andy offered a more sophisticated solution.

> *Andy:* I knew that 7 plus 3 would get us, uh, 67, plus 3 would get us to 70. I was two more than 70, and I knew that 3 and 2 was 5.

In contrast to Andy and Luis's going-through-ten solution, Hanna explained:

> *Hanna:* I just counted on my fingers, and I agree with Luis and Andy.

As other students discussed the problem, Mari continued to build a Unifix cube bar the length of the difference. When she finished, she counted the five cubes in the bar.

> *Teacher:* Mari, is that the same five as Andy?
>
> *Andy:* It's the same five. Mari did it by ones and I did it by 3 and 2 'cause it's easier to go 3 more.

In this particular episode, a variety of ways of reasoning emerged while discussing solutions to the task. As before, the teacher continued to acknowledge the differing ways of reasoning. This diversity continued to support students' ability to construct personally meaningful ways to reason mathematically.

Later in the instructional sequence, an empty number line—a line without any markings—was introduced as a means of reasoning about quantities while also providing a way for students to record their thinking. The empty number line evolved from activities with the measurement strip and was initially used to show the relationships between quantities. For instance, the teacher asked students to show *about* where 50 cans would be. They then compared that to *about* where 30 cans might be. In the process of whole-class discussions, students began to use the empty number line as a means of explaining how they reasoned about the relative magnitude of certain quantities. The emphasis in these activities was not on marking numbers in an exact place, but on using the relative positions to let the number line represent how they had reasoned about the task. In other words, students might reason that 50 is about in the middle since it is half of 100. Thirty would be a little more than halfway between the beginning of the empty number line and 50. As the sequence progressed, changes in the ways the students reasoned with the empty number line became evident. For instance, on the third day that the students used the empty number line, the following task was posed: *Maria has 87 cookies in a box. How many will be left if she eats 18 of them?* After the students had worked individually, Angie shared her solution method at the white board during whole-class discussion by first marking eight "jumps" of ten and a "jump" of seven to show 87 (see fig. 8.4). She then worked backwards from the 87 to take away eighteen cookies by removing the seven, a group of ten, and one more (see fig. 8.5). She indicated

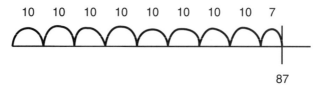

Fig. 8.4. Angie's explanation of 87 cookies

which cookies she took away by circling the eighteen that had been eaten, as shown in figure 8.5.

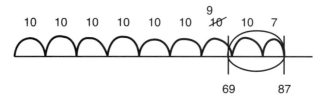

Fig. 8.5. Angie's explanation of 87 cookies and 18 are eaten

When she finished, Pat asked, "Why did you take the 1 from the 9?"

> *Angie:* I want to take away that 7 (*points*) and that 10 (*points*) and 1 more 'cause if I just took away the 10 and then 7 that would be 17, right? And it says here you want to take 18, so I need one more.
>
> *Pat:* Oh, I understand.

In response to the teacher's request for other solutions, Michael simply marked 87 on the empty number line and then drew a jump of ten to 77 and a jump of eight to 69 (see fig. 8.6).

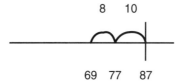

Fig. 8.6. Michael's solution for 87 cookies take away 18 cookies

In both of the examples above, the students' thinking seemed to reflect their prior activity of measuring with the Smurf bar and reasoning with the measurement strip. In Angie's case, it was important to first create the 87 by iterating the tens, whereas Michael was able to take the 87 as a given quantity.

To present the next task, the teacher showed a picture of 17 cups and 48 saucers and asked the students to determine how many more cups were needed so that there would be the same number of cups and saucers. Mari explained her solution at the white board by first drawing jumps of ten and seven and marking 17. She then continued to draw jumps of ten until she reached 47 and finally drew a jump of one to get to 48 (see fig. 8.7).

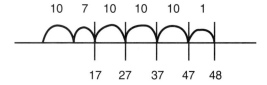

Fig. 8.7. Mari's solution to the cups and saucers problem

In discussing Mari's solution method, students questioned how what she had drawn helped solve the task.

Pat: How can this be 48? When you put the ten and seven together you only have 31.

Mari: I mean this whole thing to be the saucers, and I'm using the 17 twice. I'm using the 17 to be cups and then put it with all this (*points to entire drawing*) to make 48 saucers.

Pat: Yeah, but I can't tell them apart. How can you tell these are cups and the whole thing is saucers? I don't think you can use the same thing twice.

Hanna then volunteered that she could help Pat understand Mari's reasoning.

Hanna: I know that she has 17 cups there (*points to 17*) and altogether that's the saucers, but you have to count to 17 to get the saucers.

At this point, the teacher asked Mari to show where the cups were on her number line. In response, Mari drew the arc from the beginning of the number line to 17 and labeled it "17" as shown in figure 8.8. She then continued by drawing an arc above the line, explaining that this showed the 48 saucers (see fig. 8.8). The teacher then asked the class, "Where are the extras, the cups we need?" Evan came to the white board and marked an arc on Mari's line that he labeled "31" (see fig. 8.8).

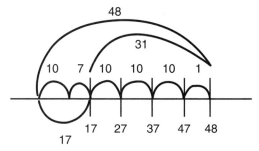

Fig. 8.8. Notating on Mari's number line

Thus for Evan, as for the other students, Mari's number line came to signify a relationship between quantities of cups and saucers. Further, the drawing served as a means of argumentation throughout the exchange. As a consequence, the discussion focused on how Mari had interpreted the problem rather than merely the calculational steps she took to produce an answer. The next student to explain his solution, Trent, took 17 as a given quantity and drew jumps from 17 to 48 to find how many more cups were needed (see fig. 8.9).

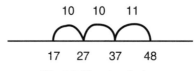

Fig. 8.9. Trent's solution

The teacher asked if someone could look at Trent's drawing and explain what he was thinking.

> *John:* You need to go from 17 to figure how many more to make it equal.

Although John did not refer to cups and saucers, his explanation indicates that Trent had calculated with the number line in order to equalize his two quantities.

These episodes indicate the value of classroom discussions in which students not only explain their own reasoning but also reason about others' solution methods. As a result, the solution process, not the answer, is what is valued. Students then come to understand the obligation to be able to represent their thinking so that others might understand. In this way, the drawings provide an opportunity for students to reflect on and discuss various ways of reasoning about the situation. It is in the course of such exchanges that students come to understand the importance of representing their thinking so that it might be comprehensible to others. These representations then make it possible for students to reflect on and compare not just different calculational processes but different ways of interpreting and reasoning about situations.

In examining the students' written work for this particular task, it is interesting to note that they used a variety of methods in addition to those shared in the whole-class discussions. For example, Susan found the difference between 17 and 48 by first making a jump of 1 to 18 and then making jumps of ten until she reached 48 (see fig. 8.10a). Mae, however, found the difference by making a jump of 20 to 37 and then a jump of eleven to 48 (see fig. 8.10b).

For her part, Hanna first made a sequence of jumps to reach 48 and used these to find the difference between 48 and 17 (see fig. 8.11a). Luis's solution did not involve the use of the number line. Instead, he wrote a series of number sentences to express his reasoning, as shown in figure 8.11b.

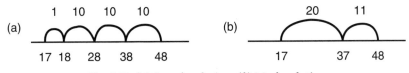

Fig. 8.10. (*a*) Susan's solution; (*b*) Mae's solution

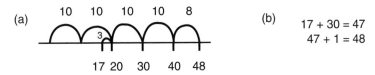

Fig. 8.11. (*a*) Hanna's solution; (*b*) Luis's solution

These examples indicate that by the end of the teaching experiment, the students had developed a range of personally meaningful ways to reason about quantities. The teacher's role in supporting discussions that focused on the meanings that the students' records of their thinking had for them was crucial to this process.

CONCLUSION

In this paper, we have highlighted students' mathematical reasoning while focusing specifically on measurement. In doing so, we have noted the importance both of discussions in which students explain and justify their thinking and of carefully sequenced instructional activities. These interrelated aspects of instruction play an essential role in supporting students' development of powerful ways of reasoning. As we have noted, the intent of the instructional sequence on measuring was that students might come to reason mathematically about space and distance, and not merely measure accurately. In other words, students would be able to reason quantitatively about their measuring activity instead of simply using measurement tools correctly. This reasoning then served as the starting point for the second instructional sequence, which aimed to support their construction of relationships between numbers to 100. In addition, students seemed to reconceptualize their understanding of what it means to know and do mathematics in school as they solved tasks and discussed their reasoning. The crucial norm that became established was that of explaining and justifying solutions in quantitative terms. We find this significant because the students' reconceptualization of mathematics went hand in hand with their development of increasingly sophisticated ways of reasoning. In particular, preliminary analysis of the data indicates that students who, at the beginning of the classroom teaching experiment, were unable to reason quantitatively with numbers up to 20 were, by the end of the experiment, able to reason in a variety of ways with numbers to 100.

In our view, the students' ability to act as increasingly autonomous members of the classroom community and their development of powerful ways of reasoning were reflexively related. Initially in this classroom, the teacher judged the value of students' contributions. By the end of the teaching experiment, the students could make these judgments and justify why their contributions were important. This is significant pedagogically and mathematically because it constitutes a change in the way many teachers perceive both their role and that of their students. This was an important part of the culture established in the project classroom and contributed to the students' development of mathematical power.

REFERENCES

McClain, Kay, and Paul Cobb. "The Role of Imagery and Discourse in Supporting Students' Mathematical Development." In *Mathematical Talk and School Learning: What, Why, and How,* edited by Maggie Lampert and Merrie Blunk. Cambridge: Cambridge University Press, in press.

Thompson, Alba, and Patrick W. Thompson. "Talking about Rates Conceptually, Part II: Mathematical Knowledge for Teaching." *Journal for Research in Mathematics Education* 27 (1996): 2–24.

9

Mathematics Is for the Birds
Reasoning for a Reason

Phyllis Whitin

David J. Whitin

A_{RE} math and science cousins?" asked Ashley, after having calculated mathematical information for a scientific study of birds. To us (the teacher and her university collaborator), her question highlighted the value of engaging children in authentic problem-solving situations. By grappling with mathematical concepts in a meaningful context, children use reasoning for a reason.

Children in this fourth-grade class watched birds daily at a small feeder that was attached to their second-story classroom window. An investigation of seed preference led the class to explore two mathematical concepts, ratio and average. Throughout the study, we adults came to appreciate more deeply the role of a shared, collaborative investigation and the natural emergence of mathematics in scientific inquiry.

When the children arrived at school in August, they found the bird feeder filled with a seed mixture purchased from a bird specialty store. The mixture, which included black oil sunflower seed, safflower seed, and white millet, was designed to attract a wide variety of birds. However, when we checked the feeder one day to add seed, we found that the millet was virtually uneaten. The sunflower seeds had completely disappeared, and a good number of safflower seeds remained. We decided to bring the problem to the class. We emptied the contents of the feeder into a clear plastic cup and filled a second cup with fresh seed for the children to compare. We asked them, "What do you notice about the way the birds are eating our seed mixture? Why do you think this is happening?"

Catherine commented, "Since all the sunflower seeds are gone, their favorite seed is sunflower seed." Colby added that he and Jesse had read that cardinals really like sunflower seeds. However, Cruz pointed out that he had seen several birds picking up the safflower seed. The children could clearly see the type of seed each bird ate as they sat at the observation table next to the window. Although children had watched individual birds selecting specific seeds, no one reported having seen a bird eat millet. Jesse offered a reason why no millet was eaten. He had observed at home that mourning doves eat millet on the ground, but they do not come to feeders. Given this information, the children decided that we should only put sunflower and safflower seed in the feeder. However, before deciding how much of each would make an ideal mixture, we needed more data. We and the children decided to track the kind of seed that each bird ate by observing the birds more systematically. In this way we would have more specific data for making our decision.

COLLECTING AND ANALYZING DATA

The next day the class collected the necessary data. With adult assistance the children took turns watching as each bird came and selected one seed at a time. They recorded the name of the species and the number of each seed eaten (fig. 9.1 shows an excerpt of this data). At the end of the day, results were typed and photocopied for the children. We then invited the students to share their observations about the chart with the class. They noticed that three different species visited the feeders: chickadees, titmice, and brown-headed nuthatches. A quick glance down the columns revealed that chickadees came more than any other bird, and more sunflower seeds were consumed than safflower. However, the titmice selected safflower seeds more often. The nuthatches ate both seeds, but preferred safflower. Intrigued, the children decided to count the total number of each kind of seed. They found that 57 safflower and 117 sunflower seeds were eaten during the entire observation period (although some children miscounted and had slightly different totals). For convenience, we rounded 57 to 60, and 117 to 120. Whitney and a few of her classmates studied the chart further and classified the data by differentiating among individual species of birds:

Chickadee	Tufted Titmouse	Nuthatch
Sun – 85	Sun – 2	Sun – 30
Saf – 8	Saf – 8	Saf – 43

This finer distinction provided us with additional information as we considered our next steps. It was clear that the sunflower seed was overwhelmingly popular, but Whitney's data helped us realize that eliminating safflower seed altogether would restrict the number of species at the feeder. For instance, the tufted titmouse and the nuthatch, which ate more safflower than sunflower, might come less frequently. Kyle provided another perspective for the decision to maintain both seeds. Since the data were assembled chronologically, he calculated seed consumption at different times. Kyle discovered that early in the day sunflower seed consumption outnumbered safflower 37 to 13 (more than three times as much), whereas later in the day the difference was quite small, with 28 sunflower seeds versus 19 safflower. Kyle's analysis showed the class a second reason to offer both varieties: to attract as many birds as possible throughout different times of the day.

The chart of bird seed consumption was particularly intriguing to Jennifer. She took the data home and spent two evenings working on a graph to display the information. When she finally brought the graph to school (fig. 9.2) the children appreciated seeing the data in a new way. Ryan commented, "You can really see how much the chickadees came, and how much the titmice and the nuthatches came." By classifying the data according to species, as well as by seed preference (as Whitney had done), Jennifer showed two layers of data simultaneously. Thus, her graph enabled us all to compare seed preference within a species and across species. For instance, Jennifer noticed the difference across species when she wrote, "The nuthatch and the titmouse like more safflower than they do the sunflower. The chickadee likes more sunflower than they do of safflower." Her graph helped the class pay more attention to the less preferred seed (safflower) and notice how it was eaten by each species. It was very easy to see that the nuthatch and titmouse actually preferred the safflower; this information reinforced our commitment to continue to offer both kinds of seeds to the birds. The other relationship that this graph highlighted was the ratio of seed preference within a species. For instance, if we wanted to attract tufted titmice only, we might try putting out a mixture of 4:1, safflower to sunflower seeds, because Jennifers's data show an 8:2 ratio of seed consumption. Jennifer's graph helped the class see that the same data displayed in a different way can reveal new relationships and invite additional interpretations. In fact, all the children's comments highlighted different features of the data, and each view contributed to an informed decision-making process. We found that reasoning is enhanced in a collaborative community.

Bird	Seed
ch	sf
ch	sf
ch	sf
ch	sf
ch	sf
ttm	sf
ch	sf
ch	sf
nt	saf
ch	sf
nt	saf
nt	saf
nt	saf
nt	sf
ttm	saf
ttm	saf
ch	sf
nt	saf
ch	sf
nt	sf
nt	saf
nt	sf
ch	sf
ch	sf

KEY
BIRD
CH = Chickadee
NT = Nuthatch
TTM = Tufted Titmouse
SEED
SF = Sunflower
SAF = Safflower

Fig. 9.1. Birdseed consumption data for one day

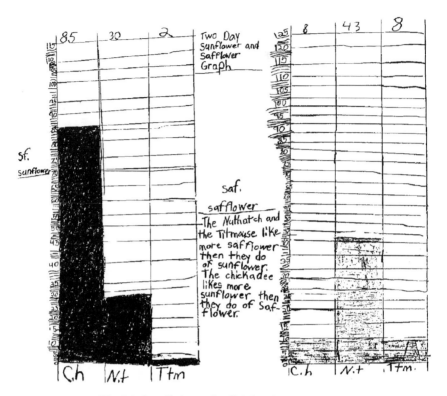

Fig. 9.2. Jennifer's graph of birdseed consumption

Determining an Appropriate Ratio

The class was concerned about attracting a variety of species but did not want to waste any seed. We challenged the children to think about how these data could help us develop a better ratio of seed. First, we asked them to describe what they noticed about the rounded numbers of 60 and 120. Ryan remarked, "I noticed something. Sixty is half of 120. Exactly half of 120, 'cause if you had 60 + 60 = 120, or 60 × 2 = 120."

David (the university collaborator) agreed. "If you took exactly half of the sunflower, that would be safflower." Since David wanted to avoid the tedious counting of individual seeds to create this mixture of 2:1, he showed the children a cylindrical liter container and asked them to consider how they could use Ryan's idea to measure. Sara suggested that we fill the entire container with sunflower seeds and half of the container with safflower seeds to show this ratio of 2 to 1. In this way she expressed the numerical proportion of 120:60 as a ratio using volume.

Ross was concerned that Sara's strategy would result in too much seed for the feeder to hold. Indicating about 1/3 of the container, he suggested, "We could fill about this much with safflower and the rest with sunflower." His explanation showed this same ratio within a single unit of measure.

After a few other children had contributed similar ideas, we asked the group to record their explanations of the ideal mixture in their journals. We wanted all the students to commit their ideas to paper so that we could better understand the thinking of each child. When we reviewed the journals, we once again realized the importance of the group conversation. Gavin drew a diagram showing one container divided into 2/3 and 1/3, as Ross had demonstrated. Like Ryan, he used a numerical relationship to strengthen his argument: "Because 4 + 4 = 8, so 40 + 40 = 80. You put 80 sunflower seeds in and put 40 safflower" (fig. 9.3).

Gavin

Because 4 + 4 = 8 so 40 + 40 = 80. You put 80 sunflower seeds in and put 40 safflower.

Fig. 9.3. Gavin's diagram and explanation of 2:1 ratio of sunflower seeds to safflower seeds

Selita also drew a single measure divided roughly into a 2/3, 1/3 proportion. She wrote, "I think it is more half of sunflower and less half of safflower." Selita was not familiar with the terminology of thirds, but her drawing and her explanation of "more half" and "less half" demonstrated her understanding of the necessary ratio. Sara, however, reiterated her explanation of one cup of sunflower and half a cup of safflower but also reasoned that this same ratio could be applied to a new set of numbers: "If we started with one hundred sunflower and fifty safflower, it would be even at the end of the day." Each child made sense of the ratio in a personal way by drawing on different aspects of the group conversation.

Despite the general agreement of the ideal ratio, however, the children realized that our decision had limitations. Sara wondered if the birds had chosen sunflower simply because there was an ample supply in the feeder. She mused, "If we put more safflower than sunflower, would [the birds] eat more safflower?" A. J. remarked that new species of birds might come if we put out more safflower seed. Our present mixture might be good for these three species, yet restrictive to other birds. Sara added that we could not tell if a single bird was choosing safflower more often, or if several birds of the same species were sharing the same preference. Maybe our generalizations of which species preferred which seed were inaccurate. All these comments illustrate that there are no clear-cut solutions to real-life problems. By choosing the ratio of 2:1, we might be restricting other possibilities. It was important, however, that the children weighed these factors as they came to a decision. Realizing that decision making is a tentative process that may not be free from doubt is a necessary part of reasoning.

DEBATING THE BENEFITS OF AN AVERAGE

Given the overall seed consumption of 2:1 (sunflower to safflower), the children finally decided to use that ratio as the guiding principle for our own seed mixture. Since our container held about 300 cubic centimeters (cm^3) of seed, the children put out 200 cm^3 of sunflower seeds and 100 cm^3 of safflower seeds. After three days the children noticed that a significant amount of seed had been eaten, so we dumped what was left into the liter container and found that 225 cm^3 of seed remained. The children calculated that 75 cm^3 had been eaten in three days. The teacher, Phyllis, then asked, "If the birds ate the same amount each day, how much of that 75 cm^3 would they have eaten each day?" After her students determined that daily amount to be 25 cm^3, Phyllis asked, "Do we know for sure that it was 25 cm^3 each day?"

Jon was the first of several students to disagree with this amount: "I don't think they did eat that amount each day. Some day they might be hungrier than another day. Like they're going to migrate soon, and they want to store up one day so they can go the next." When asked what the seed consumption might have been, Jon said, "Maybe 17 on one day and more the other days." Jon was disagreeing with the average of 25 cm^3 because it did not take into account important contextual factors, such as migratory behavior. We had been observing a ruby-throated hummingbird at our other feeder since the beginning of school, and we assumed that it had just left on its long migratory journey to South America. Although these three seed-eating birds do not migrate for the winter, Jon's reasoning made good sense. He was tying this recent experience of the hummingbird to this new problem of seed consumption. His reasoning did highlight for us the caveat that averages do not always take into account certain contextual considerations.

Ross realized that there are many three-addend possibilities for a total of 75. He used what he knew about number combinations to suggest, "Sometimes they might not have eaten anything, like 10, 65, and nothing." His example pointed out that sometimes an average cannot tell us the range of numbers that actually do occur in a given total.

Phyllis extended this skeptical attitude by asking, "So what good is it to say that about 25 cm^3 was eaten each day? How does an average help us?" Jon responded, "It's helpful because it's not exactly right and it's not exactly wrong—it's just on the borderline. It tells you what the birds did usually." Although Jon disagreed with the daily 25 cm^3 amount at the beginning of the conversation, he nevertheless felt it was more right than wrong: an average doesn't really exist (it's wrong), but it's probably fairly close to what happened (it's right). From this perspective, Jon reasoned that an average was on the borderline between right and wrong.

Kyle explained the advantage of an average in another way: "It's good because you can already tell what it's mostly of, and then if it might change, then you already know you don't have to go way up...we'd already have a jump start because we already know from last week we had 75." Jennifer used the field of science to extend Kyle's idea: "An average might help us predict what it might be. Like scientists do—they sometimes predict, and then they find out the real answer. So maybe we can probably predict, and the next person who watches out the window can see if it's 25 or not." She reasoned that an average enables people to predict so that future bird watchers could have a mathematical framework in mind as they collected new data.

The children's comments highlight slightly different benefits of an average: an average acts as a starting point, or "jump start," for understanding new data; it acts as a hypothetical point for thinking about what is "usual," as a point of comparison, and as a prediction or mental framework. Although the children had not yet been formally introduced to this concept of average, they made sense of it themselves because it was embedded in a meaningful context. They were also learning to be critical consumers of statistical information. If we strive to build democratic classrooms, then we must allow children to analyze the limitations of mathematical concepts. In this way learners develop a healthy skepticism toward statistical information (Paulos 1988).

A FINAL REFLECTION

This investigation is not merely a story about birds. Rather, it is a story of nurturing mathematical thinking in authentic contexts. It is important to step back and examine the conditions that supported this investigation in order to recognize their universal application:

1. Mathematical reasoning emerges from real contexts. Just as the children described in this article confronted the problem of devising an appropriate

seed mixture, children in other classrooms can grapple with problems that are pertinent to their own interests. In one school, for instance, children were involved in collecting data about their favorite kinds of books to help the librarian decide which books to order for the following year.

2. Mathematical reasoning is cultivated by teachers who value a skeptical stance (Whitin and Whitin 1997). It is the role of the teacher to support skepticism by raising such critical questions as these: What information are we still not sure about? What relationships do our data not reveal? What questions did we fail to ask? What information did we never track? Mathematical reasoning is enhanced when learners take nothing for granted and become vigilant skeptics of numerical information.

3. Mathematical reasoning is nurtured in collaborative communities. In this classroom children valued multiple interpretations of data, described the mathematical concept of average in their own language, and built on one another's ideas. Teachers can support this diversity of response by asking open-ended questions, such as, What do you notice about the data? What do you find interesting? What are different ways you might display these data?

We began this article with a child's question, "Are math and science cousins?" We conclude by answering emphatically, "Yes, they are." Mathematical reasoning develops best in real contexts, as children confront real issues and invent strategies for addressing them. Teachers can support this inquiring attitude by capitalizing on authentic problems and by encouraging children to be skeptical consumers as well as collaborative peers. It is in these ways that we can nurture mathematical reasoning in our classrooms.

REFERENCES

Paulos, John. *Innumeracy: Mathematical Illiteracy and Its Consequences.* New York: Hill and Wang, 1988.

Whitin, Phyllis, and David J. Whitin. *Inquiry at the Window: Pursuing the Wonders of Learners.* Portsmouth, N.H.: Heinemann Books, 1997.

10

Mathematical Reasoning during Small-Group Problem Solving

Alice F. Artzt

Shirel Yaloz-Femia

FOUR fifth graders in a New York City middle school—Brian, Caroline, Richard—and Simone, are engaged in solving the problem in figure 10.1.

A cricket is on the number line at point "1." He wants to get to point "0" but he only hop half of the remaining distance each time.

a) Where on the number line is the cricket at the first hop?
b) Where on the number line is the cricket at the second hop?
c) Where on the number line is the cricket at the tenth hop?
d) Where on the number line is the cricket at the hundredth hop?
e) Where on the number line is the cricket at the nth hop?
f) Does the cricket ever get to the point labeled 0?
   Explain why or why not.

Fig. 10.1. The Cricket Problem

As the students' discourse will show, five minutes into their problem-solving session, the students have recreated the problem in a most interesting and unexpected way:

We would like to thank Barbara Nimerofsky and Frances Curcio for allowing us to work with their fifth grade students at Louis Armstrong Middle School in East Elmhurst, New York.

Richard: But what I want to know is when it jumped halfway, how come it said it can only jump half of the remaining distance? Why didn't they make it on the next half?

Brian: Because it's still cutting it in half.

Simone: It lost most of its energy. It lost all its energy so it can only go a little. Because it's a very small, small cricket. And this cricket, every time it jumps, it loses half of its body. It's a really, really cool cricket.

Richard: So by the time it gets there it has just a head?

Simone: It has a microscopic body. Yeah!

Brian: So, let's say like it gets smaller and smaller on each hop so it can't make it all the way. Let's say that the cricket, when it got here it got really small so it couldn't go that far again. So he had to go half of what he did before and again half of that.

When we first heard this discussion, we examined it from a problem-solving perspective and thought that it was an example of students trying to *understand* the problem, and that in fact they were not doing it very well. Specifically, our initial reaction was that the students were digressing and needed a better clarification of the problem. That is, as one student, Caroline, later clarified: "*He's* not getting smaller. His *jumps* are getting smaller." However, as we have been thinking more about the meaning of mathematical reasoning, we have come to appreciate the students' ideas as a very rich example of reasoning. This episode, among others, has created our desire to revisit problem solving within small groups from a mathematical reasoning perspective.

The power of having students learn through discussing mathematics with one another has been well documented (Artzt 1996; Artzt and Armour-Thomas 1992; Curcio and Artzt 1992, 1998; Lambdin 1993; Webb 1989). In recent years research has shown many advantages of the small-group setting for problem solving (Qin, Johnson, and Johnson 1995). Artzt and Armour-Thomas (1992) have documented the fact that when students work in small groups to solve a mathematical problem, their cognitive behaviors mirror those of expert mathematical problem solvers (Schoenfeld 1987). Little work, however, has been done that specifically examines mathematical reasoning in a small group setting, and the role of mathematical reasoning as an integral part of problem solving. The purpose of this article is to examine the mathematical reasoning behaviors of a group of students solving the cricket problem and to see how these behaviors are integrated into the problem-solving process. We will also share how small groups can be used to increase the mathematical reasoning of students within classrooms.

After first defining the terms used to examine problem solving and reasoning, an overview of the students' problem-solving session will be presented.

This is followed by descriptions and examples of the dialogue of the fifth-grade students that are examined to determine where mathematical reasoning is evident within the problem-solving session. Finally, a discussion will be given of the relationship between mathematical reasoning and problem solving and how these behaviors can be enhanced through the use of rich problems assigned to students working in small groups.

MATHEMATICAL REASONING WITHIN THE PROBLEM-SOLVING PROCESS

In order to describe the students' problem-solving behaviors the following categories from Artzt and Armour-Thomas (1992) were used: *read, understand, explore, analyze, plan, implement, verify, watch,* and *listen*. In order to detect instances of reasoning within these categories we used the definition of reasoning presented by O'Daffer and Thornquist (1993): "*Mathematical reasoning* is part of mathematical thinking that involves forming generalizations and drawing valid conclusions about ideas and how they are related" (p. 43). We also used the criteria in NCTM's *Curriculum and Evaluation Standards* (1989) that indicate that mathematical reasoning is demonstrated when students (*a*) use trial and error and working backward to solve a problem, (*b*) make and test conjectures, (*c*) create inductive and deductive arguments, (*d*) look for patterns to arrive at generalizations, and (*e*) use spatial and logical reasoning.

In order to set the stage for understanding the details of how the reasoning behaviors of the students were embedded within their problem-solving endeavor, an overview follows of the four students' problem-solving session as they worked together for thirty minutes.

The students began by *reading* the problem. Each student made statements showing that he or she was trying to *understand* what the problem was asking for. They questioned the length of the given line, and they specified that the cricket would always jump one-half of the distance from its present location to the point 0. Brian, Caroline, and Simone did some *analysis* regarding the relevance of the actual length of the given line. They reasoned that it did not matter how long the line was since, after jumping half the remaining distance each time, it would end up being very close to the point 0 anyway.

Brian, Richard, and Simone then engaged in *exploration,* which led to a *plan,* which led to an *implementation,* which continued for several minutes. During their exploration, they questioned how the cricket would look each time it reached a new point. That is, they believed the cricket itself would be shrinking in size or losing part of its body. To get a better picture of what was happening, Simone suggested a *plan* to draw a long line across the room and "see if there's a pattern when it gets smaller." Richard suggested a different *plan* to draw a bar graph of each successive remaining length. The students agreed to go with Richard's idea and they all engaged in this *implementation* by contributing to the drawing of the bar graph.

As the bar graph did not lead them to their solution (details to be explained later), the students returned to more *exploration* and *analysis* of the problem until they arrived at a new *plan*. During their *exploration* the students experimented with the idea of multiplying fractions. But they got involved in the computation and strayed from the meaning of the problem. Simone brought them back on track when she tried to *analyze* some of the results of the *exploration* by looking for a pattern that would help them answer part (e) of the original question. Since during their exploration the students mistakenly ended up multiplying each successive fraction by itself, the pattern at which they arrived was "*n* times *n*." Confused by this result, Simone switched gears and suggested a *plan* to fold a piece of paper to model the hopping of the cricket.

During the remainder of the problem-solving session, the students *implemented* this *plan*, did more *analysis* of the problem, and finally *verified* their results. That is, the repeated folding suggested that even if they were not able to make the fold, there was a left-over length that *could* be folded. They engaged in an interesting *analysis* of the problem that centered on the fact that this was really a theoretical problem, not to be confused by the real context of the problem (although they did not discuss it in these terms). Basically, the students realized that in reality the cricket has an actual dimension and would therefore have to cross the point 0. But, theoretically, the cricket is represented by a point and would therefore never cross the point 0.

MATHEMATICAL REASONING DETECTED DURING THE PROBLEM-SOLVING SESSION

In order to describe the reasoning that was detected during the problem-solving session, we will give actual examples of the students' dialogue. The following problem-solving behaviors and related instances of reasoning are not necessarily presented in the order in which they occurred. These behaviors occurred intermittently throughout the session.

Understanding the problem. During the beginning minutes the students made efforts to understand that the cricket can only hop half of the remaining distance each time it hops. One example of students trying to understand the problem is provided at the beginning of the chapter.

During this episode the students used their reasoning to try to make sense of the problem by justifying *why* the cricket would only be able to jump half the distance of each previous jump. After all, there would have to be a good reason why the cricket would have such a restriction placed on it, such as it was shrinking in size because of loss of energy.

Exploring. In the middle of their problem-solving session the students began to explore some mathematical ideas involving fractions. Although students were monitoring this exploration, it was not done with the consistency needed to save the group from arriving at a meaningless solution. Caroline proposed the incorrect idea of multiplying one-sixteenth times one-sixteenth. Richard monitored her arithmetic and made the correct comment that $16 \times 16 = 256$ rather than 266. As we can see from the dialogue below, Caroline then returned to examine her reasoning and do the problem again. Brian reacted positively to her idea of multiplying by 1/2, but rather than multiplying 1/16 by 1/2, he used the previous mistaken result of 1/256, referred to it as 256, and then suggested multiplying that by 1/2.

> *Caroline:* Okay. I'm going to do this again. One-fourth, right? But I want one half of one-fourth, right? So then you'd multiply and get one-eighth. Then you keep on going like that.
>
> *Brian:* Oh. I see what you are saying. Instead of putting one hundred, I mean 256 times 256, you would put 256 times one-half.
>
> *Caroline:* Yeah!
>
> *Richard:* Oh! That's good.

Caroline used good mathematical reasoning when she returned to test her original incorrect conjecture to multiply one-sixteenth by one-sixteenth. She offered a logical argument that suggested repeated multiplying by one half. This caused Brian to revise Caroline's original conjecture and suggest that they multiply 256 times one-half. It appeared that Brian was following Caroline's line of reasoning and agreed with it. However, he acted too quickly and abandoned his reasoning when he made his incorrect suggestion that made use of a previous incorrect result. Unfortunately, when Brian suggested multiplying "256 times one-half," Caroline and Richard agreed.

Despite the erroneous result of this exploration, it is clear that in several cases the students tried to test and judge the validity of their own and each others' arguments. Had they done this more diligently, they might have had a more successful exploration. It is also interesting to note that when the students became bogged down in the multiplication of fractions, it appeared to inhibit their mathematical reasoning of the fact that 256 times one-half made no sense in terms of this problem.

Analyzing the problem. Throughout the course of the problem-solving endeavor the students critically examined the elements of the problem. In the latter part of the session the students analyzed how the crickets' size would affect their solution.

> *Simone:* Forget my theory in the beginning. What I'm trying to say is that here is the zero point. Okay. But if he is going to jump over half and this is how big he is, he'll be jumping over half.

> *Richard:* Not his head, just his feet. The feet touches the goal post just like that.
>
> *Simone:* Oh! So look. Here is the one, and here is the zero. His legs are over here, but his head is still over here.
>
> *Brian:* This is not reality. This is a math problem.
>
> *Richard:* This problem is crazy. We can't answer it!

At this point the students have used spatial reasoning to figure out that in reality, the cricket will get to the end. This is a most interesting aspect of the problem that the students have addressed. The students have, in fact, used correct reasoning when they took the dimensions of the cricket into account and concluded that the cricket would get to the end. It is fascinating to see how these young fifth graders were able to determine that this problem required them to consider the representation of the cricket as a point having no dimension. In their own way they recognized that this is a "math problem" disconnected from reality, and that the cricket's size should probably not come into play. They also rejected their original idea that the cricket was getting smaller with each jump, as that did not fit with their knowledge about reality or mathematics. Note that these are examples of how the students made and evaluated conjectures and arguments and tried to validate their own and each others' thinking.

One might interpret Richard's final comment that the "… problem is crazy. We can't answer it!" as a negative one. However, without having the facility to express himself with correct mathematical terminology, he might have used mathematical reasoning to conclude that, given the problem as written, the problem in fact could not be answered. That is, if the cricket has dimension, then it *will* get to the end. Conversely, if the cricket has no dimension, then it *will not* get to the end. Since mathematical reasoning suggests that these conclusions cannot both be true at the same time, the problem cannot be answered and, indeed, is a crazy one!

Planning. The students came up with five different plans for solving the problem. Brian suggested the idea of using the number line to look for a pattern.

> *Brian:* I was going to say that you use the number line and then just jump half and half and then if you see a pattern from one to ten that will fit. Then we can go on like to a hundred to what it says here. And then we can keep on going then to n.

Simone and Richard discussed drawing a long line or making a graph with which they could represent the problem. Brian came up with a plan to model the problem by drawing a line on the floor and jumping like a cricket himself. Simone decided to take a piece of paper and fold it in half repeatedly.

In Brian's first plan it is evident that he was preparing to use pattern recognition as a means of arriving at a generalization and solving the problem. That is, he already had an idea of how to use inductive reasoning as a viable strategy for arriving at a solution. The remaining four plans involved methods for modeling the problem.

The students created these different models as a means of explaining their thinking. As we will see during the implementation of several of the plans, some of these models worked better than others as a means of validating their arguments regarding how far the cricket would go.

Implementing. During this problem-solving endeavor, after the students arrived at a plan they usually followed it with attempts at implementation. When the students performed an implementation systematically through monitoring and regulation, they discovered that either the plan was good and led to a reasonable solution, or it was faulty and needed some adjustment. In the case of this problem, the students monitored the implementation of most of the plans.

Brian began to implement Richard's bar graph idea. The students watched Brian draw the bars, until they got so small they were not visible. Despite a few glitches, they were on the way to noticing the pattern of multiplying each successive fraction by one-half until they got distracted by other conceptualizations that Brian and Simone presented.

> *Brian:* So they are all one-fourth.
>
> *Richard:* Yeah!
>
> Simone: It is because it's all half of a half.
>
> *Caroline:* What it really is one whole then one-half, then one-fourth, then one-eighth.
>
> *Richard:* Yeah. Cool.
>
> *Caroline:* Then one-tenth and one-twelfth.
>
> *Simone:* It is?
>
> *Caroline:* Yeah, because if you see one-half and then.
>
> *Brian:* No, it's not the one-tenth and one-twelfth.
>
> *Simone:* Yeah! But did you know that actually all of these lines are really one-half?

As the students were implementing the plan, they were reasoning about the size of each successive bar. The interesting aspect of this problem is that there are many different ways of using mathematical reasoning to determine the size of each bar.

For example, Brian's statement that each bar is one-fourth is correct in some way. That is, each bar, after the second one, is one-half of one-half. Simone's final statement represents the same type of reasoning, only in this case each bar, starting from the second, is really one-half. It is interesting that Caroline, who came up with the reasoning most likely to lead to a pattern and thus a solution to the problem, got confused and gave a final suggestion that appeared to lack reasoning. That is, by continuing her sequence incorrectly, with one-tenth and one-twelfth, it appeared that she was no longer using the correct reasoning she had used previously. It seemed that she mindlessly continued with fractions having successive even numbers in the denominator. Luckily, the other students were still monitoring the implementation using sound mathematical reasoning and caught her error. However, all the students agreed that Simone's reasoning was correct when she proclaimed that each bar was really one-half. This reasoning, although correct in some way, did not contribute to the solution of the problem. Therefore, the students were unable to realize the full potential of their plan and found themselves at a dead end in search of a new plan.

Simone carried out her plan to model the problem by repeatedly folding a piece of paper in half. This plan worked well until it became difficult to keep folding the paper.

> *Simone:* And now it's getting a little bit difficult to fold (*trying to fold it in half again*).
>
> *Richard:* But, but maybe it will probably be more easier if you bend it this way (*suggests folding it lengthwise*).
>
> *Simone:* Look, I can keep on folding this. I can keep folding this till the Messiah comes! (*putting all of her energy into folding the paper into smaller and smaller pieces*).
>
> *Richard:* What Messiah?

As Simone was implementing the paper-folding plan, Richard, Brian, and Caroline were watching attentively and trying to make sense out of what she was doing. They were able to use their spatial reasoning to understand the idea of repeated jumping of half distances. The visual nature of this model helped students reason about whether the cricket would ever reach the point 0. However, this model did not facilitate their ability to address questions (a) through (e), which focused on the numerical aspects of the problem. It seems that different models evoke different types of mathematical reasoning.

Verifying. An effective verification requires the student to examine his or her final solution and check that the answer makes sense. Although the group got sidetracked and never completed answering questions (a) through (e), through their implementation of the paper-folding plan they did determine that somehow the cricket would never get to 0. In the dialogue below, we can see that after Simone made her statement regarding the solution, the group continued to verify that, in fact, she was correct. (They refer to the folding paper model throughout.)

> *Simone:* What I'm trying to say is that it's always going to have somewhere to jump. Even if it's half of an atom.
>
> *Richard:* But how do you know that?

Simone: Look, it's like what Brian was saying. I'll continue. I'll show you (*she unfolds the paper and starts over*). He has this much to jump before he can get to one (*she holds up the paper*). Now he only has this much (*she folds the paper and holds it up.*)

Richard: But it keeps getting smaller.

Brian: Exactly. But it's still never going to get there.

Simone: I can keep on folding this until I get a million paper cuts. It's pretty difficult, you see.

Brian: It will get so tiny. Like an atom. Like a neutron.

Simone: See, I can't even do it but I still have something left to fold (*she uses all of her strength to fold the paper into smaller and smaller pieces*). I might not be able to fold it.

Brian: But it's possible. Just like it is impossible to stop folding that because it will keep on going, it is impossible for the cricket to reach the 0.

Throughout this process students were seeking to validate their own and each others' thinking. They were trying to justify their remarks so that they could be sure that their answer made sense. It is interesting to note that during this validation process they encountered similar difficulties that challenged them in their analysis of the problem. That is, in each case the physical representations they used to envision or model the problem created roadblocks that they had to overcome. For example, during the analysis, when thinking of the cricket as having actual physical dimensions, they determined that, in fact, the cricket *would* cross the point 0. During the verification, by using the physical paper-folding they were unable to continue the simulation. That is, they could only fold the piece of paper a few times. In each case, the students had to use mathematical reasoning to help them cope with the abstract nature of the problem. They had to envision a cricket as a point, and they had to envision the infinite number of points between any two points. It is remarkable to think that fifth graders are capable of such reasoning.

DISCUSSION AND IMPLICATIONS FOR TEACHING

There are many issues that can be addressed as a result of dissecting the interactions and analyzing the many instances of mathematical reasoning that were evident during this small group problem-solving effort. First, one must note that the nature of the problem certainly contributed towards the rich problem-solving interactions. The cricket problem is based on a classic problem in analysis, yet, stated in terms of the cricket, it was easy enough for students to understand. Furthermore, the problem lent itself to multiple modeling techniques. The discrepancies between the ideas arrived at through the use of the concrete models and the ideas underlying the theoretical interpretations of the problem provided a fertile ground for controversy. When students are engaged in controversy they must rely on their mathematical reasoning to validate their own or someone else's arguments. Teachers need to challenge students with interesting, complex, and worthwhile mathematical tasks that provide the necessary context for mathematical reasoning.

It should be mentioned, that if these students sounded a bit sophisticated in their thinking and approaches, it is not because they were of higher ability, but rather it is because they were part of a program that inspired mathematical reasoning and problem solving. Judging from their comments, it seemed natural for these students to want to look for a pattern so as to arrive at a generalization. It is true that the students did not demonstrate an ability to find the generalization that on the nth hop the cricket would be at the $1/2^n$ spot on the number line. However, the fact that they understood the process of inductive reasoning should demonstrate to all teachers that this level of mathematical reasoning is well within the capabilities of average fifth-grade students when they are given enough opportunities to engage in such reasoning.

The students only arrived at a solution to part (f) of the original problem. This is most interesting, since parts (a) through (e) were assigned as a means of helping students to arrive at a solution to part (f). That is, these preliminary questions were designed to be more concrete in that they involved questions regarding the exact location of the cricket after the first several jumps. It was hoped that the generalization at which they would arrive in part (e) would help them determine the answer to the question regarding whether the cricket would ever reach the point 0. Although several times the students appeared to address the first parts of the problem, each time they got bogged down in difficulties associated with arithmetic operations involving fractions. It appeared that the procedural, computational aspects of the problem presented more difficulty to the students than the mathematical reasoning they needed to answer the very abstract conceptual question. Perhaps, if teachers provide students with appropriate technology (in this case a fraction calculator), the students can overcome their difficulties with the mechanics and proceed more quickly to the higher-level activities of mathematical reasoning.

It is also interesting to note that the students did not approach the problem in an organized, sequential manner. That is, for example, not one person in the group suggested that they find the answer to part (a) before they proceed to part (b), and so on. One wonders whether, in fact, the students would have thought about question (f) differently had they done the first parts first. It is also interesting to see that the problem-solving steps also did not occur sequentially. The students, similar to expert problem solvers, returned several times to the problem-solving episodes *understanding, exploring, analyzing, planning, implementing,* and *verifying.* Inherent in these transitions from one episode to another was the underlying mathematical reasoning of the students. For example, when they could not verify a solution, they determined that they had better analyze or explore the problem further to arrive at a new way of thinking about the problem. Also, the students showed flexibility in arriving at different plans for approaching this problem. Some plans worked better than others for the students, and the mathematical reasoning they used determined which plans they would pursue. Students often tend to think that problem solving and mathematical reasoning should occur in a linear and direct fashion. They therefore become frustrated when they can't solve problems using a direct, sequential approach. It might be worthwhile to have students reflect on the processes they use during their small-group problem-solving endeavors as a means to identify where, when, and how they use mathematical reasoning. Such reflection might prove helpful to students when they are called on to solve problems such as these on their own.

The use of the small group not only provided a window into the students' mathematical reasoning but it created a natural setting within which such reasoning would flourish. The small-group setting encourages spontaneous verbalizations of students. These audible comments allow the observer to examine the problem-solving behaviors and mathematical reasoning of the students. They also encourage the other students in the group to question, ask for elaboration and explanation, and give feedback to one another. Mathematical reasoning is at the heart of discourse of this nature. It is true, however, that not all students in a group contribute at the same level. For example, in the group we examined, it appeared that Caroline and Richard had the most instances of watching and listening, whereas Brian and Simone were actively involved in the discourse at all moments. At the end of the problem-solving session one would feel relatively confident that Brian and Simone understood the problem, its solution, and the reasoning involved in supporting that solution. The teacher might, however, wish to press Caroline and Richard a bit further to determine whether they could explain the reasoning behind the group's solution. At the end of a small-group problem-solving activity such as this, the teacher might be wise to require each student to write a description of the solution and the supporting mathematical reasoning.

CONCLUDING COMMENTS

Through this investigation we were able to examine how mathematical reasoning is an integral part of problem solving. That is, it appears that mathematical reasoning underlies all aspects of the higher-level components of problem solving. Students can't understand problems, analyze problems, or plan how to approach problems without engaging in mathematical reasoning. The very act of monitoring one's own or someone else's explorations, implementations, or verifications of problems coincides with one of the defining aspects of mathematical reasoning—the justification of ideas. One can safely conclude that mathematical reasoning is embedded in the process of mathematical problem solving. Moreover, one can also conclude that just as the small-group setting is a fertile environment within which rich problem solving can occur, it is also a fertile environment for mathematical reasoning.

REFERENCES

Artzt, Alice F. "Developing Problem-Solving Behaviors by Assessing Communication in Cooperative Learning Groups." In *Communication in Mathematics, K–12,* 1996 Yearbook of the National Council of Teachers of Mathematics, edited by Portia C. Elliott, pp. 116–25. Reston, Va.: National Council of Teachers of Mathematics, 1996.

Artzt, Alice F., and Eleanor Armour-Thomas. "Development of a Cognitive-Metacognitive Framework for Protocol Analysis of Mathematical Problem Solving in Small Groups." *Cognition and Instruction* 9 (1992): 137–75.

Curcio, Frances R., and Alice F. Artzt. "The Effects of Small Group Interaction on Graph Comprehension of Fifth Graders." Paper presented at the Seventh International Congress on Mathematics Education, Quebec, Canada, August 1992.

————— . "Students Communicating in Small Groups: Making Sense of Data in Graphical Form." In *Language and Communication in the Mathematics Classroom,* edited by Maria Bertolini-Bussi, Anna Sierpinska, and Heinz Steinbring, pp. 179–90. Reston, Va.: National Council of Teachers of Mathematics, 1998.

Lambdin, Diana V. "Monitoring Moves and Roles in Cooperative Mathematical Problem Solving." *Focus on Learning Problems in Mathematics* 15 (Spring and Summer 1993): 48–64.

National Council of Teachers of Mathematics. *Curriculum and Evaluation Standards for School Mathematics.* Reston, Va.: National Council of Teachers of Mathematics, 1989.

O'Daffer, Phares G., and Bruce A. Thornquist. "Critical Thinking, Mathematical Reasoning, and Proof." In *Research Ideas for the Classroom: High School Mathematics,* edited by Patricia S. Wilson, pp. 39–56. New York: MacMillan Publishing Co., 1993.

Qin, Zhining, David W. Johnson, and Roger T. Johnson. "Cooperative Versus Competitive Efforts and Problem Solving." *Review of Educational Research* 65 (Summer 1995): 129–43.

Schoenfeld, Alan H. "What's All the Fuss about Metacognition?" In *Cognitive Science and Mathematics Education,* edited by Alan H. Schoenfeld, pp. 189–215. Hillsdale, N.J.: Lawrence Erlbaum Associates, 1987.

Webb, Noreen M. "Peer Interaction and Learning in Small Groups." *International Journal of Educational Research* 13 (1989): 21–39.

11

Developing Students' Algebraic Reasoning Abilities

Carole Greenes

Carol Findell

UNTIL recently, algebra was a high school course that was reserved for those students who were successful with arithmetic and demonstrated an interest in, and a flare for, mathematics. With the publication of NCTM's *Curriculum and Evaluation Standards for School Mathematics* (1989), the College Board's Equity Project, *The Math Connection: Using Mathematics as a Lever for Education Reform* (1996), and the SCANS Report, *What Work Requires of Schools* (1991), educators have revised their thinking about who should study algebra and when that study should take place. Educators now recognize the centrality of algebraic reasoning to advanced mathematics and other academic courses, as well as to the requirements of many vocations. As a consequence, school systems throughout the country have jumped on the bandwagon and are requiring "algebra for everyone."

Most students enrolled in the formal study of algebra at the middle and high school levels come to the courses with little or no prior experience with the subject and, as a consequence, often experience difficulty making the transition from arithmetic-based programs to those that focus on the big ideas of algebra and on algebraic reasoning. This lack of experience has occurred despite the fact that several professional groups have recommended that algebra be a curricular strand in kindergarten through grade 8 mathematics programs (Educational Testing Service and the College Board 1990; NCTM 1989, 1992). What is needed is a mechanism for providing students with algebraic experiences beginning early in their educational careers and continuing throughout all stages of their mathematical development.

What are the big ideas of algebra about which students should reason? What methods could be used to develop students' algebraic reasoning abilities?

In the discussion that follows, the big ideas of deductive and inductive reasoning, representation, equality, variable, function, and proportion are defined. Problems that develop students' familiarity with these concepts and that prompt algebraic reasoning are presented. By requiring students to document in writing—or describe orally—their thinking, justify their solutions, provide multiple solution methods, or verify someone else's line of reasoning, the problems help students develop their understanding and their use of the language of algebra, as well as their abilities to communicate. Furthermore, by capitalizing on students' vast experiences with arithmetic in the elementary and middle grades, the problems serve as a connection between the studies of arithmetic and algebra.

For some of the problems that follow, solution paths described by students in grades 5, 6, and 7 are included to give the reader a sense of the nature of the reasoning required to solve the problems and the types of student performance that might be expected.

THE BIG IDEAS

Deductive and Inductive Reasoning

The process of deduction involves reasoning logically from generalized statements or premises to conclusions about particular cases. Deductive reasoning often comes into play when students solve problems containing clues in which they have to draw conclusions from facts presented in words, diagrams, graphs, or tables.

To reason inductively involves examining particular cases, identifying relationships among those cases, and generalizing those relationships. Often, the generalization is a rule or function that describes the relationship between any term or object and its position in a sequence. Rules may be in the form of words, symbols, or graphs. Typical of problems requiring inductive reasoning are those in which students are given a sequence of numbers or shapes and asked to determine "What comes next?"

Representation

Representation is the display of mathematical relationships pictorially, graphically, or symbolically. Pictorial representations include isometric drawings, schematic diagrams, scale drawings, time lines, and maps. Graphical representations include bar, circle, and line graphs, as well as pictographs, scatterplots, and stem-and-leaf plots. Symbolic representations include tables, variable expressions, formulas, functions, and prose presentations.

Representation ability has several components: (*a*) the interpretation of mathematical relationships presented in the forms cited above; (*b*) the matching of different representations of the same mathematical relationship—for example, matching an equation of a line with its graph or with its text description; (*c*) the creation of multiple representations of the same relationship; and (*d*) the recognition of how a change in one representation affects a change in a different representation of the same relationship, as, for example, how changing a coefficient of a variable in an equation alters the graph of that equation (Sierpinska 1992).

All the algebraic reasoning problems used to illustrate the important ideas in the sections that follow require the ability to interpret various representations and to reason deductively or inductively.

Equality

The concept of equality, or balance, is central to an understanding of equations and inequalities. Students must learn ways to transform expressions and equations to equivalent forms and to modify inequalities to achieve equality. They need to have opportunities to experiment with solving problems in which balance is maintained while modifications are being made (Bellman et al. 1997; McConnell et al. 1990). Modifications include adding the same amount to both sides of a balanced scale, multiplying both sides by the same positive factor, and making substitutions with equal amounts. These modification actions on equality are difficult conceptually for students. Consider, for example, the two equations $4x = 8y$ and $x = 2y$. Obviously, the two equations *look* quite different. Thus, it is not surprising that students don't believe that the same pairs of values for x and y can satisfy both equations. Students need experience with balance and the different types of "modification" techniques in preparation for solving equations and inequalities in algebra. That experience can be provided with algebraic reasoning problems like the one involving pan scales in figure 11.1.

In each pan of the scales, there are collections of objects. Using the balanced scales as clues, students have to analyze the contents of each pan, compare collections of objects, and deduce relationships about the masses of the objects. The inferred information may then be used to determine which object or objects should be placed in the pan on the left of the unbalanced scale to achieve balance.

Which block will make the scale balance?
Describe how you solved the problem.

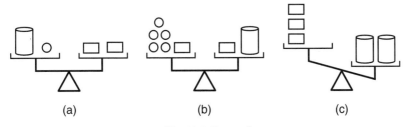

(a)   (b)   (c)

Fig. 11.1. Pan scales

To solve the problem, students may reason as shown below in the steps recorded by Bettsaly, a grade 7 student. The symbolic representation of each step is also given to help the reader see how closely the actions of the steps resemble the algebraic manipulations typically taught in first-year courses in algebra.

Bettsaly's Solution Path

Step 1:   In Scale B, subtract one box from each side.
That leaves 5 spheres (5S) balancing 1 cylinder (1C).

$5S + 1B = 1B + 1C$
$5S + 1B - 1B = 1B + 1C - 1B$
$5S = 1C$

Step 2:   In Scale A, substitute 5 spheres (5S) for the cylinder (1C).
That makes 6 spheres (6S) balancing 2 boxes (2B).
Each box (1B) is equal to (6 ÷ 2), or 3 spheres (3S).

$1C + 1S = 2B$
$5S + 1S = 2B$
$6S = 2B$
$6S/2 = 2B/2$
$3S = 1B$

Step 3:   In Scale C, put in 3 spheres for each box and 5 spheres for each cylinder.
That makes 9 spheres on the left and 10 spheres on the right.
Add one sphere to the left pan to make the scale balance.

$3B < 2C$
$3(3S) < 2(5S)$
$9S < 10S$
$9S + 1S = 10S$

Variable

> Understanding the concept [of variable] provides the basis for the transition from arithmetic to algebra and is necessary for the meaningful use of all advanced mathematics.
>
> —Schoenfeld and Arcavi 1988, p. 420

In algebra, variables are used in several ways. They may represent—

- a specific unknown number or numbers, as in the equations $5x + 3 = 13$ and $x^2 = 36$;
- a varying quantity that has a relationship with another variable, as in $y = 4x$;
- a generalization that can take on values of a set of numbers, as in $x + -x = 0$;
- a label or object, as in $3F = 1Y$ (3 feet = 1 yard).

Küchemann (1978) described several stages in the development of an understanding of the concept of variable. It is at the most advanced of these stages that students can view letters as variables having multiple values and representing relationships between two sets of values, as is required by problems involving any type of function.

Students need experience with variables that represent specific unknowns as well as variables that do indeed vary in value. In the algebraic reasoning problem shown in figure 11.2, there is only one pair of values that will satisfy both equations, A and B. If, however, during the solution process, the equations are considered separately, multiple pairs of values will satisfy each equation. Two students' solution paths are shown below. Ann and Nick are both grade 6 students.

A. $\square + \triangle + \triangle = 12$

B. $\square + \triangle = 7$

$\square = \underline{}$ $\triangle = \underline{}$

Fig. 11.2. Square and triangle

Nick's Solution Path

- I looked at B and saw that a square and a triangle equal 7.
- So I minused 12 minus 7 so then I got the triangle.
- So I wrote the numbers in.

Ann's Solution Path

- I looked at B.
- I thought of 3 and 4 in B. They don't work in A.
- I tried 5 and 2. They don't work.
- I tried 2 for the square and 5 for the triangle. It works.

The problem dealing with weight scales, shown in figure 11.3, is a more complex problem involving variables. Students have to use information provided by the scales to determine the mass of each of the four objects.

To solve this problem, Terrance, grade 7, documented his reasoning as follows:

Terrance's Solution Path

- C says that one cylinder and one box weighs 18 pounds.
- So in A one cylinder and one box is 18 of the 34 pounds. The other cylinder and the ball must be (34 – 18), or 16 pounds.
- In B the cylinder and the ball are 16 of the pounds, so the four tall boxes must be (20 – 16), or 4 pounds together, so a tall box weighs (4 ÷ 4), or 1 pound.
- So in D the tall box is 1 and the cylinder and the box are 18 (we know that from Scale C), so that means that 2 boxes are (35 – 1 – 18), or 16. One box is (16 ÷ 2), or 8.

- In C the box is 8 so the cylinder is $(18 - 8)$, or 10.
- In A, put in 8 for the box and 10 for each cylinder. That leaves the ball equal to $(34 - 10 - 10 - 8)$, which is 6.

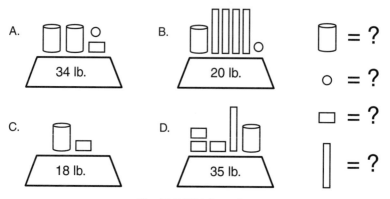

Fig. 11.3. Weight scales

Function

The concept of function is often considered to be the single most important idea in mathematics instruction at all levels (Harel and Dubinsky 1992). A function is a relationship in which two sets are linked by a rule that pairs each element of the first set with exactly one element of the second set. Prior to the formal study of functions, students must understand this one-to-exactly-one functional relationship among elements, develop ways to determine the input when given the output for a particular function, and learn how to construct inverse operation rules to "undo" what other operations "did."

One of the simplest and most concrete representations of function is that of a machine that accepts an input and returns exactly one output. If the rule is known, students can find an output value for each input number. Similarly, outputs may be given and students can determine the corresponding inputs. This latter situation requires the use of inverse operations. After students gain skill with single operation machines (e.g., $f(x) = 3x$), they can link machines to explore functions with multiple operations (e.g., $f(x) = 3x - 7$). At a more advanced level, students can be given several input numbers and their corresponding outputs and asked to identify the relationship and describe, in words, the "rule" that relates inputs to outputs. Ultimately, students should be able to identify the functional relationship between pairs of data and record that relationship symbolically with an equation.

Lattice types of problems, like the one shown in figure 11.4, require students to identify and continue patterns and generalize the relationship between the row and column labels and the numbers in the lattice.

Columns

	A	B	C	D	E	F
Row 1	1	2	3	4	5	6
Row 2	7	8	9	10	11	12
Row 3	13	14	15	16	17	18
Row 4	19	20	21	22	23	24
Row 5	25	26	27	28	29	30
.	.	.	.	.	.	.
.	.	.	.	.	.	.
.	.	.	.	.	.	.

In what row and column is the number 100 located?

Fig. 11.4. Lattice

To determine the row and column in which the number 100 is located, some grade 6 students continued the lattice entries to 100. Other students noticed that the numbers in Column F are all multiples of 6. By continuing Column F and listing consecutive multiples of 6, students were able to "trap" 100 between two contiguous multiples (96 and 102) and identify the row and column labels. Still other students observed that there are six entries in each row; that 100 is the 100th entry; and that $(100 \div 6)$ gives 16 complete rows of six with four entries left over. Thus, the number 100 is in Row 17 and is the fourth entry from the left, which locates it in Column D. Some grade 7 students generalized this procedure and pointed out that each number, x, may be represented as $6k + r$ where k is the quotient and r is the remainder when x is divided by 6. Thus, if r equals zero, then k represents the row number. If r is not equal to zero, then the row number is represented by $(k + 1)$. The column is determined by the value of r; $r = 1$ corresponds to Column A, $r = 2$ corresponds to Column B, ..., $r = 0$ corresponds to Column F.

Proportion

We have singled out one particular type of function, a proportion, for special attention because of its prevalence in so many of the mathematical topics students study at the elementary and middle school levels. Fractions, unit costs, rates, percents, similar triangles, and right triangle relationships are all examples of proportions that students confront in their mathematics programs. For this reason, proportion has historically held a "privileged place" among mathematical relationships (Sierpinska 1992).

Proportion is also a big idea in other areas of the curriculum. In geography and history, students reason proportionally when they interpret map scales and time lines. In science, in the study of simple machines, students explore the proportional relationships illustrated by gears, pulleys, and levers. In art, students make use of proportions when drawing the human figure or constructing scale models. In music, students use proportions to transpose melodies from one key to another.

Students encounter proportions very early in their mathematical careers but often have difficulty both in understanding the multiplicative nature of proportional relationships and in distinguishing relationships that are proportional from those that are not. Students assume that since all proportions are linear relationships, then all linear relationships are proportional. This is not so. When two quantities are in a direct proportional relationship, they vary in such a way that one quantity is always a constant multiple of the other quantity. That means that only relationships of the form $y = kx$, where x and y are variables and k is a constant, are proportional. All proportions are represented by straight line graphs that contain the origin.

To develop students' abilities to reason proportionally, we present two different types of problems. In the first problem, Icies and Fridgies, students have to determine the better buy. In the second, Losing Your Marbles, students have to remove marbles from a collection of marbles in order to achieve a specified ratio between the colors of the remaining marbles.

In the design of the Icies and Fridgies problem shown in figure 11.5, we chose numbers that are compatible to facilitate the invention of different types of solution methods. Regardless of the approach taken, students must either equate the numbers of flavored ices and compare the costs or equate the costs and compare the numbers of flavored ices. For their first methods, the majority of fifth-grade students computed and compared unit costs of the Icies and Fridgies. For their second and third methods, students applied concepts from number theory. For example, for his second method, Timothy identified the greatest common factor of 12 and 18 and used that number as the basis for the comparison of costs. He wrote, "6 Icies are $1.25 and 6 Fridgies are $1.00." For his third method, he recognized the 2 to 3 relationship between 12 and 18 and wrote, "There are 2/3 as many Icies (as Fridgies) so, $2.00 is better (2/3 of the cost of the Fridgies)."

Other students identified common multiples of the numbers of flavored ices or of the prices and used those numbers to facilitate the comparison

Cold Ice makes identical flavored ices under two different brand names.
Which brand is the better buy?
Describe three methods for deciding.

| 12 Icies | $2.50 |
| 18 Fridgies | $3.00 |

Fig. 11.5. Icies and Fridgies

process. Anita wrote, " If you buy 36 Icies you would spend $7.50, but if you buy 36 Fridgies you would spend $6.00. So, Fridgies are better." Heather wrote, " I found the number of Icies and Fridgies you could buy for $15. You can get $6 \times 12 = 72$ Icies and $5 \times 18 = 90$ Fridgies. So get Fridgies."

Bradley graphed the points (12, $2.50) and (18, $3.00), connected each of the points to the origin with a straight line, and then compared the slopes of the lines. "The line with the point (18, $3.00) is not as steep as the other line, so it stands for the better buy."

Losing Your Marbles in figure 11.6 requires students to interpret the language of proportions. Students have to understand the meaning of the phrase *for every* and then construct tables of values, generate equivalent ratios, make drawings, or manipulate objects representing the marbles, in order to solve the problem.

In the box, there are 8 red marbles (R), 8 black marbles (B), and 8 white marbles (W). What is the fewest number of marbles you can remove from the box so that for every three red marbles left in the box, there are two white marbles and one black marble left in the box?

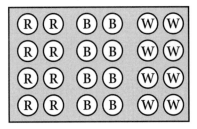

Fig. 11.6. Losing Your Marbles

HOW CAN THESE PROBLEMS BE USED?

Algebraic reasoning problems may be used to introduce and stimulate a discussion of the big ideas or to provide practice and fine-tune reasoning skills. When used to introduce a key idea, the teacher might begin by working through a couple of the problems with the whole class. Using prompting questions, the teacher can guide the students through the solution process and draw attention to related concepts and skills. Thereafter, students might work on their own or in pairs to tackle additional problems of the same type.

At other times, the teacher might choose not to discuss the key ideas until after students have had opportunities to wrestle with problems that embody those ideas. After allowing sufficient time for independent exploration, the teacher could engage the students in group discussions and elicit from them what they have learned and what still needs to be clarified or explored.

If designated for practice involving the big ideas, algebraic reasoning problems should be inserted into the curriculum to support or extend existing topics. Practice problems may be assigned for in-class work or for homework

Because algebraic reasoning problems have multiple solution paths, they are amenable to creative approaches. Students should be encouraged to consider and explore alternative solution methods and, once they have solved the problems, to reflect on their own solution methods and to compare solution paths with other students. Having students follow one another's line of reasoning in the solution of a problem is a good way to develop logical reasoning and verification skills.

Many of the problems presented in this paper have mathematical relationships that can be represented symbolically, as was done for the pan scales (fig, 11.1). Once students have experience describing solution paths in prose, the symbolic representations of the steps may be presented for discussion. Students should be assisted in understanding how the equations and modifications of those equations represent actions with the objects. In this way, students will come to better understand the "words to symbols" translation process.

CONCLUSION

To alleviate many of the difficulties students experience when they begin the study of algebra at the middle or high school level, we concur with recommendations of the various professional groups that students must have experience in algebraic reasoning beginning with their first days in school. One mechanism for providing such experience is the use of algebraic reasoning problems that focus on representation, balance, variable, proportionality, function, and inductive and deductive reasoning; that can be represented symbolically; and that can be solved in a number of different ways.

Because the problems have multiple solution paths, they can be used to reveal students' creativity in the design of solution plans, as well as their strengths in mathematical reasoning. As they describe their thinking, justify their solution methods, and evaluate classmates' solution processes, students will not only develop their communication skills but also will develop their facility with the language of algebra.

REFERENCES

Bellman, Allan, Sadie C. Bragg, Suzanne H. Chapin, Theodore J. Gardella, Betty C. Hall, William G. Handling, Sr., and Edward Manfrey. *Algebra*. Needham, Mass.: Prentice Hall, 1997.

Educational Testing Service and the College Board. *Algebridge: Concept Based Instructional Assessment*. Dedham, Mass.: Janson Publications, 1990.

The EQUITY 2000 National Mathematics Technical Assistance Committee. *The Math Connection: Using Mathematics as a Lever for Education Reform*. New York: College Entrance Examination Board, 1996.

Harel, Guershon, and Edward Dubinsky, eds. Foreword to *The Concept of Function: Aspects of Epistemology and Pedagogy*. MAA Notes 25 of the Mathematical Association of America. Washington, D.C.: Mathematical Association of America, 1992.

Küchemann, Dietmar. "Children's Understanding of Numerical Variables." *Mathematics in School* 7, no. 4 (1978): 23–26.

McConnell, John, Susan Brown, Susan Eddins, Margaret Hackworth, Leroy Sachs, Ernest Woodward, James Flanders, Daniel Hirschhorn, Cathy Hynes, Lydia Polonsky, and Zalman Usiskin. *The UCSMP Algebra.* Glenview, Ill.: Scott Foresman & Co., 1990.

National Council of Teachers of Mathematics. *Algebra for the Twenty-first Century: Proceedings of the August 1992 Conference.* Reston, Va.: National Council of Teachers of Mathematics, 1992.

———. *Curriculum and Evaluation Standards for School Mathematics.* Reston, Va.: National Council of Teachers of Mathematics, 1989.

Secretary's Commission on Achieving Necessary Skills. *What Work Requires of Schools: SCANS Report for America 2000.* Washington, D.C.: U.S. Department of Labor, 1991.

Schoenfeld, Alan, and Abraham Arcavi. "On the Meaning of Variable." *Mathematics Teacher* 81 (September 1988): 420–42.

Sierpinska, Anna. "On Understanding the Notion of Function." In *The Concept of Function: Aspects of Epistemology and Pedagogy,* edited by Guershon Harel and Edward Dubinsky. MAA Notes 25 of the Mathematical Association of America. Washington, D.C.: Mathematical Association of America, 1992.

Additional Reading

Edwards, Edgar, ed. *Algebra for Everyone.* Reston, Va.: National Council of Teachers of Mathematics, 1990.

Greenes, Carole, and Carol Findell. *Algebra: Puzzles & Problems, Grade 4, Grade 5, Grade 6, Grade 7.* Mountain View, Calif.: Creative Publications, 1998.

Heid, Kathleen, Jonathan Choate, Charlene Sheets, and Rose Mary Zbiek. *Algebra in a Technological World.* Addenda Series , Grades 9–12. Reston, Va.: National Council of Teachers of Mathematics, 1995.

Meiring, Steven P., Rheta N. Rubenstein, James E. Schultz, Jan de Lange, and Donald L. Chambers. *A Core Curriculum: Making Mathematics Count for Everyone.* Addenda Series, Grades 9–12. Reston, Va.: National Council of Teachers of Mathematics, 1992.

National Council of Teachers of Mathematics. *Assessment Standards for School Mathematics.* Reston, Va.: National Council of Teachers of Mathematics, 1995.

———. *Professional Standards for Teaching Mathematics.* Reston, Va.: National Council of Teachers of Mathematics, 1991.

12

Innovative Tasks to Improve Critical- and Creative-Thinking Skills

Stephen Krulik

Jesse A. Rudnick

The teaching of thinking skills has become a major focus in our schools. This is not to say that teachers in prior years did not concern themselves with the teaching of thinking skills; in fact, we can trace such efforts back to the time of Socrates. But now, the improvement of thinking skills has acquired a high priority in mathematics instruction. The big question is, "How do we teach children to be better thinkers and problem solvers?" Fortunately, much has been written during the past five years that deals with this question. In fact, a review of textbooks, particularly those from the elementary school, will reveal significant instructional time devoted to problem solving and reasoning.

In this article, we will offer some specific suggestions for making the mathematics classroom a place where children will be able to improve their thinking skills. When it comes to teaching thinking skills, there are two main philosophies. One is to develop a separate "course" in thinking; the other is to incorporate thinking activities into the everyday curriculum. In other words, thinking skills should be developed with, and as part of, the ongoing mathematics lessons. We strongly believe that thinking skills can be substantially improved by helping students become better problem solvers. To do so, we should include problems that require the students to use their higher-order-thinking skills. These are the skills that large-scale assessments have revealed to be seriously lacking, or at least underdeveloped, in our young people.

The lowest level of thinking is *recall*, which includes those skills that are almost automatic or reflexive. These might include some of the basic arithmetic facts (e.g., $3 \times 4 = 12$, $5 + 4 = 9$, etc.) or even remembering an address or telephone number. In their early years, students make a conscious effort to commit these facts to memory. The next level of thinking is *basic*, which includes the understanding and recognition of mathematical concepts like addition, subtraction and so on, as well as their application in problems. An illustration of *basic* thinking is recognizing that finding the total cost of twelve ice-cream cones at 95 cents each is an example of the multiplication concept. Of course, the line between these categories is not always easily determined. What is "basic" for one person might be "recall" for another. It is the final two categories, *critical thinking* and *creative thinking*, that are of particular concern to us in this article and that are the ones we believe can and must be enhanced.

Critical and Creative Thinking

Critical thinking is thinking that examines, relates, and evaluates all aspects of the situation or problem. It includes gathering, organizing, remembering, and analyzing information. Critical thinking includes the ability to read with understanding and to identify extraneous and necessary material. It also means being able to draw proper conclusions from a given set of data and being able to determine inconsistencies and contradictions in a set of data. Critical thinking is analytical and reflexive (Krulik and Rudnick 1993).

Creative thinking is thinking that is original and reflective and that produces a complex product. It includes synthesizing ideas, generating new ideas, and determining their effectiveness. Creative thinking includes the ability to make decisions and usually involves the generation of some new end product (Krulik and Rudnick 1993).

In order to improve their students' thinking skills, classroom teachers need to find ways to integrate opportunities for increasing critical and creative thinking into regular mathematics lessons. One specific suggestion for involving students in critical and creative thinking encourages teachers to expand the content of George Polya's final heuristic, *Looking Back* (Polya 1973). (Polya's four-step heuristic plan recommends understanding the problem, devising a plan, carrying out the plan, and looking back.) Polya's method includes checking the results of the problem and using those results in some other problem situations, but he does not go far enough. We believe that *the problem should never end just because the answer has been found.* One way for students to expand their critical and creative thinking skills is for teachers to extend the problems beyond the answer. As a result, we have renamed this last heuristic *Reflect* and have expanded it to include four additional areas, namely: "What's another way?", "What if … ?", "What's wrong?", and "What would you do?"

What's Another Way?

After the answer to a problem has been found and checked, the teacher should challenge the students: "What's another way to solve this problem?

Can you find another solution?" This challenge encourages them to find another path to the answer. Since none of the given conditions have been changed in any way, the students can focus on the problem itself—time need not be spent in rethinking the given conditions. The students are forced to think of other ways to approach the problem. This activity is an excellent way to practice *creative thinking.* Although contrived, the following problem elicits solutions that provide insight into students' reasoning.

Problem 1

A factory makes three-legged stools and four-legged matching tables. It uses the same kind of legs to make both items. For next month, it has ordered 340 legs to fill an order for a total of 100 pieces of furniture. How many of each item will it be making?

Student's Solution 1

The most typical solution allows algebra students to apply their knowledge of algebra:

Let x = the number of three-legged stools
Let y = the number of four-legged tables
$x + y = 100$
$3x + 4y = 340$

Solving these equations simultaneously gives the answer: sixty three-legged stools and 40 four-legged tables. At this point, the teacher should ask the students if they can solve the problem in another way. That is, use another method to arrive at the same results.

Student's Solution 2

Students often use the *guess and test* strategy:

	Tables		Stools		Total Legs
	Number	Legs	Number	Legs	
(First guess)	80	320	20	60	380 (too many)
(Second guess)	70	280	30	90	370 (too many)
(Third guess)	60	240	40	120	360 (too many)
	50	200	50	150	350 (too many)
	40	160	60	180	340 (right!)

They will be making forty tables and sixty stools. Notice that the second guess is based on the results of the first guess, the third guess is based on the results of the second guess, and so on, until the correct answer has been found.

Students' Solution 3

Some students reduce the complexity of the problem (100 and 340 become 10 and 34) and make a drawing. They begin by drawing the ten pieces of furniture as ten circles. Since there must be at least three legs on either type of furniture, they place three legs on each object (fig. 12.1a). Four legs remain and they are placed on the objects, one at a time, until there are no more (fig. 12.1b).The results show 4 four-legged objects and 6 three-legged objects. Multiplying by 10, the students obtained the answer: 40 tables and 60 stools.

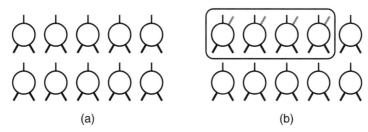

(a)   (b)

Fig. 12.1

WHAT IF ... ?

In "What's another way?" the given conditions of the problem remained the same. The students were able to focus on creativity in finding alternative solutions. However, in "What if ... ?" the given information is changed. This modification permits the students to reexamine the problem and see what effect these changes have on the solution process as well as the answer. In this way, students are reinforcing their critical thinking as they analyze what is taking place. Here is an example of a "What if ... ?" problem and some of the results that occurred.

Problem 2

Jan hit the dart board shown [fig. 12.2] with four darts. She scored 31, 5, 9, and 10. What was her total score?

This is obviously a simple addition problem, and the student merely adds 31, 5, 9, and 10 to get the answer, 55. Now, however, let's play "What if ... ?"

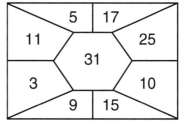

Fig. 12.2

What If...? 1

What if Jan hit the dart board with four darts and scored 55? What numbers might she have hit?

The student must add many combinations of four numbers and see which ones provide a sum of 55. Obviously, there is more than one correct answer. (For example, 31, 10, 9, and 5; or 25, 15, 10, and 5; 25, 10, 10, and 10; and so on.) This *new* problem requires a little more analysis on the part of the students, as well as some practice in addition. The fact that there can be multiple answers to a single problem is another point that should be emphasized.

What If...? 2

What if we remove the number "10" from the dart board, so that it now appears the same as figure 12.3? If Jan scored 55 with exactly four darts, what numbers might she have hit?

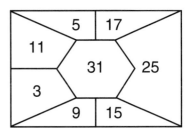

Fig. 12.3

This problem requires even more analysis on the part of the students. After sufficient time to try several different combinations of four numbers which sum to 55, the students should realize that it cannot be done. Now, however, the teacher should investigate with the students *why* it cannot be done. Is there a mathematical explanation? This is an excellent opportunity for a discussion on the properties of even and odd numbers and their sums. The students should realize that, without the 10, the dart board contains only odd numbers. The sum of four odd numbers will always be even. Thus, there is no way to arrive at a sum of 55 with exactly four darts.

By asking the appropriate "What if … ?" questions, it is quite easy to change a routine problem into an excellent activity that provides students with the opportunity to use their critical thinking.

WHAT'S WRONG?

In "What's wrong?" the students have another opportunity to use their critical thinking skills. They are presented with a problem and its solution. However, the solution contains an error, either conceptual or computational. The student's task is to discover the error, correct it, and then explain what was wrong, why it was wrong, and what was done to correct the error.

Problem 3

Mario wanted to put three shelves over his desk; each shelf was to be 3 feet long. He went to the lumber yard and bought a 9-foot board to be cut into three equal pieces. The lumber yard charged $1.50 per foot for the board and $2.00 for each cut. Mario received this bill:

```
              LUMBER EMPORIUM
   1   9-foot board . . . . . . . . . . . $13.50
   3   cuts @ $2.00 each . . . . . . . . . 6.00
                                      $19.50
   Tax . . . . . . . . . . . . . . . . . . . . . . 1.17
   Total . . . . . . . . . . . . . . . . . . . $20.67
```

Mario was angry and said that they had charged him too much. What's wrong?

Student's Solution 1

The error lies in the number of cuts for which Mario was charged. By means of a drawing, a student found that only two cuts are needed to obtain three pieces. The charge of $20.67 is $2.00 too much and should be $18.67. (This student unfortunately failed to consider the tax on the $2.00 discrepancy.)

Student's Solution 2

A group of students discovered the same error that appeared in the previous solution. However, these students included the idea that once the price for the number of cuts changed, the tax charged must also change. This now required them to find the rate of tax (6%) and recompute it based on the new total, $17.50. The tax is now $1.05, making the total bill $18.55. (Not only were these students using critical thinking skills, but they were using creative thinking as well.)

WHAT WOULD YOU DO?

This extension is designed to stimulate creative thinking skills. After to resolving a problem situation mathematically, the student is faced with a decision. This decision can be based on personal ideas, personal experiences, or whatever the student wishes to call into play. However, the student must explain what mathematics influenced the decision he or she made. This explanation can often be expressed in a paragraph format, providing an excellent opportunity for students to practice their communication skills as well.

Problem 4

Your local telephone company has just begun to offer a choice of the folowing two service plans to meet the needs of teenage callers. Which plan would you select? What would you do?

LIMITED SERVICE	UNLIMITED SERVICE
Basic Cost . . . . $14.95 First 30 calls free Each additional call. . . . . . . .09¢	Unlimited number of calls Complete Price $18.25

Student's Solution 1

$$\$18.25 - \$14.95 = \$3.30$$
$$\$3.30 \div .15 = 22$$

I make more than 22 calls, so the Unlimited Service is my choice.

(This student neglected to take into consideration the first 30 calls for the original $14.95 rate. In addition, she divided by .15 instead of by .09. We have no idea where the .15 came from)

Student's Solution 2

40 calls using Unlimited Service = $18.25
40 calls using Limited Service = $15.85

100 calls using Unlimited Service = $18.25
100 calls using Limited Service = $21.25

70 calls using Unlimited Service = $18.25
70 calls using Limited Service = $18.55

Since I make fewer than 70 calls, I would select Limited Service.

(This student made a choice based upon the number of calls he makes and only used approximations.)

Student's Solution 3

$$\$14.95 + .09x = 18.25$$
$$.09\,x = 3.30$$
$$x = 37$$
$$37 + \text{first 30 calls} = 67 \text{ calls.}$$

If I make more than 67 calls, I will choose Unlimited Service.

(This student used algebra, and was able to draw her conclusion based on the calculations she made.)

Conclusion

These are only a few examples of how we can turn an ordinary, everyday lesson into a critical- and creative-thinking lesson. This activity demonstrates that almost any problem can serve as the vehicle. All that is needed is the desire to go forward and the willingness to go beyond the printed page. The task of classroom teachers is clear. They must help their students develop critical- and creative-thinking skills. Teaching is a thinking profession, and teachers are creative people. We are certain that, if we take the time, put our minds to the task, and our shoulders to the wheel, we will achieve this objective.

Bibliography

Costa, Arthur L., and Lawrence F. Lowery. *Techniques for Teaching Thinking.* Pacific Grove, Calif.: Midwest Publications, 1989.

Feldhausen, John F., and Donald J. Treffinger. *Teaching Creative Thinking and Problem Solving.* Dubuque, Iowa: Kendall Hunt Publishing Company, 1984.

Krulik, Stephen, and Jesse A. Rudnick. *Reasoning and Problem Solving: A Handbook for Elementary School Teachers.* Needham Heights, Mass.: Allyn and Bacon, Inc., 1993.

Nicely, Robert F. Jr. "Higher Order Thinking Skills in Mathematics Textbooks." *Educational Leadership* 42 (April 1985): 26–30

Polya, George. *How to Solve It.* 2nd ed. Princeton, N.J.: Princeton University Press, 1973.

Swartz, Robert J., and D. N. Perkins. *Teaching Thinking: Issues and Approaches.* Pacific Grove, Calif.: Midwest Publications, 1989.

13

Understanding Students' Probabilistic Reasoning

Graham A. Jones

Carol A. Thornton

Cynthia W. Langrall

James E. Tarr

Jeff Soucek Photography

Ms. Ostrander moved among her third-grade students as they began the gum-ball experiment. The task was to determine which gum-ball color, red or blue, was most likely to come out of the gum-ball shakers they had made. Each gum-ball shaker contained four blue and two red gum balls. She smiled when she overheard Elaine's prediction and the discussion it promoted in her group.

Elaine: I predict it'll be red.

Michelle: No, it's going to be blue because there are more blue.

Martin: Yeah, it will be blue because the blue are at the bottom.

Elaine: Red is my favorite color. It always comes up for me.

- Do all young children reason like Elaine or Martin? Is Michelle's reasoning more typical?
- What kind of change can we facilitate in students' probabilistic reasoning?
- How can teachers' understandings of students' probabilistic reasoning help them to make assessments and set reasonable expectations for instruction?

THE vignette above focuses on differences in students' probabilistic thinking and reflects the kind of diversity in mathematical reasoning that teachers typically encounter on a day-to-day basis. The purpose of this article is to describe and illustrate the range of probabilistic thinking exhibited by elementary and middle school students and, in essence, to respond to questions like those raised in the vignette. These descriptions and illustrations are intended to provide a background that will help teachers understand and foster students' probabilistic reasoning.

PROBABILISTIC REASONING: KEY CONCEPTS

In order to capture the manifold nature of probabilistic reasoning, we have conducted a series of teaching experiments with elementary and middle school students over a three-year period. By systematically observing their thinking, we have identified six key concepts: sample space, experimental probability of an event, theoretical probability of an event, probability comparisons, conditional probability, and independence. These concepts, illustrated by the tasks in figure 13.1, are outlined below.

The concept of *sample space* is fundamental to all probabilistic reasoning. It involves listing the outcomes of a one-stage experiment (e.g., tossing one coin) or a two-stage experiment (e.g., tossing two coins). The sample space task for Miss Pierce's class (fig. 13.1) illustrates a one-stage experiment with five outcomes.

Although experimental probability and theoretical probability are related, the relationship is not immediately apparent to elementary and middle school students. The *experimental probability of an event* is based on experimentation or simulation and uses relative frequency to determine the likelihood of an event. For example, in the experimental probability task (fig. 13.1), the relative frequency or experimental probability for Sergio based on 20 draws is 8 out of 20. The *theoretical probability of an event* is based on an analysis of the sample space and uses symmetry, number, or simple geometric

Probability Tasks in the Context of Classroom Elections

It was class election time.

- In Miss Pierce's class, five students—Jennifer, Martina, Monica, Philip, and Sergio—tied for president.
- In Mr. Rubin's class, four students were tied: Amanda, Boris, Jamal, and Mary Jo.

In each class the teacher decided to break the tie by putting the names in a box, shaking them up, and drawing one name for president.

Sample Space Task	In Miss Pierce's class, what names could be drawn?
Experimental Probability Task	Miss Pierce did 20 practice draws before she did the draw to decide the president. Her results were as follows: Jennifer, 3 times; Martina, 3; Monica, 4; Philip, 2; and Sergio, 8. • On the basis of these results, who has the best chance for president, or is it not possible to say? Explain your thinking. • Suppose Miss Pierce did 100 practice draws; what do you think the result would be? Give a number for each student and justify your thinking.
Theoretical Probability Task	In Miss Pierce's class, is it more likely that a boy will be drawn for president? Explain. Does Martina have a better chance of being president than Sergio? Why?
Probability Comparison Task	In which class, Miss Pierce's or Mr. Rubin's, is a girl more likely to be drawn? How do you know?
Conditional Probability Task	In Miss Pierce's class, Monica is elected president. Miss Pierce then draws for vice-president, leaving Monica's name *out* of the box. Has the probability of drawing another name starting with *M* changed? Has Sergio's chance of being drawn changed? Explain.
Independence Task	Mr. Rubin decides to do five draws from the box, with the fifth name being the class president. Each time, he replaces the name he has drawn. The first four draws are *girl, boy, boy, boy.* Do the girls have a better chance than boys on the fifth draw? Explain.

Fig. 13.1. Tasks illustrating the six probability concepts

measures to determine the likelihood of an event. The relationship between the two concepts results from the fact that for a given event, experimental probability will more closely approximate theoretical probability as the number of trials increases. This relationship is highlighted in the experimental probability task (fig. 13.1) when the students are challenged to consider what would happen if Miss Pierce did 100 practice draws rather than only 20.

Probability comparisons require students to determine which of two probability situations is more likely to produce a specified (target) event or whether the two situations offer the same chance for the target event. *Conditional probability* involves recognizing whether the probability of an event has been changed by the occurrence of another event, and *independence* requires students to be able to recognize events for which the probability of one is not changed by the occurrence of the other. The latter three problem tasks in figure 13.1 illustrate how contextual situations associated with probability comparisons, conditional probability, and independence can reflect either experimental probability or theoretical probability.

CONCEPTUAL FRAMEWORK

As a result of our observations, we have generated and validated a framework (fig. 13.2) that describes and predicts students' probabilistic reasoning through the middle grades (Jones et al. 1997; Tarr and Jones 1997). This framework indicates that students' reasoning in probability grows over time and encompasses four levels. Level 1 is associated with subjective or non-quantitative reasoning; level 2 is seen to be transitional between subjective and naive quantitative reasoning; level 3 involves the use of informal quantitative reasoning; and level 4 incorporates numerical reasoning.

In what follows, we discuss and illustrate the four levels of probabilistic reasoning and suggest how students' reasoning can be expected to change as their thinking is challenged. We continue to use the classroom election scenario (fig. 13.1) as the context for our illustrations.

Level 1

Students exhibiting this kind of reasoning adopt a restricted perspective when considering probability situations. They seldom provide a complete listing of the outcomes of the sample space and tend to focus subjectively on what is more likely to happen rather than what is *possible*. In situations involving experimental probability, theoretical probability, probability comparisons, conditional probability, and independence, these students—like Elaine in the opening vignette—typically use subjective rather than quantitative reasoning. Jason's reasoning, which is illustrated below, is typical of level 1 thinkers.

When asked what names could be drawn in Miss Pierce's class (Sample Space Task, fig. 13.1), Jason said: "Sergio, because I think he's going to win." Notice that he made this judgment even when the teacher emphasized what names *could* be drawn. When the teacher probed further, Jason eventually gave the complete listing, but he did not do this spontaneously, and later he reverted again to incomplete listings. Similarly, in tasks related to the other key concepts, Jason's reasoning was typically driven by subjective judgments or other irrelevant aspects of the task. For example, in both the experimental and theoretical

Construct	Level 1 Subjective	Level 2 Transitional	Level 3 Informal Quantitative	Level 4 Numerical
Sample Space	• Lists an incomplete set of outcomes for a one-stage experiment	• Lists a complete set of outcomes for a one-stage experiment and *sometimes* for a two-stage experiment	• Consistently lists the outcomes of a two-stage experiment using a partially generative strategy	• Adopts and applies a generative strategy to provide a complete listing of the outcomes for two- and three-stage cases
Experimental Probability of an Event	• Regards data from random experiments as irrelevant and uses subjective judgments to determine the most or least likely event • Indicates little or no awareness of any relationship between experimental and theoretical probabilities	• Puts too much faith in small samples of experimental data when determining the most or least likely event; believes that any sample should be *representative* of the parent population • May revert to subjective judgments when experimental data conflict with preconceived notions	• Begins to recognize that more extensive sampling is needed for determining the event that is most or least likely • Recognizes when a sample of trials produces an experimental probability that is markedly different from the theoretical probability	• Collects appropriate data to determine a numerical value for the experimental probability • Recognizes that the experimental probability determined from a large sample of trials approximates the theoretical probability • Can identify situations in which the probability of an event can be determined only experimentally
Theoretical Probability of an Event	• Predicts most or least likely event on the basis of subjective judgments • Recognizes certain and impossible events	• Predicts most or least likely event on the basis of quantitative judgments but may revert to subjective judgments	• Predicts most or least likely events on the basis of quantitative judgments • Uses numbers informally to compare probabilities	• Predicts most or least likely events for one- and simple two-stage experiments • Assigns a numerical probability to an event (a real probability or a form of odds)
Probability Comparisons	• Uses subjective judgments to compare the probabilities of an event in two different sample spaces • Cannot distinguish "fair" probability situations from "unfair" ones	• Makes probability comparisons on the basis of quantitative judgments—not always correctly • Begins to distinguish "fair" probability situations from "unfair" ones	• Uses valid quantitative reasoning to explain comparisons and invents own way of expressing the probabilities • Uses quantitative reasoning to distinguish "fair" and "unfair" probability situations	• Assigns a numerical probability and makes a valid comparison
Conditional Probability	• Following one trial of a one-stage experiment does not always give a complete listing of possible outcomes for the second trial • Uses subjective reasoning in interpreting with and without replacement situations	• Recognizes that the probability of *some* events changes in a without replacement situation; however, recognition is incomplete and is usually restricted only to events that have previously occurred	• Recognizes that the probability of all events changes in a without replacement situation • Can quantify changing probabilities in a without replacement situation	• Assigns numerical probabilities in with replacement and without replacement situations • Uses numerical reasoning to compare the probability of events before and after each trial in with replacement and without replacement situations
Independence	• Has a predisposition to consider that consecutive events are always related • Has a pervasive belief that one can control the outcome of an experiment	• Begins to recognize that consecutive events may be related or unrelated • Uses the *distribution* of outcomes from previous trials to predict the next outcome (representativeness)	• Can differentiate independent and dependent events in with and without replacement situations • May revert to strategies based on representativeness	• Uses numerical probabilities to distinguish independent and dependent events

Fig. 13.2. A framework describing students' probabilistic reasoning

probability tasks, Jason said, "Sergio has the best chance for president because I think a boy is going to win." Interestingly, in the experimental probability task (fig. 13.1), the small sample of twenty trials resulted in Sergio being drawn eight times—twice as many as expected—and this produced an experimental probability that actually vindicated Jason's subjective reasoning. This apparent anomaly illustrates one of the difficulties associated with experimental probability; namely, that students at less mature levels of reasoning have a tendency to put too much reliance on small-sample data that may appear to validate their reasoning rather than challenge it.

Level 2

Students who demonstrate reasoning at this level are in transition between subjective and informal quantitative judgments. Although they consistently identify a complete set of outcomes for a one-stage experiment, they make tenuous connections between sample space and probability and often revert to subjective reasoning. For example, when faced with the theoretical probability task in figure 13.1, "Does Martina have a better chance than Sergio?" Jenny responded, "No, because Martina's in the box once and Sergio's in the box once. But Martina might be closer to the top."

In conditional probability tasks, level 2 thinkers usually recognize that the probabilities of some, but not all, events change when the sample space has been reduced. For example, in the conditional probability task (fig. 13.1), Miss Pierce asked two questions: "Now that Monica has been drawn for president, has the probability of drawing another name starting with *M* changed? Also, has Sergio's chance of being drawn changed?" To the first question, Jenny correctly said, "The chance of getting another name starting with *M* has gone down because only Martina is left." However, she added, "Sergio's chance hasn't changed, because there's still only one Sergio in the box."

Jenny is typical of level 2 thinkers, who tend to concentrate only on the event that has been drawn the first time—in this instance, a name starting with *M*. Even though she was correct in recognizing that there is only one Sergio for the next draw, she did not realize that Sergio's chance had improved in the second draw because there were fewer names in the box.

Subsequently, when Jenny was faced with the independence task (fig. 13.1) involving Mr. Rubin's five draws from the box, she said, "I predict a girl because it's a long time since a girl came up." She didn't really examine the ongoing probabilities but looked at the outcomes of the first four draws and decided on a girl in order to correct the imbalance between the number of boys and girls drawn.

Level 3

Students at level 3 use more systematic strategies when listing the outcomes of one- and two-stage experiments. However, the major change in their thinking is a more consistent use of quantitative reasoning when determining probabilities and conditional probabilities. Although conventional probabilities or odds are not always expressed, students use comparisons like *more of, less of,* and *same chance* and sometimes invent representations like "3 out of 5."

For example, in the theoretical probability task (fig.13.1) concerning the likelihood of a boy's name being drawn for president, Corey said, "No. A girl is more likely because there are three girls and only two boys." Linda, another level 3 thinker, went even further in her reasoning on the conditional probability task. She said, "No. The chance of getting another girl whose name starts with *M* has gone down because now it's only 1 out of 4." More important, in the same conditional probability task, Linda also conjectured that Sergio's probability had changed in the second draw. She said, "Sergio's got a better chance because there are not as many against him in the second draw." Although Linda didn't use numerical probabilities consistently, her reasoning was strongly quantitative and also valid.

Level 4

Students exhibiting level 4 reasoning use systematic strategies to generate the outcomes of an experiment and to determine numerical probabilities in both experimental and theoretical situations. For example, Peter not only reasoned that Martina and Sergio had the same theoretical probability of being elected ("1 out of 5") but also predicted that Sergio should come up about 20 times out of 100 in the experimental probability task. He made this response in spite of the fact that Sergio's proportion in the smaller sample— 8 out of 20—was much higher than expected (fig. 13.1).

Level 4 students' facility with numerical reasoning also operates in conditional probability and independence. Lakethia's response to the last part of the conditional probability task in figure 13.1 illustrates this and also brings out one of the major differences between level 3 and level 4 thinkers. Unlike Linda, who did not use numerical probability to justify her conjecture about Sergio's chances, Lakethia said, "Sergio's chance has improved. It was 1 out of 5. It's now 1 out of 4." Similarly, in the independence task where Mr. Rubin made five draws (fig. 13.1), Lakethia was not influenced by the sequence of outcomes occurring in the first four draws. She stated, "The fifth draw is just the same. Both the boys and the girls have a fifty-fifty chance." In essence, Lakethia focused on the composition of the sample space for each draw and justified her conclusions using appropriate numerical probabilities.

USING THE FRAMEWORK TO FOSTER PROBABILISTIC REASONING

Insights into students' thinking, like those captured in the framework and the illustrations above, provide vital background for assisting teachers to understand and foster students' probabilistic reasoning. Moreover, we have found that this background knowledge of students' probabilistic reasoning can be effectively used in three phases of the instructional process: planning, implementation, and evaluation (Tarr 1997; Jones et al. 1996).

With respect to *planning*, the framework presented in this article offers teachers a robust picture of students' probabilistic thinking—both their conceptions and their misconceptions. Informed with this knowledge, teachers are in a better position to construct problem tasks that fit the levels of probabilistic reasoning identified in the framework. The set of tasks outlined in figure 13.1 was generated from the framework, as were the two sets of sample tasks provided in figure 13.3. Each of these sample tasks is linked with one of the six key concepts and is intended to capture the thinking of students at all levels of the framework. For example, in the Sample Space task involving the rolling of two dice (fig. 13.3, Set 2), a level 1 thinker might list "1, 2, 3, 4, 5, 6," *twice*— ignoring the fact that the two dice will produce *pairs* of numbers like (1, 1), (1, 2), (1, 3) that in turn produce sums of 2, 3, and 4, respectively. By way of contrast, a level 4 thinker might list all the possible ways of finding each sum and recognize that sums are not equally likely. Such a student might reason that 7 is the most likely sum and that its chance of being rolled is 6 out of 36.

During *implementation*, the framework can serve as a filter for analyzing and classifying students' oral and written responses during instruction. We have found that this systematic monitoring of students' thinking in whole-class and group situations enhances and enriches teachers' knowledge. In particular, it enables teachers to design questions and written tasks that accommodate the diversity in students' reasoning and move them to more mature levels of probabilistic thinking. For example, in the Sample Space task involving the roll of two dice (fig. 13.3, Set 2), the level 1 thinker described in the previous paragraph might be asked, "Can you get a sum of 1 when you roll two dice?" By way of contrast, the level 4 thinker might be asked, "Can you find a pattern between sums and probabilities?"

Finally, we have found the framework descriptors to be helpful benchmarks for assessing growth in students' probabilistic thinking and *evaluating* the effectiveness of instruction. For example, in the experimental probability task involving Jenny and Pete (fig. 13.3, Set 1), several students in a class may respond at level 2, that is, argue that heads has a better chance than tails because heads came up 12 times out of 20. In order to challenge this reasoning, the teacher might suggest that pairs of students toss a coin twenty times, record the number of heads out of twenty, and then compare their results with that of the pooled results of all pairs—a pooling of data that could involve more than 200 tosses. In fact, the teacher might even want to make comparisons after each pair's results are "added" to the pool. An instructional activity like this will allow many opportunities for the teacher to explore students' reasoning by posing questions such as "Why didn't every pair come up with the same number of heads?" "What seems to be happening to the pooled class data as we include the

Construct	Set 1	Set 2
Sample Space	In a game at the school fair, you flip a coin and roll a die at the same time. You win a prize if you get a head and a 6. What are all the possible outcomes? How do you know you thought of them all?	When playing a racecar game, you roll two dice, find the sum, and move your car that number of spaces. List all the possible sums. Are they all equally likely? Explain.
Experimental Probability of an Event	Jenny and Pete had been playing a game in which they tossed a coin twenty times. Pete said, "It came up heads twelve times, so that means heads has a better chance than tails." Jenny says, "But everyone knows that the chance of getting a head is 1/2 so they both have the same chance." What do you think? Explain your response.	Miho and Iva are playing a game with a spinner that has seven equal sectors—three red and four blue. Miho gets a point whenever blue is spun and Iva gets a point for red. The winner is the first to reach 5 points. Miho won the first game 5-3, and Iva won the second game 5-3. Could this happen with the spinner they're using? Why or why not? • Does it make any difference to Miho's chance of winning the game if the winner is the first to score 1 point? 5 points? 10 points? 100 points? Why? • What do you estimate is the chance of getting blue on the spinner? Explain.
Theoretical Probability of an Event	In many games players get an extra turn when a double is rolled. *Predict:* How many doubles would you expect in fifty rolls of two dice? *Experiment:* Roll two dice fifty times and keep a tally of the doubles. How many doubles did you roll? *Analyze:* How do these results compare with your prediction? Make a class graph to compare your results with your classmates'.	It costs ten cents to play the carnival game "dicey doubles." A player rolls a pair of dice ten times. Every time a double is rolled, the player receives five cents. Every time an outcome other than a double is rolled, the player loses one cent. To win the game, a player must finish with fifteen cents after ten rolls of the dice. Can this be done? Is this a fair game?
Probability Comparisons	There are two shake-up gum-ball machines. One has one raspberry and four blueberry gum balls. The other has two raspberry and three blueberry. If you want raspberry, which gum-ball machine is best, or do they both give you the same chance of getting raspberry?	There are two shake-up gumball machines. One has three raspberry and three blueberry gum balls. The other has one raspberry and one blueberry. If you want raspberry, which gum-ball machine is best, or do they both give you the same chance of getting raspberry?
Conditional Probability	Pete is thinking of a number between 1 and 10 and challenges Fred to guess it. Right before Fred guesses, however, Pete slips and gives Fred the clue that the number is greater than 6. How does the hint affect Fred's chances of guessing the number? Has his chance of guessing the right number changed? Explain.	Stuart's trick-or-treat bag had three Milky Way, one Snickers, and two Butterfinger candy bars. He really wants the Snickers. On his first try he pulls out a Milky Way and decides to eat it anyway. If he tries again, has his chance of drawing a Snickers changed, or is it the same chance as before?
Independence	Suppose I flip a red-white chip five times and keep track of the result. Which of the following sequences is the *most likely* result of five flips, or are all four sequences equally likely? • RRRWW • WRRWR • WWWWW • RWRWR Justify your response.	In a TV game, there is a secret three-digit number. • The first digit can be 1 or 2. • The second digit can be 3 or 4. • The third digit can be 5 or 6. What's your chance of picking the first digit correctly? Suppose you correctly pick the first digit. Has your chance of picking the second digit changed? Explain.

Fig. 13.3. Sample probability tasks based on the framework

results of more and more pairs?" "Which data are best for determining the chance of getting a head—the pooled class data or the data of just one pair? Why?" Such questions will enable the teacher to assess the impact of instruction on students' reasoning and to evaluate how effective such an activity has been in provoking level 2 thinkers to recognize the necessity of basing experimental probabilities on larger samples and in helping them to develop more effective strategies for determining experimental probabilities. Moreover, on the basis of experiences like those described above, teachers can use the framework descriptors to build ongoing profiles of students' learning that will assist them in the continuing instructional cycle of planning, implementation, and evaluation.

SUMMARY AND CONCLUSION

The NCTM *Curriculum and Evaluation Standards for School Mathematics* (1989) claims that mathematical reasoning is fundamental to the knowing and doing of mathematics. Consistent with this position, we believe that probabilistic reasoning has a special place within the broader picture of mathematical reasoning because it involves reasoning that is associated with a context of uncertainty.

Developing reasoning within such contexts presents special challenges to teachers because students' probabilistic reasoning is diverse, idiosyncratic, and even subject to a certain mystique. However, within these variations there is a pattern of growth in probabilistic reasoning that we have sought to describe and illustrate in this article. Moreover, we believe that the pattern of growth described and illustrated in our probabilistic reasoning framework can be used by teachers to construct appropriate probability tasks, to monitor and assess students' reasoning, and to adapt instruction accordingly.

REFERENCES

Jones, Graham A., Cynthia W. Langrall, Carol A. Thornton, and A. Timothy Mogill. "A Framework for Assessing and Nurturing Young Children's Thinking in Probability." *Educational Studies in Mathematics* 32 (February 1997): 101–25.

Jones, Graham A., Carol A. Thornton, Cynthia W. Langrall, and A. Timothy Mogill. "Using Children's Probabilistic Thinking to Inform Instruction." In *Proceedings of the Twentieth Conference of the International Group for the Psychology of Mathematics Education,* vol. 3, edited by Luís Puig and Angel Gutierrez, pp. 137–44. Valencia, Spain: Universitat de Valencia, 1996.

Tarr, James E. *Using Knowledge of Middle School Students' Thinking in Conditional Probability and Independence to Inform Instruction.* Doctoral diss., Illinois State University, 1997.

Tarr, James E., and Graham A. Jones. "A Framework for Assessing Middle School Students' Thinking in Conditional Probability and Independence." *Mathematics Education Research Journal* 9 (May 1997): 39–59.

14

Analyzing Mathematical Reasoning in Students' Responses across Multiple Performance Assessment Tasks

Dominic Peressini

Norman Webb

MATHEMATICS teachers around the world are engaged in efforts to enhance their classrooms so that they are places where teachers and students engage in rich discourse about significant mathematics and explore interesting problems situated in meaningful contexts. These efforts are grounded in reform-based visions of schooling that include helping all students learn to value mathematics, have confidence in their mathematical ability, become mathematical problem solvers, communicate mathematically, make connections within mathematics and among other content areas, and reason mathematically in a variety of content areas and problem situations. An essential aspect of this reform movement is the development and use of rich tasks that elicit mathematical reasoning, and of frameworks that facilitate analyses of students' responses to these tasks for purposes of instruction and assessment. This article presents an *analytic-qualitative* process for examining and describing students' mathematical reasoning and other knowledge based on their responses to multiple performance assessment tasks.

MATHEMATICAL REASONING AND THE ROLE OF ASSESSMENT TASKS

Our understanding of mathematical reasoning is rooted in a dynamic conceptualization of mathematically powerful students. From this perspective, we view mathematical power as the integration of (*a*) a positive disposition toward mathematics; (*b*) knowledge and understanding of the nature of mathematics, including concepts, procedures, and skills; (*c*) the ability to analyze and reason mathematically; (*d*) the ability to use mathematical language to communicate ideas; and (*e*) the ability to apply mathematical knowledge to solve problems in a variety of contexts and disciplines (NCTM 1989). Mathematically powerful students should be able to draw on this myriad of dimensions in order to bring to bear a variety of mathematical methods that will assist them in solving nonroutine problems and navigating a changing society dependent on information and technology.

In a similar manner, mathematical reasoning can also be viewed as a dynamic activity that includes a variety of modes of thinking. We see mathematical reasoning situated in this notion of mathematical power, as well as an integral component of mathematical thinking. In particular, "mathematical thinking involves using mathematically rich thinking skills to understand ideas, discover relationships among the ideas, draw or support conclusions about the ideas and their relationships, and solve problems involving the ideas" (O'Daffer and Thornquist 1993, p. 43). Accordingly, mathematical reasoning—which plays an imperative role in this thinking process—involves gathering evidence, making conjectures, establishing generalizations, building arguments, and drawing (and validating) logical conclusions about these various ideas and their relationships. To this end, the variety of modes of mathematical reasoning include, but are not limited to, inductive (including the identification and extension of patterns), deductive, conditional, proportional, graphical, spatial, and abstract reasoning.

With these notions of mathematical power, thinking, and reasoning in mind, one of the most important activities that the mathematics teacher can engage in is providing students with a variety of rich tasks that expose students to situations in which they must invoke their mathematical power and demonstrate their ability to think and reason in problem-solving situations. Hence, it becomes paramount that teachers be able to identify, develop, and present appropriate mathematical tasks in both instructional and assessment situations (NCTM 1991, 1995). One such task that provides students with the opportunity to illustrate their mathematical reasoning is the performance assessment task (Lesh and Lamon 1992). These open-ended tasks are characterized by the following criteria: they are engaging, mathematically significant, rich, active, feasible, and equitable (Stenmark 1991; Wiggins 1993). Through the observation and analysis of students' performances, mathematics teachers are able to attain robust accounts of their students' mathematical reasoning and understanding and can in turn use this information to guide their classroom instruction.

Not only have mathematics teachers tapped into the power of these tasks, but states and districts have also recognized the value of performance-based assessments as they turn toward open-ended assessments to provide information about the mathematics students know and can do. However, since performance assessment activities require more time to complete and are more complex than traditional short-answer tasks or multiple-choice items, fewer activities can be given to a student in a limited period of time. Moreover, since efficiency and time management are essential in school environments, these complex student responses are often scored using a holistic rubric and assigned one score to each student's response for each task (Herman, Aschbacher, and Winters 1992). These scores are usually aggregated over tasks for each student to give some indication of the students' overall performance for the group of tasks. Because any one performance assessment task produces more information about a student than a single-response item, it can be argued that an abundance of information is lost by giving a single score to each task and then summing or aggregating the scores in some way across tasks. The question then becomes: What form of analyses can be applied, using the full range of information produced across tasks, to maximize the inferences that can be made about a student's set of responses to a group of tasks?

AN ANALYTIC-QUALITATIVE APPROACH TO ASSESSING MATHEMATICAL REASONING

The recent debate concerning the applicability of traditional test theory to alternative forms of assessment, such as performance assessments, is particularly relevant to our analytic-qualitative method for interpreting students' responses to mathematics performance assessment tasks. The argument is made that traditional scoring techniques, reliability formulas, and generalizability claims may not be appropriate for these more open-ended, and less standardized, forms of assessment (Mislevy 1993; Moss 1994). Rather, what is needed is an approach that takes into consideration the unique characteristics of these alternative assessments.

In particular, we have developed an analytic framework, and a four-stage qualitative process, for analyzing students' responses to a series of mathematics performance assessment tasks. The first stage of the process involves an in-depth analysis of the student's response to each individual performance task. It is at this stage that we employ the analytic framework that we have developed. The framework consists of three broad categories: foundational knowledge, solution process, and communication (fig. 14.1).

Note that we conceptualize mathematical reasoning and analysis as forming the primary components of what we call the student's "solution process." In addition, the dimensions of "mathematical power" that we outlined earlier are transparent in this framework—indeed, the three broad categories of the framework (foundational knowledge, solution processes, and communication) are respectively the second, third, and fourth dimensions of mathematical power. The framework also reflects a variety of research in mathematics education:

Analytic Mathematics Scoring Framework

I. **Foundational Knowledge—Foundation of mathematical working knowledge possessed by the individual that is brought to bear on the assessment situation**
   A. Concepts, facts, and definitions
   B. Procedures and algorithms
   C. Misconceptions

II. **Solution Process—The analytical skills and reasoning abilities that the student demonstrates in solving the assessment task**
   A. Analysis—The mental operations and tendencies that an individual employs in the process of solving the assessment task
      1. Understanding
         a) Restate problem
         b) Separate/summarize data
         c) Identify/separate conditions
         d) Draw diagram
         e) Simplify problem
         f) Examine special cases
      2. Exploration
         a) Exploratory manipulation
         b) Extend information
         c) Initiate solution
            (1) Systematic
            (2) Random
         d) Work backward

   3. Verify solution
      a) Try a different method/approach
      b) Check solution (reasonable)
   B. Reasoning—The modes of reasoning the student exhibits while approaching and solving the tasks. (This includes tendencies associated with the student's reasoning capabilities.)
      1. Inductive (patterns)
      2. Deductive
      3. Spatial
      4. Proportional
      5. Abstracting/generalizing

III. **Communication—Individual's interpretation and understanding of the assessment task, and the corresponding expression of the solution process and final conclusions**
   A. Language
   B. Symbols/notation
   C. Dimensions/labels (specificity)
   D. Argument (concise and logical)

*** **Summary of the Student's Response:** The scorer should provide a holistic-qualitative description of the individual's overall response to the task. This includes a summary of the three major categories above and a discussion on the overall appropriateness of the solution.

Fig, 14.1. A framework for analyzing responses to performance assessment tasks

Polya's (1945) work on problem solving and heuristics, Schoenfeld's (1985) research on mathematical behavior and problem solving, and Pimm's (1987) work in mathematical communication. On completion of this stage, the teacher has a number of written qualitative analyses for the student's responses to the performance tasks—one analysis for each task.

The next stage requires a critical comparison of each individual analysis in order to determine consistencies and discrepancies in the student's responses across performance tasks. It is at this point that we are attempting to make inferences about the consistency of the information that the student has provided. This stage results in a one- to two-page written synthesis of the mathematical knowledge, problem-solving strategies, mathematical reasoning, and communication skills the student has demonstrated across the performance tasks.

The third stage is best described as a distillation process. It is at this stage that we transform the synthesis from the previous stage to a condensed form that best describes what the student has demonstrated across the performance tasks. We believe that this condensed form is a more manageable form that will be both appropriate and meaningful to share with students, parents, and the public. And most important, this qualitative description of students' mathematical power—as opposed to a single score or grade—will assist teachers in monitoring students' progress and in making instructional decisions. Using this qualitative information to guide an individual student's instruction delineates the fourth and final stage of the process.

Opening a Window to View Mathematical Reasoning

The remainder of this article examines—through the application of the four-stage process—students' responses to a series of tasks that teachers have created and used to assess their students' mathematical understanding. In particular, two individual students' responses to four different mathematics performance assessment tasks—which collectively represent a performance assessment instrument—are analyzed to reveal the mathematical power demonstrated in the students' solution processes. Although we apply the entire framework and four-stage process to the collection of students' work, we pay particular attention to the students' mathematical reasoning.

The students, Paul and Ben, were tenth graders from Wisconsin. The examples of their work have been taken from an instrument developed as part of the Wisconsin Performance Assessment Development Project (WPAD) at the University of Wisconsin—Madison, which provided information for the development of mathematics performance assessment instruments for the state of Wisconsin. The instruments were designed to be administered to all students in the state at three grade levels—grades 5, 8, and 10. Each instrument consists of a multiple of tasks—up to six—and is administered over three class periods. During the course of this project we gathered more than 8000 completed instruments from students across Wisconsin during the pilot-testing of the instruments. The tasks that compose this instrument are a few of the many performance assessment tasks that have been written, developed, pilot-tested, and scored by mathematics teachers across Wisconsin.

The Assessment Instrument

The assessment tasks that make up the instrument that Paul and Ben responded to, along with their actual written work, are included in figures 14.2 through 14.6. These tasks, and the students' corresponding responses, serve as the focus of our discussion. For the purposes of the WPAD, each task was developed in conjunction with a profile sheet that guided the scoring of students' responses with a traditional holistic rubric. These profile sheets identified the goals of each assessment task, the NCTM Standards that it addressed, the Wisconsin Learner Outcomes that it emphasized, the significant mathematics that it was intended to elicit from students, and possible aspects of students' responses (e.g., actual numeric solutions as well as likely mistakes and misconceptions). However, for the purposes of this discussion, we have not included these profile sheets and the traditional holistic rubric. Rather, since we are focusing on an alternative approach to analyzing and interpreting students' responses from the perspective of the classroom teacher, we will limit our discussion to the application of our framework and process. Yet, it is beneficial to understand the nature of the three tasks that frame our discussion, and consequently, we will briefly examine these tasks that collectively form the performance assessment instrument.

All three of these authentic tasks have been crafted around problem-solving situations that are located in contexts familiar to students. Indeed, students are asked to (*a*) figure out a "fair share" of pay for three friends who are doing yardwork, (*b*) examine a set of data for ticket sales in order to determine the success of rock 'n' roll bands, and (*c*) determine a geometric or algebraic pattern and its generalization. Activities such as these naturally provide all students with a gateway into the task and engage students in mathematics activity by establishing connections between the students' experiences and interests and the discipline of school mathematics.

Moreover, these tasks are constructed around significant mathematics—as outlined in the NCTM *Standards* (1989). The big mathematical ideas represented in this collection of tasks include building mathematical models for problem-solving situations; computing and estimating with integers, fractions, and ratios; manipulating algebraic equations; analyzing data; using data to make conjectures and justify conclusions; calculating measures of central tendency; generating permutations of numbers and relating these calculations to the probability of events; identifying and comparing absolute sizes; recognizing and generalizing patterns; connecting geometry and algebra while calculating perimeter and area; and identifying the terms of arithmetic and geometric sequences. This diverse mathematical content serves as the academic context in which the students are asked to demonstrate their mathematical power.

In addition, many of these tasks are open-ended in the sense that not only do they have multiple solution methods but also some of the tasks have different solutions that can be mathematically justified (see, for example, fig. 14.4—the Rock 'n' Dough task). The open-ended nature of the tasks, in conjunction with the authentic problem situations and the significant mathematical content, provides a rich problem-solving experience that actively engages students and allows them to explore and extend the problem space. Inherent in this process is that students communicate their mathematical knowledge and reasoning in a variety of forms. Indeed, students can use charts, graphs, tables, numbers, calculations, pictures, and written prose to communicate their mathematical reasoning.

Finally, the tasks are feasible in that they can be completed within school time and most students will be able to respond to the requirements of the tasks in an appropriate fashion. The feasibility of the tasks is associated with the familiar contexts in which they are set, and by efforts to ensure that these contexts are equitable across all students. In particular, most students are familiar with getting paid for work, music bands, and dealing with patterns. These aspects of the tasks ensure that all students can become engaged in the activity and begin to respond to the requirements of each performance task.

Applying the Analytic Scoring Framework

The following sections include examples of how classroom teachers could apply the analytic framework (fig. 14.1) to actual examples of students' work—stage of the four-stage process. In particular, we have used the framework to analyze Paul's and Ben's responses to the three performance assessment tasks that they took over a period of three days. We are including the relevant notes that we took as we used the framework to guide our examination of Paul's and Ben's work, and as the reader will see, we have focused on the students' "solution process" (the second category of the framework in fig. 14.1), which includes his mathematical reasoning. (Note that in focusing on mathematical reasoning, we are not including a summary of the student's response that would discuss the overall appropriateness of the student's solution—indicated by "***" in fig. 14.1.)

All in a Day's Work

The analysis of Paul's (fig. 14.2) and Ben's (fig. 14.3) responses to the All in a Day's Work task is as follows:

Analysis of Paul's work

Foundational Knowledge:
- Performs basic operations on numbers
- Performs operations on fractions and is able to manipulate fractions
- Familiar with the concept of cost
- Familiar with the notion of part versus whole (proportional reasoning)
- Uses mathematical modeling to represent a problem situation

Solution Process:
Analysis
- Uses the provided diagram
- Approaches the problem using two methods (as required by the task)
- Organizes data in tables
- Verifies the solutions found with the two methods by indicating that the two solutions are the same—they match and are correct

Reasoning
- The use of the two methods indicates the student's ability to reason proportionally
- First, uses the drawing with money as the unit of analysis; splits into two different jobs
- Second, uses amount of work as the unit of analysis and considers the job as one complete event; calculates the money as a last step (proportional reasoning with respect to part versus whole—focuses on the whole)
- Uses mathematics to justify the results of each method

Communication:
- Uses the "$" symbol to indicate money (dollars)
- Leaves a clear paper trail of work
- Uses written prose to communicate mathematical reasoning
- Communication is clear and makes sense

ALL IN A DAY'S WORK

Our neighbor hired you and two of your friends to rake leaves. The house has a back yard and a front yard that are about the same size. The neighbor agreed to pay the three of you $60 for the entire job. On the day of the job you and one friend arrived to start the job at 9 a.m. By the time the third friend came, the two of you had finished the front yard. Then the three of you finished the back yard together.

How should the money be split up? Each person must be paid based on the amount of the yard raked by that person. Justify your solution in two ways. In one of the ways, use the following sketch.

1. Explain your first way:

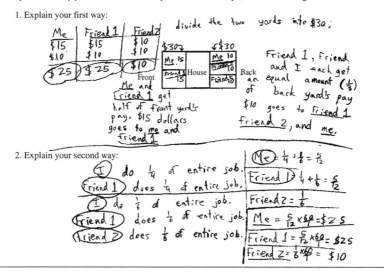

2. Explain your second way:

Fig. 14.2. Paul's response to the All in a Day's Work task

Analysis of Ben's work

Foundational Knowledge:
- Performs basic operations on numbers
- Applies the notion of unit-cost
- Strong understanding of part versus whole and able to apply this knowledge (proportional reasoning)
- Uses mathematical modeling to represent a problem situation

Solution Process:
Analysis
- Identifies and separates the conditions of the problem
- Uses the provided diagram
- Approaches the problem using two methods (as required by the task)

Reasoning
- The use of the two methods indicates the student's ability to reason proportionally

- First, uses the drawing with money as the unit of analysis; splits into two different jobs
- Second, divides the entire yard into 12 parts and assigns parts based on the problem statement; calculates the money as a last step (proportional reasoning with respect to part versus whole—focuses on the whole)
- Uses mathematics to justify the results of each method

Communication:
- Uses variables to represent people in the first method
- Uses the "$" symbol to indicate money (dollars)
- Leaves a paper trail of work—could be more complete

- Does label multiplication operation in second part
- Uses written prose to communicate mathematical solution
- Communication is clear but needs more detail—especially for the second method in that it is not clear why Ben chose 12 or how he arrived at the specific numerators that represent the amount of the yard raked.

ALL IN A DAY'S WORK

Our neighbor hired you and two of your friends to rake leaves. The house has a back yard and a front yard that are about the same size. The neighbor agreed to pay the three of you $60 for the entire job. On the day of the job you and one friend arrived to start the job at 9 a.m. By the time the third friend came, the two of you had finished the front yard. Then the three of you finished the back yard together.

How should the money be split up? Each person must be paid based on the amount of the yard raked by that person. Justify your solution in two ways. In one of the ways, use the following sketch.

1. Explain your first way:

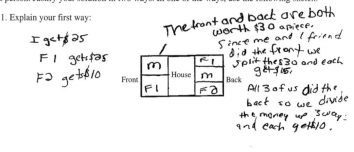

2. Explain your second way:

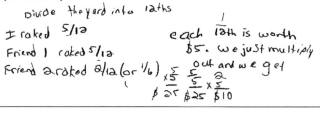

Fig. 14.3. Ben's response to All in a Day's Work task

Rock 'n' Dough

The analysis of Paul's and Ben's responses (fig. 14.4) to Rock 'n' Dough is as follows:

Analysis of Paul's work

Foundational Knowledge:	*Solution Process:*
• Performs basic operations on numbers	*Analysis*
• Understands and is able to calculate averages	• Separates the conditions of the task as well as the data
• Interprets data in tabular form	• Creates a table
• Understands the relation between ratios and averages	• Reorganizes and extends the data
	• Considers three related aspects of the data and compares these aspects

Rock 'n' Dough

"Have you seen this? This is great!" said Erin.

"No, what is it?" asked Josh.

Erin replied, "ZZ Top is my favorite rock group and according to this table, they are really successful."

"Hey, wait a minute. The way I see the numbers, Guns N' Roses is more successful than ZZ Top," said Josh

TOP-GROSSING CONCERT TOURS

Act	Total Gross	Total Attendance	# of Shows	Sellouts
1. Grateful Dead	$35,243,237	1,560,087	79	76
2. New Kids on the Block	29,395,491	1,195,498	89	84
3. ZZ Top	25,977,394	1,274,654	105	94
4. Paul Simon	21,439,096	886,516	78	24
5. The Judds	19,370,212	1,019,038	120	49
6. Bell Biv DeVoe, Keith Sweat, and Johnny Gill	18,572,895	870,747	78	11
7. AC/DC	17,876,445	904,726	72	35
8. Rod Stewart	13,902,562	591,589	35	24
9. Guns N' Roses	13,224,931	545,141	29	24
10. Clint Black	12,624,722	648,895	71	46

Source: Amusement Business Magazine

1. Which student do you agree with? Make several comparisons to support your conclusion.

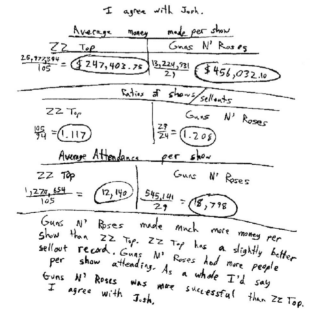

Paul's Response to the Rock 'n' Dough Task

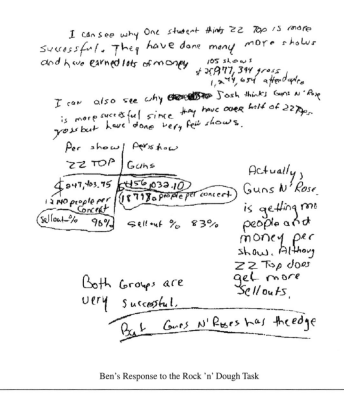

I can see why One student think ZZ Top is more successful. They have done many more shows and have earned lots of money   105 shows
$25,977,394 gross
1,244,654 attendance

I can also see why ~~one student~~ Josh thinks Guns N' Rose is more successful since they have over half of 2ZTops shows but have done very few shows.

Per show	Per show
ZZ TOP	Guns
$847,403.75	$456,033.10
12 NO people per Concert	(18,778 people per concert)
Sellout-% 96%	Sellout % 83%

Actually, Guns N' Rose is getting mo people and money per show. Although ZZ Top does get more Sellouts.

Both Groups are very successful.

But Guns N' Roses has the edge

Ben's Response to the Rock 'n' Dough Task

Fig. 14.4. Paul's and Ben's responses to the Rock 'n' Dough task

Reasoning
- Uses proportional reasoning to investigate three different aspects of the data by calculating several different ratios (the "ratio of shows/sellouts" indicates an understanding of part versus whole)
- Uses averages and proportions to make comparisons and arrive at a conclusion and justify that conclusion

Communication:
- Uses tables to communicate data and mathematical calculations
- Uses mathematical language as headings for the table
- Uses written prose to clearly communicate explanation and justification
- Includes mathematical findings in the written prose
- Does not consistently label units

Analysis of Ben's work

Foundational Knowledge:
- Performs basic operations on numbers
- Understands and is able to calculate averages
- Interprets data in tabular form
- Understands the relation between ratios and averages (uses percents)
- Understands the concept of absolute size

Solution Process:
Analysis
- Separates the conditions of the task as well as the data
- Creates a table
- Reorganizes and extends the data
- Considers three related aspects of the data and compares these aspects

Reasoning
- Uses proportional reasoning to investigate three different aspects of the data by calculating several different ratios using "shows" as the per-unit measure (these ratios "gross/show," "attendance/show," "sellouts/show" indicate a strong understanding of part versus whole)
- Uses averages and proportions to make comparisons and arrive at a conclusion and justify that conclusion

Communication:
- Uses written prose to describe how he understands the initial problem

- Uses tables to communicate data and mathematical calculations (does not show work to justify these calculations)
- Uses mathematical language as headings for the table
- Uses written prose to communicate explanation and justification
- Includes mathematical findings in the written prose
- Labels units ($, $,%)
- Usually indicates ratio ("people per show," "sellout %,"—did not do this for gross sales per show

Steps and Squares

The analysis of Paul's (fig. 14.5) and Ben's (fig. 14.6) responses to Steps and Squares is as follows:

Analysis of Paul's work

Foundational Knowledge:
- Performs basic operations on numbers
- Recognizes and calculates correct perimeter and area
- Understands the application of formula for perimeter and area
- Uses variable representation in applying formulas

Solution Process:
Analysis
- Does not use a written diagram or picture (instead immediately abstracts the pattern)
- Summarizes data in an efficient and organized fashion
- Extends the information (focuses on the developing pattern in this extension)
- Verifies solution and indicates that for the special cases of $n = 1$, $n = 2$, $n = 3$, the formula he has devised does not work (identifies the exception to the rule)

Reasoning
- Uses inductive reasoning to recognize and extend patterns

- Uses inductive reasoning to generalize an explicit formula in terms of n to calculate perimeter
- Uses inductive reasoning to generalize a recursive formula in terms of n to find area
- Uses deductive reasoning in determining that the generalized formula for area and perimeter applies to the 50th figure and then uses those formulas to calculate the correct area and perimeter for the 50th figure
- Uses abstract reasoning with variables and symbolic notation

Communication:
- Uses variables and symbolic notation
- Leaves a clear paper trail of work
- Uses written prose to communicate mathematical reasoning
- Communication is clear and makes sense

STEPS and SQUARES

Study the figures below.

1st figure   ⌗   A = 1   P = 4

2nd figure   ⌗   A = 3   P = 8.

3rd figure   ⌗   A = 6   P = 12

Assume the area of the first square is 1 and that the length of each side of the square is one unit long.

Use tiles to help determine the pattern that has been started.

1. Use the patterns that you discover to find the perimeter and area of the 50th figure.

A

1	4
3	8
6	12
10	16
15	20
21	24
28	28
36	32
45	36
55	40

n = The number of the figure

$$A = (\ n\ ) + (n - 1) + (n - 2) + (n - 3) + \dots$$
$$+ (\cdot n\ - (n - 1))$$

Area of 50th figure = (1275)
$50 + 49 + 48 + \dots + 1 = 1275$

$P = 4n$ n = the number of the figure

Perimeter of 50th figure = (200)
$4 \cdot 50 = 200$

2. Describe the perimeter and area of the nth figure where n can represent any whole number.

Area = $n + (n-1) + (n-2) + (n-3) + \dots + (n - (n-1))$
If the number reaches "$n - (n-1)$" before "$n-3$" as in the above formula, then the adding stops. The area of the 0th figure is zero.

Perimeter = $4n$

Fig. 14.5. Paul's response to the Steps and Squares task

Analysis of Ben's work

Foundational Knowledge:
- Performs basic operations on numbers
- Recognizes and calculates correct perimeter (adds up all sides)
- Understands the application of formula for area (understands the concept of perimeter but does not indicate the use of the formal algorithm)
- Use of area for algorithm leads to incorrect area for 50th figure

Solution Process:
Analysis
- Uses a picture or diagram in both parts of the problem (does not complete the second diagram), but does not attend to the details of the diagram
- Does exploratory calculations
- Extends the information
- Uses two approaches to calculate area (algorithm and "adds up all squares")

Reasoning
- Recognizes and extends patterns (for perimeter; does not do this for area)
- Does not generalize or abstract a representation of the perimeter or area of the nth figure (instead, calculates the area and perimeter for 4th figure)
- Instead of generalizing, relies on the concrete aspects of the specific figures

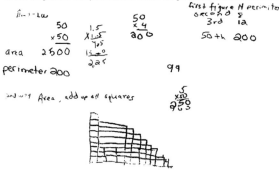

STEPS and SQUARES

Study the figures below.

1st figure

2nd figure

3rd figure

Assume the area of the first square is 1 and that the length of each side of the square is one unit long.

Use tiles to help determine the pattern that has been started.

1. Use the patterns that you discover to find the perimeter and area of the 50th figure.

2. Describe the perimeter and area of the nth figure where n can represent any whole number.

Fig. 14.6. Ben's response to the Steps and Squares task

- Seems to have a misunderstanding in part two of this problem

Communication:
- Very little communication in this response

- Labels perimeter and area for some figures
- Written explanation is not complete and not detailed
- No apparent argument other than the mathematical work

Integrating and Distilling the Analyses

On the basis of the analyses of Paul's and Ben's work in stage 1, we can move on to stages 2 and 3 by beginning to describe what Wiggins (1993) calls the "habits of the mind." At this point we are ready to look across their three responses in order to describe the consistency of mathematical reasoning, or as Wiggins (1993) says, to "search for patterns of response in diverse settings" (p. 207). It is during these stages that we are reflecting on the individual analyses of each student's responses so that we can make inferences about the consistency of information that they have demonstrated.

Foundational knowledge

As we examine Paul's work, it is clear that he has a strong foundation of mathematical knowledge including basic skills, algorithms, and conceptual knowledge of a variety of mathematical domains. In addition, he can appropriately apply this diverse knowledge of mathematics to a variety of open-ended problem-solving situations.

Ben also demonstrated a solid understanding of the necessary computational skills, mathematical ideas, and concepts as required by the tasks. In addition, he has a facility for numbers and can apply this facility, as well as his other mathematical knowledge, to a variety of problem-solving situations.

Mathematical reasoning and analysis

As we turn our attention to Paul's mathematical reasoning, it is apparent that he can abstract mathematical ideas and representations. Indeed, Paul has provided several examples, in different situations and mathematical contexts, of his ability to reason inductively by recognizing, extending, and generalizing patterns. In addition, Paul consistently revealed his capacities for abstract reasoning as he used variables and symbols to represent a variety of mathematical terms. Not only did Paul use inductive reasoning to arrive at generalizations, but he also demonstrated the ability to reason deductively as he identified the necessary conditions for a generalized formula to be applicable and then applied this formula to the problem-solving situation (an example of this was when he found the area and perimeter of the 50th figure in the Steps and Squares task). Paul also demonstrated the ability to reason proportionally (part versus whole) and geometrically. In addition, it is interesting to note that Paul is not bound to pictorial-concrete examples of mathematical relations as he demonstrated the ability to visualize relationships and make comparisons (see, for example, his solution process to the Steps and Squares task). In short, Paul was able to rely on his mathematical reasoning to make conjectures, build arguments, draw logical conclusions, and justify his overall arguments. Moreover, Paul considers multiple approaches—on demand and at his own incentive—in order to verify his solutions and support his conclusions.

Ben, however, almost always approached the tasks in a deductive manner and used deductive reasoning throughout the entire instrument; his response to the Steps and Squares task demonstrates the deductive reasoning that seems to characterize his work. Although Ben did use variables to represent certain quantities, he did not demonstrate an ability to abstract or generalize across these tasks and his reasoning seemed to be primarily deductive as he relied on specific cases and concrete examples to structure his responses (e.g., his reliance on the pictorial diagrams for the Steps and Squares task). Ben also used both proportional (part versus whole) and spatial reasoning and was able to recognize and extend patterns. Ben was able to rely on his mathematical reasoning to make an argument and arrive at a conclusion; however, his arguments were often not complete and lacked the detail to completely justify his conclusions.

Communication

Paul can also communicate his mathematical knowledge and reasoning in a clear and logical fashion. He is comfortable using mathematical notation, variables, and language, and when asked to provide written descriptions, Paul can incorporate mathematics into his prose. In addition he uses tables, graphs, and charts to organize his work and mathematical communication.

Ben was able to communicate mathematically but frequently did not include enough detail in his solutions or justification of these solutions. He also seemed comfortable using mathematical notation and variable representations, but his overall work often lacked detail and it was at times difficult to follow his reasoning on the basis of his written work. In addition, Ben seemed not to understand parts of the tasks (e.g., the second part of Steps and Squares).

A condensed summary of Paul's and Ben's mathematical power

Paul has provided confirming evidence that he can apply appropriate mathematical knowledge to problem situations. He demonstrated the ability to use multiple methods in solving a problem and then used the results to verify each solution. Paul showed the ability to reason in several modes (inductive, deductive, proportional, and geometric) and can abstract mathematical ideas and representations. Paul effectively communicates his mathematical solution processes. In addition, he is able to support his mathematical arguments; however, the overall construction of his arguments could include more detail.

Ben has shown sufficient evidence of understanding the necessary computational skills, mathematical ideas, and concepts as required by the tasks. Ben tended to use deductive reasoning in his mathematical work and relies on concrete examples to support his thinking. In addition, he demonstrated the ability to reason proportionally and was able to recognize and extend patterns. He was able to communicate mathematically but frequently did not include enough detail. Ben was able to make comparisons and arrive at conclusions, but he often did not provide the necessary detail in responding to the requirements of the task.

Guiding Instruction

The condensed summary of Paul's and Ben's mathematical power can now be used in a formal reporting of the assessment process. Indeed, this qualitative description of the students' mathematical abilities could be included in their report cards or shared with their parents during parent-teacher conferences. In addition, if a traditional grade is required, then the application of a traditional analytic or holistic scoring rubric to Paul's and Ben's work could be easily accomplished. However, the value of this four-stage analytic scoring process is now realized during the final stage as the teacher uses this wealth of information about the individual student to make instructional decisions.

With this perspective in mind, we are now ready to individualize Paul's and Ben's instruction so that we can build on the mathematical knowledge and reasoning that they already possess. As a first step, some of our observations may need to be further verified so that as classroom teachers we are certain of the two students' abilities. This can be accomplished in a number of ways. We can ask Paul and Ben to complete similar tasks that elicit the same types of reasoning skills. A more direct approach may be to sit with the individual students and ask them questions about the work that they have already accomplished in responding to these three tasks. This allows us to truly integrate the assessment and instruction processes, since they are no longer discrete events but, rather, occur simultaneously as we try to obtain an accurate picture—a picture that is holistic in nature—of Paul's and Ben's mathematical power by relying on multiple sources of information.

In addition, we can begin to push Paul's mathematical thinking by building on his foundation of mathematical knowledge and reasoning abilities. For example, it seems that Paul is able to reason inductively in a variety of situations. We can now begin to introduce Paul to the special case of inductive reasoning that we know as "proof by induction." Paul, of his own accord, has already demonstrated the ability to use most of the components of an inductive proof, and he seems ready to be introduced to the formal method. With Ben, we can begin to introduce him to problems that focus on his ability to abstract and generalize so that his inductive reasoning abilities can be strengthened. We may also want to present both Ben and Paul with tasks that elicit modes of mathematical reasoning that they seemed to possess but did not clearly demonstrate (e.g., spatial reasoning, conditional reasoning, geometric reasoning).

As classroom teachers, we may also want to work with both Paul and Ben so that they develop more complete arguments. During the analysis phase of this process, it was apparent that Paul and Ben usually understood what they were doing and that they were using mathematical reasoning to support their arguments. However, as readers of his responses, we often were forced to make subtle inferences about both students' thinking—this is especially true for Ben—and how their mathematical work fit into their overall justification of conclusions. Some instructional time would be well spent assisting both students in more clearly communicating the process through which they make conjectures, test those conjectures, build an argument, and justify their conclusions. This process would allow Paul and Ben to communicate more effectively their mathematical reasoning that they have developed during the course of their mathematics experiences.

SUMMARY AND CONCLUDING REMARKS

Even though this analytic approach for interpreting students' responses to performance assessments offers a promising alternative to traditional techniques, it also presents significant challenges for students and teachers alike. Undoubtedly, we must provide students with ample opportunities to become familiar with these types of assessments and to be comfortable performing on demand. Students must also become aware of the importance of communicating their mathematical reasoning in a variety of forms and leaving clear trails of their mathematical work. Teachers need to be confident in their mathematical expertise as they analyze their students' responses to these complex assessment items. The analysis process we have outlined is also somewhat time-consuming. As teachers begin to use this process, we would recommend that they focus on different parts of the rubric—and complete condensed analyses depending on their schedule and needs—so that they can be more time-efficient. In addition, tasks such as these will often result in responses that contain false starts, exploration, mistakes, and unexpected solutions that are often insightful and more than viable. Hence, classroom teachers must be continually open to unconventional responses and attempt to perceive the problem-solving situation through the eyes of their students.

In conclusion, the structure of this interpretive process and analytic framework provides an alternative way to view, and hence to examine in detail, students' responses to mathematics performance assessment tasks. This process moves away from traditional ways of perceiving assessment and approaches the interpretation of students' mathematical work from a different perspective. By analyzing a collection of performances by individual students and synthesizing our interpretations in a qualitative summary, we are embracing Moss's (1994) hermeneutic approach— "A hermeneutic approach to assessment would involve holistic, integrative interpretations of collected performances that seek to understand the whole in light of its parts" (p. 7). As this approach is integrated with classroom instruction as well as observations of, and interviews with, students, we will arrive at more robust and complete understandings of students' mathematical power.

REFERENCES

Herman, Joan L., Pamela R. Aschbacher, and Lynn Winters. *A Practical Guide to Alternative Assessment.* Alexandria, Va.: Association for Supervision and Curriculum Development, 1992.

Lesh, Richard, and Susan J. Lamon, eds. *Assessment of Authentic Performance in School Mathematics.* Washington, D.C.: American Association for the Advancement of Science, 1992.

Mislevy, Robert J. "Foundations of a New Test Theory." In *Test Theory for a New Generation of Tests,* edited by Norman Frederiksen, Robert J. Mislevy, and Isaac I. Bejar, pp. 19–39. Hillsdale, N.J.: Erlbaum Publishers, 1993.

Moss, Pamela A. "Can There Be Validity without Reliability?" *Educational Researcher* 18(9) (1994): 5–12.

National Council of Teachers of Mathematics. *Assessment Standards for School Mathematics.* Reston, Va.: National Council of Teachers of Mathematics, 1995.

————. *Curriculum and Evaluation Standards for School Mathematics.* Reston, Va.: National Council of Teachers of Mathematics, 1989.

————. *Professional Standards for Teaching Mathematics.* Reston, Va.: National Council of Teachers of Mathematics, 1991.

O'Daffer, Phares G., and Bruce A. Thornquist. "Critical Thinking, Mathematical Reasoning, and Proof." In *Research Ideas for the Classroom: High School Mathematics,* edited by Patricia S. Wilson, pp. 39–56. Reston, Va.: National Council of Teachers of Mathematics, 1993.

Pimm, David. *Speaking Mathematically: Communication in Mathematics Classrooms.* New York: Routledge & Kegan Paul, 1987.

Polya, George. *How to Solve It: A New Aspect of Mathematical Method.* Princeton, N.J.: Princeton University Press, 1945.

Schoenfeld, Alan H. *Mathematical Problem Solving.* New York: Academic Press, 1985.

Stenmark, Jean K. *Mathematics Assessment: Myths, Models, Good Questions, and Practical Suggestions.* Reston, Va.: National Council of Teachers of Mathematics, 1991.

Wiggins, Grant. "Assessment: Authenticity, Context, and Validity." *Phi Delta Kappan* 75 (November 1993): 200–214.

15

Mathematical Reasoning
In the Eye of the Beholder

Peggy House

TEACHING is a complex operation, and there is a danger that teachers, especially less-experienced teachers, will lose sight of the fact that much of mathematics and mathematical reasoning is in the eye of the beholder. The ways in which students structure a problem and, consequently, the strategies they use to formulate a solution can differ markedly from the teacher's approach. The teacher who tries to impose his or her own reasoning pattern, rather than understanding and accepting diverse methods from the students, will almost surely miss a rich opportunity to further students' learning of mathematics. This realization that it is essential for teachers to understand and accept different ways of conceptualizing and solving problems came to light in a dramatic way for a group of preservice secondary mathematics teachers during a course on teaching geometry; it was subsequently repeated in other classes of in-service teachers and high school students as well.

The stimulus for the lesson was the following problem that had been assigned for homework: *ABCD* is a square (fig. 15.1), and *E, F, G,* and *H* are midpoints of the respective sides. Each midpoint is joined to the two opposite vertices. What is the area of the shaded region?

You are encouraged to think about the problem above before continuing. In particular, it will be most useful if you describe for yourself what you see in the diagram and the general approach that you would use in solving the problem so that you can compare your reasoning with that of others, for it is in such comparison that the richness of the problem lies.

After working on the problem for a few days, twenty-four students submitted their solutions. As is often the case when one grades assignments, the instructor instinctively began sorting the solutions into piles according to the approach used by the solver. To her surprise, when all the papers had been read, the instructor found herself surrounded by thirteen piles representing distinct solution paths. These different approaches proved to be far more interesting and instructive than any lesson about area that might have derived from the problem per se. The next class period was spent examining and discussing the views of the problem and the resulting lines of reasoning that students employed.

Preliminary Observations

Before proceeding, it will be useful to examine the problem and establish some preliminary results that will appear later in various students' solutions.

Observation 1

Segment EG joining opposite midpoints divides the square into two equal rectangles ($AEGD$ and $EBCG$ in fig. 15.2) with diagonals that intersect at the center of each rectangle (e.g., DE and AG in rectangle $AEGD$); segment HF produces an analogous result. The symmetries of the figure lead to the observation that segments HQ, QO, OL, LF, EJ, JO, ON, and NG all have length $s/4$, where s is the length of the side of $ABCD$.

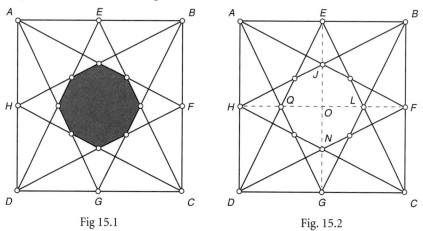

Fig 15.1   Fig. 15.2

Observation 2

Less obvious is the fact that lines drawn perpendicular to the sides of the original square through points R, K, M, and P trisect the sides of the original square (see fig. 15.3). A proof of that relationship, done by a high school student, is illustrated in figure 15.4. She argued that a perpendicular from K to segment OF (KK_3 in fig. 15.4) forms $\triangle KK_3L$ similar to $\triangle EOL$. Since $OL = s/4$ and $OE = s/2$, then $K_3L = KK_3/2$. But K lies on the diagonal BD, so $\triangle KK_3O$ is isosceles and similar to $\triangle BCD$; hence $KK_3 = K_3O = 2K_3L$ and $OL = K_3O + K_3L = 3K_3L = s/4$. This yields $K_3L = s/12$, from which it follows that $K_3O = s/4 - s/12 = s/6$. From the symmetry of the figure we know that $RK = KM = MP = PR = 2(s/6) = s/3$.

Observation 3

Another important set of relationships can be derived by considering figure 15.5, also the result of one student's insight. In this instance, the four light-colored triangles from the original figure are rotated about the midpoints

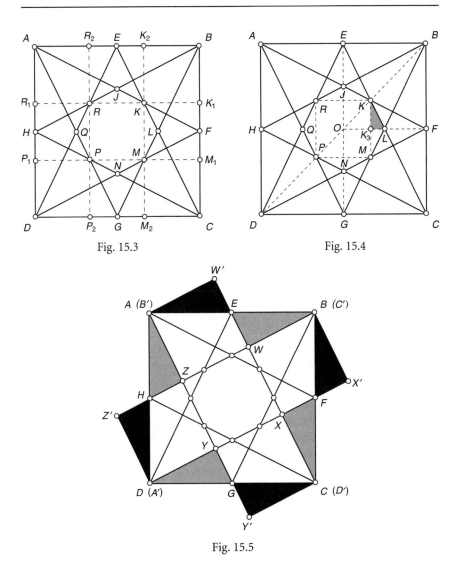

Fig. 15.3

Fig. 15.4

Fig. 15.5

of the sides of the square ($\triangle AZH$ to $\triangle A'Z'H$; $\triangle DYG$ to $\triangle D'Y'G$; $\triangle CXF$ to $\triangle C'X'F$; $\triangle BWE$ to $\triangle B'W'E$). The resulting concave figure consists of five congruent squares, each with area x^2, whose total area is equal to the area of the original square $ABCD$. Thus, $5x^2 = s^2$, and consequently the side of each small square is $x = \left(s\sqrt{5}\right)/5$.

Observation 4

Within the original figure there are numerous similar right triangles, all with sides in the ratio $1:2:\sqrt{5}$. Figure 15.6 shows one representative of each of

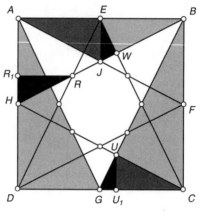

Fig. 15.6

eight families of such triangles; it is possible to find at least eight congruent members of each family somewhere within square *ABCD*. Table 15.1 summarizes the dimensions of these eight families of triangles.

Table 15.1
Dimensions of Families of Similar Triangles

Family Defined by:	Short Leg	Long Leg	Hypotenuse	Area
$\triangle ADG$	$s/2$	s	$s\sqrt{5}/2$	$s^2/4$
$\triangle BUC$	$s\sqrt{5}/5$	$2s\sqrt{5}/5$	s	$s^2/5$
$\triangle AEJ$	$s/4$	$s/2$	$s\sqrt{5}/4$	$s^2/16$
$\triangle BWE$	$s\sqrt{5}/10$	$s\sqrt{5}/5$	$s/2$	$s^2/20$
$\triangle CU_1U$	$s/5$	$2s/5$	$s\sqrt{5}/5$	$s^2/25$
$\triangle HR_1R$	$s/6$	$s/3$	$s\sqrt{5}/6$	$s^2/36$
$\triangle EWJ$	$s\sqrt{5}/20$	$s\sqrt{5}/10$	$s/4$	$s^2/80$
$\triangle GU_1U$	$s/10$	$s/5$	$s\sqrt{5}/10$	$s^2/100$

Observation 5

Finally, we establish a result that escaped the notice of the vast majority of persons who attempted to solve this problem. The eight small triangles whose hypotenuses form the sides of the shaded octagon are 3–4–5 right triangles (e.g., $\triangle JWK$ in fig. 15.7). This result can be confirmed by referring back to figure 15.5 from which it can be shown that, in

$$\triangle HWC,\ HW = \frac{3}{2} \cdot \frac{s\sqrt{5}}{5},\ WC = \frac{4}{2} \cdot \frac{s\sqrt{5}}{5},\ \text{and}\ CH = \frac{5}{2} \cdot \frac{s\sqrt{5}}{5}.$$

Since $\triangle JWK$ is similar to $\triangle HWC$, the sides of $\triangle JWK$ are likewise in the ratio of 3:4:5. From table 15.1, $JW = s\sqrt{5}/20$ $= 3s\sqrt{5}/60$, so $WK = 4s\sqrt{5}/60 = s\sqrt{5}/15$ and $JK = 5s\sqrt{5}/60 = s\sqrt{5}/12$.

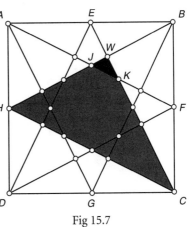

With these observations established, it is possible to consider the diverse lines of reasoning that were exhibited by different students and teachers when solving the given problem. Each solution seemed to depend on what the problem solver saw in the given diagram, and the way the solver conceived the problem dictated the line of reasoning that followed.

Fig 15.7

SOLUTIONS 1 AND 2: "ADD-ONS"

Two groups of solvers viewed the octagon as a square surrounded by four triangles, although the component parts were different in the two cases. For these solvers, the solution required summing the areas of the parts as shown in figure 15.8. The arguments given are typical of the reasoning used by the persons who chose one of these two approaches.

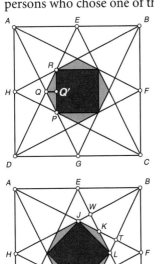

1. "Square Plus"

Argument:

$QQ' = (s/3 - s/4) = s/12.$
$RP\ = s/3.$
Area of octagon $= (s/3)^2 + 4(1/2)(s/3)(s/12)$
$= s^2/9 + s^2/18 = s^2/6.$

2. "Diamond Plus"

Argument:

Since $\triangle JWK$ and $\triangle LTK$ are 3-4-5 right triangles, area of
$\triangle JKL = $ (area of $\triangle JTL$) − (area of $\triangle KTL$)
$= (1/2)(3x)(9x) - (1/2)(3x)(4x)$
$= (3/2)(9x^2 - 4x^2) = (3/2)(5x^2)$
where $x = s\sqrt{5}/60$ (see Observation 5).
Area $\triangle JKL = (15/2)(5s^2/60^2) = (s^2/2)(1/4)(1/12)$
$= (1/24)(s^2/4)$
Further, $JL^2 = (3x)^2 + (9x)^2 = 90x^2 = 90(s\sqrt{5}/60)^2 = s^2/8$
[or $JL^2 = (s/4)^2 + (s/4)^2 = 2s^2/16$] and $JL = s\sqrt{2}/4.$
[or area of square = product of diagonals/2 $= (1/2)(s/2)^2$]
Area of octagon $= (s\sqrt{2}/4)^2 + 4(1/24)(s^2/4) = s^2(1/8 + 1/24)$
$= s^2/6$

Fig. 15.8. Solutions 1 and 2—"Add-ons"

Solutions 3 and 4: "Cutouts"

The solvers in these groups viewed the octagon as the residue of a square from which the corners were removed. In the case of solution 3, this amounted to removing four triangular pieces, whereas solution 4 required removal of eight triangles. These views and the resulting lines of reasoning are shown in figure 15.9.

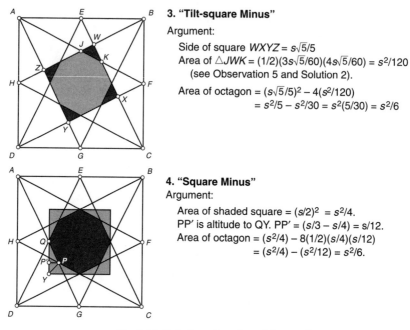

3. "Tilt-square Minus"

Argument:

Side of square $WXYZ = s\sqrt{5}/5$

Area of $\triangle JWK = (1/2)(3s\sqrt{5}/60)(4s\sqrt{5}/60) = s^2/120$ (see Observation 5 and Solution 2).

Area of octagon $= (s\sqrt{5}/5)^2 - 4(s^2/120)$
$$= s^2/5 - s^2/30 = s^2(5/30) = s^2/6$$

4. "Square Minus"
Argument:

Area of shaded square $= (s/2)^2 = s^2/4$.
PP′ is altitude to QY. PP′ $= (s/3 - s/4) = s/12$.
Area of octagon $= (s^2/4) - 8(1/2)(s/4)(s/12)$
$$= (s^2/4) - (s^2/12) = s^2/6.$$

Fig. 15.9. Solutions 3 and 4—"Cutouts"

Solution 5: "Between"

A few solvers seemed to combine the views in solutions 1 and 4, viewing the octagon as nested between two squares. For them, the solution required both the addition of regions to the inner square and the removal of regions from the outer square. The reasoning for this view is summarized in figure 15.10.

SOLUTION 6: "LAYERS"

Quite a different view of the problem is represented in a dissection of the octagon into two trapezoids and two triangles whose areas must be summed. Figure 15.11 shows this approach.

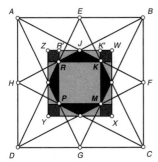

5. "Between Squares"

Argument:

Area of $WXYZ = (s/2)^2 = s^2/4$.

Area of $KMPR = (s/3)^2 = s^2/9$.

Area of each small corner square $= (s/12)^2 = s^2/144$.

Area of $RR'K'K = (1/4)(s^2/4 - s^2/9 - 4s^2/144)$
$= (1/4)(s^2/9) = s^2/36$

Area of black triangle $= (1/2)(s^2/36) = s^2/72$

Area of octagon $=$ Area $KMPR +$ area 4 black triangles
$= s^2/9 + 4(s^2/72) = 3s^2/18 = s^2/6$.

Fig. 15.10. Solution 5—"Between Squares"

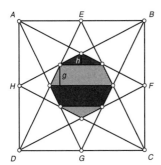

6. "Trapezoids and Triangles"

Argument:

$h = (3/4)s - (2/3)s = s/12$.

Area of each triangle $= (1/2)(s/3)(s/12) = s^2/72$.

$g = (2/3)s - (1/2)s = s/6$.

Area of each trapezoid $= (1/2)(s/6)(s/2 + s/3) = 5s^2/72$.

Area of octagon $= 2s^2/72 + 10s^2/72 = s^2/6$.

Fig. 15.11. Solution 6—"Layers"

Solutions 7 and 8: "Pinwheels"

Another approach to the problem arose from a view of the octagon as consisting of eight triangles emanating as a pinwheel from the center. A somewhat less-common variation viewed it as four "kites" rather than eight triangles. The first of these two approaches, always one of the most common solution strategies, was also the one most likely to lead the solvers down an incorrect path.

The error frequently made by students, including by seasoned geometry teachers, is to assume that the shaded region is a regular octagon; hence, it is assumed that the eight triangles in the pinwheel are isosceles as well as congruent. Among the erroneous statements made by geometry teachers themselves were the following:

- "Since *ABCD* is a regular polygon, the octagon created is a regular polygon ..."
- "Since the octagon is equilateral, it is regular ..."
- "Since the octagon is equilateral and the central angles are congruent, the octagon is regular ..."
- "Since a polygon inscribed in a square is a regular polygon ..."

Figure 15.12 can be used to illuminate the source of the misconception. It has already been established that $QO = s/4$, $RR'' = s/6$, and $QR'' = s/12$. From this we know that $OR'' = s/4 - s/12 = s/6$. Applying the distance formula, we find that

$$OR = \sqrt{\left(\frac{s}{6}\right)^2 + \left(\frac{s}{6}\right)^2} = \frac{s\sqrt{2}}{6} \approx 0.236 \cdot s.$$

But $OQ = 0.25s$, proving that the small triangles are not isosceles, from which it follows that the angles of the octagon are not congruent, and hence the octagon is not regular. A nice demonstration of the fact that an equilateral octagon with central angles of 45° is not necessarily regular is outlined in figure 15.13. The demonstration uses dynamic geometry software such as the Geometer's Sketchpad. Figure 15.14 presents correct reasoning paths for the two cases of pinwheel solutions.

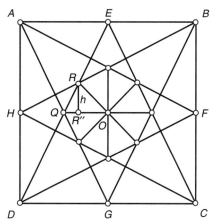

Fig. 15.12. Counterexample: Central angle hypothesis

Solutions 9–12: "Surroundings"

The final groups of problem solvers focused not on the octagon itself but on the *unwanted* portions of the square surrounding the octagon. The common thread in these solutions was to dissect the outer region into sets of triangles whose areas could easily be calculated and then to subtract the sums of those areas from the whole. Figure 15.15 portrays four approaches using the surround strategy.

Discussion

Teachers are encouraged to ask their students, "Could you solve the problem another way?" Often, that "other way" amounts to substituting a different

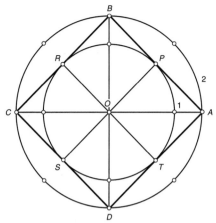

Concentric circles, 1 and 2, with central angles of 45°. *APBRCSDT* is the octagon constructed with vertices *A,B,C,D* on Circle 2 and vertices *P,R,S,T* on Circle 1. Figures below show variations in the octagon as the relative radii of the two circles change. Only when the radii are equal (fig. 15.13d) is the octagon regular, although it begins to appear regular as the radii approach equality (fig. 15.13c)

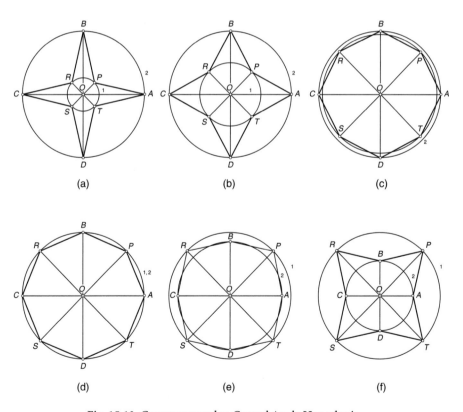

Fig. 15.13. Counterexamples: Central Angle Hypothesis

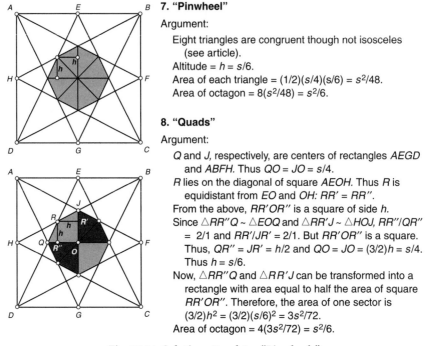

7. "Pinwheel"

Argument:

Eight triangles are congruent though not isosceles (see article).

Altitude = $h = s/6$.

Area of each triangle = $(1/2)(s/4)(s/6) = s^2/48$.

Area of octagon = $8(s^2/48) = s^2/6$.

8. "Quads"

Argument:

Q and J, respectively, are centers of rectangles $AEGD$ and $ABFH$. Thus $QO = JO = s/4$.

R lies on the diagonal of square $AEOH$. Thus R is equidistant from EO and OH: $RR' = RR''$.

From the above, $RR'OR''$ is a square of side h.

Since $\triangle RR''Q \sim \triangle EOQ$ and $\triangle RR'J \sim \triangle HOJ$, $RR''/QR'' = 2/1$ and $RR'/JR' = 2/1$. But $RR'OR''$ is a square. Thus, $QR'' = JR' = h/2$ and $QO = JO = (3/2)h = s/4$. Thus $h = s/6$.

Now, $\triangle RR''Q$ and $\triangle RR'J$ can be transformed into a rectangle with area equal to half the area of square $RR'OR''$. Therefore, the area of one sector is $(3/2)h^2 = (3/2)(s/6)^2 = 3s^2/72$.

Area of octagon = $4(3s^2/72) = s^2/6$.

Fig. 15.14. Solutions 7 and 8—"Pinwheels"

but equivalent equation or to establishing a different pair of congruent triangles. That did not seem to be what was happening in this lesson. Rather, different groups of students appeared to be solving quite different problems, depending on what they perceived in the original figure.

Class discussion the next day focused on comparing the different interpretations of the problem that arose from the class. Not only were the students amazed at the number and diversity of solutions, but in some cases they admitted that they were quite incapable of seeing what others had seen. Much like the well-known perception tests that ask whether one sees one vase or two faces, this problem appeared to present different figure-ground patterns to different viewers. So, for example, a person who conceptualized the problem as a pinwheel of eight triangles might not be able to see the surrounding triangles in some of the later solutions.

The pedagogical implications of the lesson are significant. Often in mathematics classes, the teacher or a student displays one solution to a problem assuming that all listeners see and follow what he or she is explaining. But a person presenting, for example, solution 1 to this problem and describing the addition of four triangles to a square might not communicate at all with the student who is focused on solution 3 and the need to subtract, not add, the areas of four triangles—or with the person

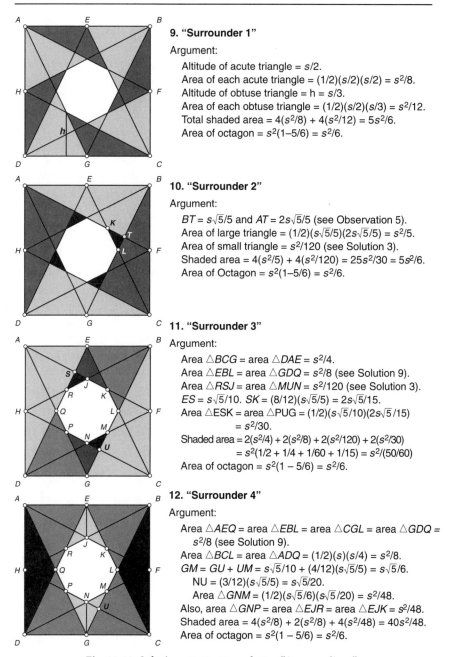

9. "Surrounder 1"

Argument:

Altitude of acute triangle = $s/2$.
Area of each acute triangle = $(1/2)(s/2)(s/2) = s^2/8$.
Altitude of obtuse triangle = h = $s/3$.
Area of each obtuse triangle = $(1/2)(s/2)(s/3) = s^2/12$.
Total shaded area = $4(s^2/8) + 4(s^2/12) = 5s^2/6$.
Area of octagon = $s^2(1–5/6) = s^2/6$.

10. "Surrounder 2"

Argument:

$BT = s\sqrt{5}/5$ and $AT = 2s\sqrt{5}/5$ (see Observation 5).
Area of large triangle = $(1/2)(s\sqrt{5}/5)(2s\sqrt{5}/5) = s^2/5$.
Area of small triangle = $s^2/120$ (see Solution 3).
Shaded area = $4(s^2/5) + 4(s^2/120) = 25s^2/30 = 5s^2/6$.
Area of Octagon = $s^2(1–5/6) = s^2/6$.

11. "Surrounder 3"

Argument:

Area $\triangle BCG$ = area $\triangle DAE = s^2/4$.
Area $\triangle EBL$ = area $\triangle GDQ = s^2/8$ (see Solution 9).
Area $\triangle RSJ$ = area $\triangle MUN = s^2/120$ (see Solution 3).
$ES = s\sqrt{5}/10$. $SK = (8/12)(s\sqrt{5}/5) = 2s\sqrt{5}/15$.
Area $\triangle ESK$ = area $\triangle PUG = (1/2)(s\sqrt{5}/10)(2s\sqrt{5}/15)$
$= s^2/30$.
Shaded area = $2(s^2/4) + 2(s^2/8) + 2(s^2/120) + 2(s^2/30)$
$= s^2(1/2 + 1/4 + 1/60 + 1/15) = s^2/(50/60)$
Area of octagon = $s^2(1 – 5/6) = s^2/6$.

12. "Surrounder 4"

Argument:

Area $\triangle AEQ$ = area $\triangle EBL$ = area $\triangle CGL$ = area $\triangle GDQ$ = $s^2/8$ (see Solution 9).
Area $\triangle BCL$ = area $\triangle ADQ = (1/2)(s)(s/4) = s^2/8$.
$GM = GU + UM = s\sqrt{5}/10 + (4/12)(s\sqrt{5}/5) = s\sqrt{5}/6$.
$NU = (3/12)(s\sqrt{5}/5) = s\sqrt{5}/20$.
Area $\triangle GNM = (1/2)(s\sqrt{5}/6)(s\sqrt{5}/20) = s^2/48$.
Also, area $\triangle GNP$ = area $\triangle EJR$ = area $\triangle EJK = s^2/48$.
Shaded area = $4(s^2/8) + 2(s^2/8) + 4(s^2/48) = 40s^2/48$.
Area of octagon = $s^2(1 – 5/6) = s^2/6$.

Fig. 15.15. Solutions 9, 10, 11, and 12—"Surroundings"

who has viewed the octagon as a pinwheel of eight triangles and has not see a square at all. The discussion occasioned by the problem helped the participating teachers realize the importance of listening carefully and understanding what a student is seeing and communicating, a challenge that is often easier to state than to accomplish.

In one class of experienced teachers who had worked on the problem, the vast majority submitted incorrect solutions because they had made the assumption that the octagon was regular. They were surprised later, when confronted with their own misconceptions, at the ease with which they had fallen into those misconceptions even when they "knew better." Many admitted having taught lessons about regular polygons, yet not being able to apply their knowledge in an unfamiliar context. A number of teachers discovered that the assumption that the octagon was regular led them to a value for the area of the shaded region that did not check when put back into the problem, and although they could recognize that "something was wrong," they continued to trace their same line of reasoning over again, never questioning the validity of their assumption.

Another interesting outcome was the attitude of the preservice teachers toward the problem and what constituted an appropriate solution. In addition to the dozen solutions outlined earlier, a few students recognized that the problem could be solved using analytic geometry. If, for example, the square is placed on a coordinate grid with one vertex at the origin and each side equal to unity, as shown in figure 15.16, one can write the equations of the eight line segments emanating from the midpoints and solve pairs of equations to determine the coordinates of the points of intersection. This information is sufficient to determine the necessary dimensions for finding

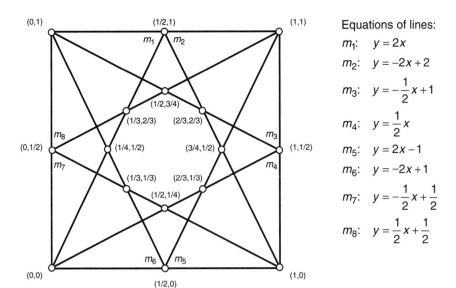

Equations of lines:

m_1: $y = 2x$

m_2: $y = -2x + 2$

m_3: $y = -\dfrac{1}{2}x + 1$

m_4: $y = \dfrac{1}{2}x$

m_5: $y = 2x - 1$

m_6: $y = -2x + 1$

m_7: $y = -\dfrac{1}{2}x + \dfrac{1}{2}$

m_8: $y = \dfrac{1}{2}x + \dfrac{1}{2}$

Fig. 15.16. Coordinate Solution

the area of the octagon. But students tended to shun the analytical-geometry approach on the grounds that it was not a "real proof." For example, when two students were becoming frustrated because their attempts at a solution seemed to be leading nowhere, the instructor suggested that perhaps a coordinate approach would give them a fresh perspective on the problem. They acknowledged that they would have no trouble doing it that way but rejected the suggestion, insisting that there had to be a "real geometric way" to reason it out.

CONCLUSION

The problem discussed here has provided rich insights into the different ways that students have constructed meaning in this setting and to the lines of reasoning that flowed from their conceptions of the problem. It illustrates the importance of finding out what students see and understand and listening to them describe their lines of reasoning, rather than trying to impose one perspective (often presented as the "right way" to do the problem). The outcomes first noted in a preservice course on teaching geometry have been replicated every time the problem has been given, not only to preservice teachers but to in-service teachers and to high school students as well. In every case, individuals have viewed the problem from very different perspectives, leading to different lines of reasoning.

It is not surprising that the perspectives described in this article do not form an exhaustive list. A physicist who was present during one discussion of the problem noted afterward that the approach he would use would be to construct a square with one shaded area from a uniform sheet of material, weigh it, then cut it apart and weigh the shaded region. The ratio of the weights would equal the ratio of the areas. A statistician suggested throwing a large number of darts in a random fashion at a square target and noting what proportion of them hit inside the shaded region. A computer scientist decided to program the computer to throw the darts for him. Are these, also, valid solutions?

It's all in the eye of the beholder.

16

The Language of Quantification in Mathematics Instruction

Susanna S. Epp

As a relatively young college professor in 1979, I began teaching mathematics courses whose primary aim was to help students improve their ability to assess the truth and falsity of mathematical statements. At the outset, I had a lot of good intentions and much personal experience doing mathematics myself, but I had very little background in the formal aspects of mathematical thought. It soon became clear that the unconscious instincts for logic and language that had enabled me to succeed were not shared by the large majority of my students (Epp 1986). Moreover, my lack of knowledge about the formal basis for those instincts made it difficult for me to communicate with them to help correct their errors and build their capacity for abstract reasoning.

As I attempted to gain insight into my students' problems, I consulted the work of cognitive psychologists and researchers in mathematics education and discovered that the kinds of mental processing problems my students exhibited are extremely common in the population at large. This discovery helped reconcile me to the existence of these problems in the young people in my classes and inspired me to try to invent remedies. My efforts were aided by continual interaction with my students, by a few of my own experiments, and by acquiring some technical knowledge about logic and language. My approach was influenced by my increasing awareness about the use of language outside of mathematics and the realization that some of my students' problems may have resulted from confusion between the way certain words are used in everyday speech and their more-technical meanings in mathematics.

When I began incorporating instruction in the logic and language of mathematics as a theme running through my courses, students' performance improved significantly. Nevertheless, I was struck by how much effort was required for many of them to overcome the linguistic habits that were leading them into mathematical error. Since the ability to acquire language is greatest in the young, cultivating students' sensitivity to logic and language in the precollege years could check the formation of these habits before they become deeply ingrained. The success of programs such as TexPREP, run by Manuel Berriozábal in San Antonio, provides objective support for such a conclusion. (Berriozábal 1995).

SOME FORMALISM

At the heart of mathematical discourse are words referring to quantity: *all* and *some*, along with variations such as *every, any,* and *no*. Almost all important mathematical facts contain at least one of these words. For example, consider the following list of statements:

1. For all pairs of real numbers a and b, $a + b = b + a$.
2. In every right triangle, the square of the hypotenuse equals the sum of the squares of the other two sides.
3. No integers a and b have the $\sqrt{2} = \dfrac{a}{b}$.
4. Given any integer, there is some integer that is larger.
5. Some positive integer is less than or equal to all positive integers.
6. For all real numbers $\varepsilon > 0$, there is some integer N such that for all integers $n > N$, $\left| a_n - L \right| < \varepsilon$.

In order to work effectively with such statements, students need to have a sense for their logical form. For instance, how can we figure out if a given *all* statement is true? What does it mean for an *all* statement to be false? What are other, equivalent ways of expressing an *all* statement? If a given *all* statement is true, what can be deduced?

A *universal statement* is one that can be written in the form "All A are B." To deal capably with such statements, one needs to be able to express them in a variety of equivalent ways. For instance, "All squares are rectangles" can also be stated as "Every square is a rectangle," "Any square is a rectangle," "For all squares x, x is a rectangle," "If something is a square, then it is a rectangle," and "For all x, if x is a square, then x is a rectangle." The fact that universal statements can be expressed as *if–then* statements is of particular importance in mathematics.

An *existential statement* is one that can be expressed as "Some A are B." Such statements also have alternate, equivalent formulations. For instance, "Some rational numbers are integers" can also be written, "There is at least one rational number that is an integer," "For some rational number, that number is an integer," or "There exists a rational number x such that x is an integer."

A beautiful duality governs the truth and falsity of universal and existential statements. To say "It is false that all A are B" is equivalent to saying "Some A are not–B," or "Some A have the property that they are not B." And to say "It is false that some A are B" is equivalent to saying that "All A are not–B," or "All A have the property that they are not *B*." For example, the statement "It is false that all people are honest" means that "Some people are dishonest," and the statement "It is false that some doors are locked" means that "All doors are unlocked."

In general, to establish the truth of a statement of the form "All *A* are *B*," we suppose we have a particular but arbitrarily chosen (or generic) object that is an *A*. Let's call this object *x*. We then show *x* is a *B*. This method of reasoning is sometimes called *generalizing from the generic particular* because since we make no special assumptions about *x* that do not apply equally to every other *A*, everything we deduce *x* applies equally to every other *A*. For instance, to show that the square of any odd integer is odd, we suppose *x* is any particular but arbitrarily chosen odd integer. By definition of odd, $x = 2k + 1$ for some integer *k*. It follows that $x^2 = (2k + 1)^2 = 4k^2 + 4k + 1 = 2(2k^2 + 2k) + 1$, which is odd (because it can be written in the form 2 • (an integer) + 1.

WHAT RESEARCH SHOWS

The abilities to rephrase statements in alternative, equivalent ways, to recognize that other attractive-looking reformulations are not equivalent, and to have a feeling for the truth and falsity of universal and existential statements are crucial mathematical problem-solving tools. Yet numerous studies show that students do not acquire these abilities spontaneously.

For instance, there is much evidence that a majority of people perceive the statements "If *A* then *B*" and "If *B* then *A*" as equivalent and do not readily deduce that "If *A* then *B*" implies "If not *B* then not *A*." (Anderson 1990, 292–97). Furthermore, I've found that approximately 70 percent of students select "No mathematicians wear glasses" as the sentence that "*exactly* expresses what it means for the sentence 'All mathematicians wear glasses' to be false," whereas only about 20 percent choose the correct negation "Some mathematicians do not wear glasses" (Epp 1986). Recently, Dubinsky and Yiparaki (1996) have collected evidence showing that a significant fraction of students interpret a statement of the form "There is a ✶ such that for all Δ, □" to mean the same as "For all Δ, there is a ✶ such that □." Both Epp (1986, 1997) and Selden and Selden (1995, 1996) have documented some of the ways in which students' inability to "unpack the logic of mathematical statements" impairs their ability to understand and construct mathematical arguments.

Table 16.1 illustrates how some of these misconceptions manifest themselves inside the mathematics classroom.

CONFUSION BETWEEN MATHEMATICAL AND EVERYDAY LANGUAGE

One reason students may have problems using logic correctly in mathematics and other technical situations is that in informal settings certain

TABLE 16.1

Just because it's true that	it doesn't follow that
1. All irrational numbers have nonterminating decimal expansions	All numbers with nonterminating decimal expansions are irrational.
2. For all positive numbers a, there is a positive number b such that $b < a$.	There is a positive number b such that for all positive numbers, a, $b < a$

Just because it's false that	it doesn't follow that
3. All rational numbers are integers.	No rational numbers are integers.

Because it's true that	it *does* follow that
4. For all positive numbers x, if $x^2 < x$ then $x < 1$.	For all positive numbers x, if $x \not< 1$ then $x^2 \not< 1$.

forms of statements are often interpreted in ways that differ from their formal meanings. The following is one example.

Imagine that a teacher promises a class: "All those who sit quietly during the test may go out and play afterwards." Also imagine that this teacher then allows noisy students to go outside and play along with the students who were quiet. From the point of view of formal logic, the teacher's actions are perfectly consistent with the teacher's words. After all, the teacher only said what would happen to students who sat quietly during the test; nothing was said about students who made noise. Most observers of the scene, however, would judge such a teacher lacking in resolve. Presumably, the teacher would not have made the statement without intending students to infer the converse: "All those allowed to go out and play after the test will have sat quietly during it," or equivalently, "All those who do not sit quietly during the test may not go out and play afterwards."

Even mathematicians sometimes take advantage of people's perception that "All A are B" and "All B are A" are equivalent. For example, a text might define an even integer by stating: "Any integer with a factor of 2 is *even*," or equivalently, "An integer is *even* if it has a factor of 2." Yet later, when showing why the sum of two even integers is even, the text would assume the truth of the converse statement, "Any integer that is even has a factor of 2" (or "If an integer is even, then it has a factor of 2").

The problem is, of course, that situations arise regularly in mathematics and other technical fields where "All A are B" is true whereas "All B are A" is false. Item 1 of Table 16.1 is one such instance. So, despite the many times we can get away with being imprecise about the logical relationship between the two types of statements, in order to be really successful, we need to develop an awareness that it is possible for the statements to have different truth values and as teachers, to be on the lookout for situations where this occurs.

The example cited above is just one of many. In fact, Wells (1997) has made available on the Internet an entire lexicon of grammatical usages whose everyday meanings differ somewhat from their mathematical ones.

SUGGESTIONS FOR MATHEMATICS INSTRUCTION

1. As a result of the NCTM *Standards* (1989), many teachers are now asking students to explain their reasoning or to justify their answers to various problems. Critiquing students' work, though time-consuming, gives teachers an excellent opportunity to point out fallacies in a student's own reasoning or to show that more evidence is needed to support a student's conclusion adequately. When given by teachers with a solid command of mathematical language and logic, such feedback can be of enormous benefit to students' intellectual development.

2. Logical puzzles are both fun and almost unbeatable at helping students learn that deductive reasoning consists of chains of inferences. They are also a marvelous introduction to the concept of reasoning by contradiction because, to solve many of them, it is necessary to show that certain possibilities lead to contradictions and can therefore be eliminated. Logical puzzles suitable for all K–12 grades are widely available. If every math teacher devoted just a few hours a year to having students work such puzzles, a marked improvement in students' reasoning abilities might result.

3. Even in the earliest grades, students can be given activities to increase their sensitivity to the language of quantification. Consider, for instance, showing them the following picture:

Fig. 16.1

One could ask whether each of the following statements is true or false:

a. All the white objects are squares.

b. All the square objects are white.

c. No square objects are white.

d. There is a white object that is larger than every gray object.

e. Every gray object has a black object next to it.

f. There is a black object that has all the gray objects next to it.

g. All objects that are not small are not gray.

Observe that statements a–g address all the logical difficulties illustrated in Table 16.1. Perhaps if students became accustomed at an early age to dealing with such statements in simple situations, they might develop a feeling for the deep grammar of mathematics that would lead them, as more mature students, to avoid the kinds of misunderstandings shown in Table 16.1. A recent study indicates that the way the human brain processes the deep grammar of a language differs depending on whether fluency in the language was developed from infancy or at about age eleven (Kim et al. 1997).

4. As soon as letters have been introduced to stand for unknown or unspecified quantities, teachers can ask questions involving variables. The following two problems are taken from the Russian Mathematics series translated as part of the University of Chicago School Mathematics Project (Moro et al. 1992).

Problem 1

For what values of the letters are the following equalities true? (Grade 3, age 9)

(a) $36 \cdot b = b$ (b) $10 \cdot c = 10$ (c) $12 \cdot a = a \cdot 12$ (d) $a \cdot a = a$

(e) $49 \cdot a = 0$ (f) $c + c = c$ (g) $b + b = b + 6$ (h) $b \cdot 0 = 0$

Problem 2

It is given that x and y are positive numbers with $x < y$. Replace each asterisk with the symbols $<$, $>$, or $=$ so as to obtain a true equality or inequality. (Grade 5, age 11)

(a) $0 * x$ (b) $-y * 0$ (c) $-x * x$ (d) $y * -x$

(e) $|x| * -x$ (f) $|y| * y$ (g) $-x * |x|$ (h) $|-x| * |-y|$

Note that for each of these problems students are only asked to give an answer, not to justify it. However, in order to answer the questions correctly, students need to imagine substituting various values for the variables and testing the resulting expressions for the truth and falsity. This is an excellent way for them to start thinking about the issue of the truth and falsity of general mathematical statements. Even if such special questions are not added to the curriculum, teachers can improve students' understanding by asking them to "find all numbers that make this equation true" rather than always phrasing the request as "solve this equation for x," which many students come to see as a purely mechanical procedure involving the mysterious "x."

5. As early as prealgebra, one can introduce the idea of disproof by counterexample. One could start by using the kind of exercise suggested in item 3 above. Or, one might invite the class to discuss whether a statement like "All eighth-graders are lazy" is true or false. Since students have a personal interest in this statement, it should not be hard to get general agreement that the existence of just one nonlazy eighth-grader is enough to falsify it. One could then

go on to ask: Sam claims the equation $(a + b)^2 = a^2 + b^2$ is true for all values of a and b. Ann disagrees. Who is right? Justify your answer.

6. At about the same time as one introduces disproof, one can have students justify statements by simply citing a universal property such as the commutative, associative, or distributive law or one of the laws of exponents. For instance, one could pose the following question: Dan claims the equation $k(k +5) = 5k$ is true for all values of k. Jan disagrees. Who is right? Justify your answer.

Or, more challengingly (from a step in a mathematical induction problem): Dan claims the equation

$$(k)\left(2^{k+2}\right)+(k+2)\left(2^{k+2}\right)=\left[k+(k+2)\right]\left(2^{k+1}\right)$$

is true for all values of k. Jan disagrees. Who is right? Justify your answer.

Of course, the hoped-for answer in both cases is something like "Dan is right. This equation is true for all values of k because of the distributive law." As one asks about more and more complicated expressions, students develop an increased mastery and appreciation for the power of universal properties.

7. Stating universal properties in words as well as in symbols also enhances students' ability to apply them in a broad range of situations. For instance, one can express one of the distributive laws by saying that "one number times the sum of two others equals the sum of the first times the second plus the first times the third" while pointing to the various parts of the expression as one refers to them. This seems to have a positive effect on students who get stuck identifying the law with the particular letters used to symbolize it. If, for example, we only express this distributive law using the formula $a(b + c) = ab + ac$, many students have difficulty applying it to the $b(a + c)$.

8. Once students have developed a little more experience with algebra and the concept of the truth and falsity of mathematical statements, one can introduce the notion of proof proper, asking students to tackle a question like the following: Is the equation $a^2 +b^2 = -1$ true for all values of a and b, for some values a and b, but not for others, or for no values of a and b? Justify your answer.

Assuming that students answer the question correctly, the main problem they have in justifying it is realizing that citing a few examples is not sufficient to establish its truth. However, previous experience in thinking about properties that are true for some values of the variables and false for other values virtually forces them to agree that the fact that a property holds in a certain number of cases does not imply it must hold in all cases.

Of course, the justification we would like students to give is something like: "Since the square of any real number is never negative and the sum of any two numbers that aren't negative is not negative, it is impossible for the sum $a^2 +b^2$ to be negative regardless of the choice of a and b." Students who answer correctly and give a few examples as support can be complimented for seeing part of the picture, but it should be made clear that their justification is incomplete.

9. At about the same time as one introduces the concept of proof, one can pose problems to help resolve the kinds of common misconceptions listed in Table 16.1. For example, one can give students the following exercises and provide them with feedback individually, in small groups, or in class discussions.

Exercise 1

Given that all irrational numbers have nonterminating decimal expansions, does it follow that all numbers with nonterminating decimal expansions are irrational? Explain your answer.

Exercise 2

Consider the set $S = \{-2, -1, 1, 2\}$. For each statement below, determine whether it is true or false. Explain your answers.

a. For all x in S, there exists a y in S such that $x + y = 0$.
b. There exists a y in S such that for all x in S that $x + y = 0$.

Exercise 3

a. Show it is false that all rational numbers are integers.
b. Is it true that no rational numbers are integers? Explain your answer.

Exercise 4

The following statement is true: For all positive numbers x, if $x^2 < x$ then $x < 1$.

a. Suppose x is a positive number for which $x \not< 1$. Could x^2 be less than x? Explain your answer.
b. Is the following statement true or false? For all positive numbers x, if $x < 1$ then $x^2 \not< x$

Exercise 2 gives students a relatively simple environment in which to explore the truth and falsity of statements with the same syntax as those in item 2 of Table 16.1. Exercise 4 probes the relation between a conditional statement and its contrapositive.

10. Clever teachers at all levels of instruction have devised methods for enabling students to obtain correct answers to problems in ways that circumvent their difficulties with logic and language. The problem is that using these methods deprives students of the opportunity to improve those aspects of their reasoning skills that more traditional methods require. Epp (1997) gives several examples of this phenomenon: solving inequalities using test points rather than the logic of *and* and *or*; using the vertical line test without an adequate tie-in to the definition of function; and finding the inverse of a function without explicitly using the definition of inverse.

Another example is the presentation of polynomial multiplication. Since it would take more time to teach students to appreciate the power and usefulness of the universal rule for multiplying polynomials (multiply each term of one by each term of the other), many teachers just present FOIL, which is effective only for finding the product of two binomials. The problem is that not only does the use of FOIL result in college students' not being able to multiply general polynomials, but more important, the use of this method fails to give students the chance to broaden their understanding about how to apply universal statements in general.

11. A number of bright, capable students become disillusioned with mathematics because the rules they are taught seem so mysterious. It is understandable that as teachers we don't want to alienate our students by burdening them with explanations they cannot understand. But we may have gone overboard and may now be underexplaining. Even when students don't follow every detail, many are reassured to hear reasons for rules that would otherwise seem arbitrary. So, for instance, if students ask why $1/0$ is undefined, we can say it is because in general, a/b is that number, when multiplied by that b, gives a. So, since there is no number that when multiplied by 0, gives 1, $1/0$ is not a number. Similarly, if students ask why $-(-1) = 1$, we can say it is because in general $-a$ is that number, which when added to a, gives 0. Then we can ask what number, when added to -1, gives 0. The answer, of course, is 1. So $-(-1) = 1$. Note that a sentence like "a/b is that number, which when multiplied by b, gives a" is linguistically complex but mathematically important because every inverse relationship is defined by a sentence with a similar grammatical structure.

BENEFITS FOR STUDENTS' GENERAL INTELLECTUAL DEVELOPMENT

The linguistic framework used for mathematics consists of a small set of terms and rules. Most of these are part of the language we use everyday, but everyday language contains additional rules and conventions that are occasionally at odds with those used in mathematics. In ordinary discourse, we use context to resolve ambiguity. Indeed, a small number of children appears to be able to use this method to sort out differences between ordinary and mathematical usages without apparent assistance from their mathematics teachers. Whatever the reason for the success of this small number, the ability of the large majority of children to make effective use of the language of mathematics could be improved through explicit instruction in their mathematics classes. Surely, one of the most valuable roles schools can play in society is to level the playing field for students from different backgrounds and abilities.

The precision of thought and clear deductive reasoning that has traditionally been associated with mathematical thinking has value far beyond the classroom.

The same deductive logic used in careful mathematical reasoning is used to tackle tough problems in all fields. As mathematics teachers, we should strive to help our students improve their abilities not only to come up with correct answers to traditional mathematical problems (though that is important) but also to use the language and logic of mathematics in ways that will potentially transfer to benefit their performance in many different areas of their lives. This may well be the most significant contribution we can make to society.

References

Anderson, John R. *Cognitive Psychology and Its Implications*, 3rd ed. New York: Freeman, 1990.

Berriozábal, Manuel. "The Texas Prefreshman Engineering Program: Filling the Pipeline for Workforce Diversity." *Proceedings of the National Symposium and Career Fair of the Society of Mexican-American Engineers and Scientists*. 1995: B1–B14.

Dubinsky, Ed, and Olga Yiparaki. "Predicate Calculus and the Mathematical Thinking of Students." *International Symposium on Teaching Logic and Reasoning in an Illogical World*. Center for Discrete Mathematics and Theoretical Computer Science, Rutgers University. <www.cs.cornell.edu/Info/People/gries/symposium/symp.htm> (1996)

Epp, Susanna S. "The Logic of Teaching Calculus." In *Toward a Lean and Lively Calculus: Report of the Conference/Workshop to Develop Curriculum and Teaching Methods for Calculus at the College Level*, edited by Ronald G. Douglas, pp. 41–59. Washington, D.C.: Mathematical Association of America, 1986.

——— . "Logic and Discrete Mathematics in the Schools." In *Discrete Mathematics in the Schools: Making an Impact*, edited by Deborah Franzblau and Joseph G. Rosenstein. Providence, R.I.: American Mathematical Society, 1997.

Kim, Karl H. S., Norman R. Relkin, Kyoung-Min Lee, and Joy Hirsch. "Distinct Cortical Areas Associated with Native and Second Languages." *Nature* 388 (10 July 1997): 171–74.

Moro, M. I., M. A. Bantova, et al. *Russian Grade 1 Mathematics, Russian Grade 2 Mathematics, Russian Grade 3 Mathematics*. Translated by Robert Silverman. Chicago: University of Chicago School Mathematics Project, 1992.

National Council of Teachers of Mathematics. *Curriculum and Evaluation Standards for School Mathematics*. Reston, Va.: National Council of Teachers of Mathematics, 1989.

Selden, Annie, and John Selden. "Unpacking the Logic of Mathematical Statements." *Educational Studies in Mathematics* 29 (February 1995): 123–51.

——— . "The Role of Logic in the Validation of Mathematical Proofs." In *International Symposium on Teaching Logic and Reasoning in an Illogical World*, Center for Discrete Mathematics and Theoretical Computer Science, Rutgers University. <www.cs.cornell.edu/Info/People/gries/symposium/symp.htm> (1996).

Wells, Charles. *The Handbook of Mathematical Discourse*. <www–math.cwru.edu/~cfw2/aboutbk.htm> (1997).

17

Mathematics Journal Articles
Anchors for the Guided Development and Practice of Reasoning Skills

Robert Gerver

STUDENTS naturally wonder how mathematics can be extended beyond what they have been taught. Fortunately, throughout their schooling, students build mathematical *toolkits*—a collection of all the mathematics they have internalized. Since it may be difficult for students to explore new mathematical territory without guidance and sufficient experience in mathematical reasoning, helping them learn to use their toolkits properly is an important way to promote mathematical reasoning. This paper describes what North Shore High School's Mathematics Research Program has done to provide students with opportunities to tap into their mathematical toolkits and engage in solid, yet accessible, mathematics.

JOURNAL ARTICLES—PROVIDING A FOCUS

Well-written mathematics journal articles present students with a playing field on which they can develop and practice their reasoning skills. Typically, each article solves a specific problem and includes *some* information that is essential to the solution of that problem. Most of the best articles are only three to six pages long, but the topics they discuss can be built into yearlong projects for individual students or groups. The strength of the journal articles is that they offer the basic skeletal guidance high school students need to begin their own mathematical exploration and research. The student adds the *flesh*—extensions, explanations, examples, tests of claims, counterexamples, conjectures, and proofs as the project grows. The cornerstone of North Shore High School's Mathematics Research Program is a set of articles from back issues of the *Mathematics Teacher* and other mathematics journals. These articles are a gold mine of excellent materials for developing and practicing reasoning skills. With teacher assistance, students look through back issues of journals to find a topic. They soon realize that interest in the topic and experience with its prerequisites are essentials in choosing a research idea. Appropriately, students often favor articles on the Pythagorean theorem, circles, factoring, and quadratic equations. Most researchers start with problems they are familiar with and have an interest in. Teachers may also want to find a few dozen articles to recommend to students. Different articles are appropriate for different grade levels because of the associated prerequisites. Articles can be continued in subsequent years and combined with other article ideas to create new, original results. Back issues of the *Mathematics Teacher* and readily available publications can help teachers implement mathematics as reasoning well into the twenty-first century!

The benefits of working through journal articles are numerous. As students read through their articles, they must follow the arguments presented by the authors. They must check that the arguments are valid and that they understand the logic used by testing the claims and working through the proofs, step-by-step. They formulate ideas based on patterns or their mathematical intuition. Most proofs in the articles are presented in paragraph form, without explanations for certain steps. As students follow these arguments, they need to verify each step. Making conjectures also requires reasoning because conjectures are hypotheses that, whether true or false, are reasonable to test. Mathematicians make many conjectures that turn out to be false. Students may find counterexamples or may read a statement that is not proven and decide to construct a proof on their own. Some of these articles present ideas without proof. Some of them even give hints for proofs.

Teachers may have students write research papers based on their readings. At North Shore High School, students have written papers that were 20 to more than 100 pages long based on short journal articles. Of course, the depth and quality of the research—the questions, trials, testing of claims, conjectures, proofs, extensions, explanations, and the like—affect the length of the paper. We have found that the value of this type of research paper far exceeds that of the math "book report" that is condensed from several library books into an expository paper. (See also article 20 by Boldt and Levine in this volume.)

A SAMPLE JOURNAL ARTICLE AND A SAMPLE OF THE REASONING REQUIRED TO READ IT

Figure 17.1 shows the first page of a three-page article written by Amos Nannini for the November 1966 issue of the *Mathematics Teacher*. The article, entitled "Geometric Solution of a Quadratic Equation," is one example of the articles available to the high school student that provide excellent exercises in reasoning. The article explains a construction that can be used to find the roots of a quadratic equation.

GEOMETRIC SOLUTION OF A QUADRATIC EQUATION

By **AMOS NANNINI**

Milan, Italy

MAY I remind the reader of an elegant construction, discovered by Descartes, whereby it is possible to find both solutions of a quadratic equation $ax^2 + bx + c = 0$, geometrically? [1][1]

Given a rectangular coordinate system, mark off on the y-axis a segment OA of length 1; on the x-axis a segment OB of length $\dfrac{-b}{a}$ (of course in the same unit chosen for the y-axis), and, on the perpendicular to the x-axis through B, lay off a segment

BC of length $\dfrac{c}{a}$. (Fig. 1.)

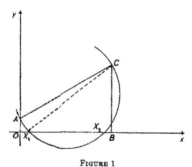

FIGURE 1

We assert that, if the circle having AC as its diameter intersects the x-axis in the

points X_1, X_2, then the lengths of OX_1, OX_2 are the solutions of equation

$$ax^2 + bx + c = 0.$$

Indeed, since angle AX_1C is right (being inscribed in a semicircle), right triangles OAX_1, X_1BC are similar, because they have angle $AOX_1 =$ angle X_1BC (right angles), and angle $OAX_1 =$ angle CX_1B (both complements of angle AX_1O); remember that, since angle $AX_1C = 90°$, it is necessary that angle $AX_1O +$ angle $CX_1B = 90°$.

Hence the proportion between corresponding sides,

$$OA : OX_1 = X_1B : BC,$$

or, keeping in mind their measures,

$$1 : OX_1 = \left(\frac{-b}{a} - OX_1\right) : \frac{c}{a},$$

whence, equating the product of extremes to the product of means and transposing all terms to the left,

$$(OX_1)^2 + \frac{b}{a} OX_1 + \frac{c}{a} = 0,$$

and, multiplying through by $a(\neq 0)$,

$$a(OX_1)^2 + b \cdot OX_1 + c = 0,$$

which proves our statement.

An analogous argument holds for OX_2, and also for coincident X_1 and X_2. In this latter case, the circle would be *tangent* to the x-axis, and the equation would have

a double solution $OX_1 = OX_2 = \dfrac{-b}{(2a)}$.

(Fig. 2.)

[1] Numerals in brackets indicate references given at the end of the article.

Fig. 17.1. First page of a three-page article from *Mathematics Teacher*, November 1966

Before reading the article, students should review the ways they already know to solve a quadratic equation. These may include factoring, using the quadratic formula, and finding the x-intercepts of the graph employing a graphing calculator. If unknown to them, students can learn how to complete the square by following the steps in an algebra textbook or using algebra tiles. At this point, they can study the derivation of the quadratic formula, which involves completing the square. They can be given the steps for completing the square and asked for the reasons for each step or be given nothing but a few hints about the process.

Students can also be asked to find the roots of $y = x^2 - 7x + 12$ and $y = 2x^2 - 14x + 24$ by factoring. They usually notice that these equations have the same two roots, 3 and 4. Then they are asked to graph the parabolas. Sometimes students say, "They are the same." After some discussion, however, they can be led to realize that the graphs are different but have the same x-intercepts. In the article, students are going to find a circle that has the same x-intercepts as a given parabola. They should realize that they are doing something similar when they use $y = x^2 - 7x + 12$ in its factored form to find the roots of $y = 2x^2 - 14x + 24$.

Often, the article's title alone will spawn lots of discussion. This discussion should be used to prime students as quadratic equation *experts* before they actually read the article. After reviewing the methods they already know to solve a quadratic equation, the students should be then asked for advantages and disadvantages of each method, which ones they prefer, and why. Now, they are ready to read and take notes on the article.

REASONING "BETWEEN THE LINES" IN MATHEMATICS

Read the first page of the article in figure 17.1. Notice that instructions are given without any reasons. Determining the *why* behind each one of the steps is a terrific exercise in reasoning. Students might need hints, to different degrees, for some steps. All this reasoning is "between the lines." A comprehensive reading of the article will require much student input and teacher feedback. Since the target audience of the article has a mathematics background and any article may have space limitations, not everything in the article is explained. In Nannini's article, take note of some of the explanatory material that needs to be inserted to produce an article that makes more sense to a high school student:

1. The article uses the problem-solving strategy "work backward" to build the construction. The construction is used to *find* the roots, yet the roots themselves are plotted early in the construction, as explained in the second paragraph.

2. The two x-intercepts do not determine a unique circle, therefore three noncollinear points must be used. How do three noncollinear points determine a unique circle? This will require students to tap into what they know about chords and perpendicular bisectors.

3. Where do the expressions $-b/a$ and c/a come from? Teachers can direct students to pick several quadratic equations—first some with leading coefficient 1; then others without—and find the roots. If a spreadsheet is available, then students can look for the patterns suggested by the sum and product of the roots, using the data in the spreadsheet. After making conjectures about the sum and product of the roots, students can prove their conjectures using the form of the roots as expressed in the quadratic formula.

4. The coordinates of B and C can be determined if the axes are viewed as secants to the circle. *If two secants are drawn to a circle from a common point, the product of one secant and its external segment is equal to the product of the other secant and its external segment.* Students unfamiliar with the theorem and students who need to revisit the theorem can read about it in a geometry textbook.

5. The other point where the circle intersects the y-axis can be called point D. The coordinates of D, $(0, c/a)$, can be found using the properties of secants. The image of D over a vertical line reflection that bisects the circle is point C. Therefore, C's y-coordinate, c/a, can now be determined. Students will need to recall information on inscribed angles to see why AC is a diameter, as claimed in the bottom of column 1 of the article. The coordinates of point B can be found using the reflection of the origin in the same line and the sum of the roots.

6. The construction claims to find the roots by using the sum and product of the roots. Is it possible that two *other* numbers, besides the roots, can yield the same sum and product as the roots do? If s and p represent the sum and the product respectively, an examination of the graphs $s = x + y$ and $p = xy$ is necessary. Using a graphing calculator, students can see that one gives a negatively-sloped line and the other a rectangular hyperbola. There are 0, 1, or 2 intersection points, as shown in figure 17.2. Only the roots will yield the given sum and product.

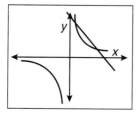 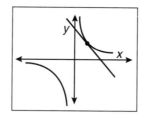 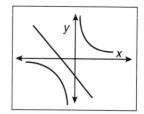

Fig. 17.2. Possible intersections for the rectangular hyperbola $xy = k$ and a line with slope -1

7. Students need to use their algebra and plane geometry tools to follow a logical argument as they read the material in the second column.

Notice how much reasoning was required to do a comprehensive interpretation of every facet of just the first page of this article. Observe how technology (spreadsheets and graphing calculator) and manipulatives (algebra tiles) enhanced the treatment of the article. The article presents the one-root case, the negative/positive-root case, and the imaginary-root case. Students must create new, analogous, but different diagrams and proofs for these cases. These proofs are *guided*—they are not 100 percent original—since they are rooted in the first proof in the article. However, there are differences. Students must be able to understand and use the building blocks of previous proofs before attempting original proofs from scratch. Many articles can be attacked in a similar fashion, and some recommended articles on which students have based their research are included at the end of this article.

EXTENDING THE ARTICLE WITH ORIGINAL RESEARCH

Students who work quickly or want to continue their research beyond the initial article (even in subsequent school years) can read two articles that have some common thread and attempt to combine the results. With the help of all of the guided reasoning exercises in which they were engaged while reading their first article, the second article and the combination of two articles can be handled with much more independence. Many students have taken this route in the past. Here are two examples of how students extended the same initial article in different directions:

1. Tenth grader Julianne and eleventh grader Michael both read, on their own, the article "On the Radii of Inscribed and Escribed Circles of Right Triangles" from the September 1979 *Mathematics Teacher*. This article derives expressions for the radii of the inscribed and one escribed circle to a right triangle in terms of the sides of the right triangle. (Escribed circles are tangent to one side of a triangle and the extensions of the other two sides.)

Julianne and Michael extended the results to include circumscribed circles and the two other escribed circles. This was a natural extension since the article gave formulas for the radii of the other two escribed circles but did not show how these formulas

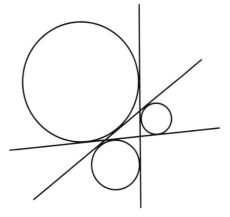

Fig. 17.3. A triangle has three escribed circles

were derived. Julianne read a second article, "Pythagoras Meets Fibonacci," from the April 1989 *Mathematics Teacher*. This article shows how Pythagorean triples can be generated from four consecutive Fibonacci numbers. Julianne intuitively felt that she could combine both articles to find a relationship between the original Fibonacci numbers used to create a right-triangle triple and the resulting radii of the escribed circles to the same right triangle. First she decided to see if she could notice a relationship between the Fibonacci numbers and the radii by trying about a dozen numerical examples and looking for a pattern. She did her work on a spreadsheet and made conjectures about the formulas based on several patterns she found. She proved her conjectures using algebraic substitution and found that they were, indeed, correct. This line of reasoning is typical of many undertakings in the mathematics research arena—students find a pattern by creating and analyzing numerical examples; they make a conjecture about a general relationship based on the pattern; and they set out to prove or disprove their conjecture.

2. Some mathematical intuition and curiosity helped Michael notice that the expressions for the radii of the inscribed and escribed circles somewhat resembled the formula for the semiperimeter of a triangle. (For example, r_a, the radius of the escribed circle to side a is, in terms of the sides a, b, and c, equal to $[a-b+c]/2$).

Based on Heron's formula, he proceeded to use algebra to create a new (for him and his teacher) formula for the area of a right triangle, in terms of its inscribed and escribed circles. If r_I, r_a, r_b, and r_c represent, respectively, the radii of the inscribed circle and the three escribed circles to sides a, b, and c, then the area of a right triangle is $\sqrt{(r_I)(r_a)(r_b)(r_c)}$. Michael also showed this was equivalent to $ab/2$, which he knew was the area of a right triangle with legs a and b. This strategy of using algebraic manipulation to achieve a conjectured result is also commonplace in the mathematics research program. Additionally, students often examine the value of using algebraic steps *in reverse* to help construct parts of the proof of a converse of a theorem they have already proven.

Notice that the articles first provide a foundation and then act as a springboard for research and exploration. The experience of tinkering in uncharted mathematical territory (uncharted at least for the student and, very likely, the teacher) brings about a unique combination of challenge and exhilaration. Furthermore, there is tremendous latitude in the journal article assignments. Some students can read four articles in one school year, whereas others might not finish one. Periodic discussions about an article with the teacher systematically and gradually give the students a chance to think about and discuss their reasoning. The teacher facilitates the discussion, whether it is with one student, a group, or the whole class, by asking questions, requesting explanations, giving hints, making corrections, and suggesting other reading assignments.

PERIODIC DISCUSSIONS TO MONITOR PROGRESS

How the journal articles are used is up to the teacher. Students may read their journal articles as part of a research course requirement or independent study assignment. They may read and report on their article as part of a graduation-by-exhibition or honors-by-achievement requirement. Students can read journal articles as an ancillary part of their core mathematics course, individually or cooperatively. The journal articles can also be treated as topics to be studied by a whole class. The goal, in all instances, is to make sure the students make consistent, gradual progress on their articles. Students need guidance and deadlines to accomplish these goals. They need to consult with the teacher on a regular basis. The consultation aspect of a project requires the student to engage in research activities between each consultation sessions and prepare material for the session. Newly-completed work must be brought to each consultation. Students discussed their new work at each consultation. As a result, over the course of the entire project, students have worked on their articles in many separate sittings. The strength of the consultation period is in the one-on-one communication—the accountability raises the students' persistence, their level of responsibility, and their expectations of themselves.

Entire articles are usually not read at once. After each discussion, the teacher assigns appropriate amounts of further reading from the article. Typically, students come to the next discussion with the material read, underlined, and annotated right on their copy of the article. They should have notes on which they have asked questions, explained material from their article, made a conjecture, tested a claim, tried a proof, or extended the reading passage. At the beginning of each discussion, the teacher can revisit the students' progress using the article and copies of their written work. Teachers should review students' work, ask questions, answer questions, and so forth. By requiring students to be explicit in their explanations, their oral communication skills will improve. The depth and breadth of a student's coverage of a journal article has no bound. The students really get a chance to explore—to *play with* mathematics. Mathematics journal articles give students the chance to practice reasoning in a guided format that can help them gradually develop more sophisticated reasoning ability.

REFERENCES

Boulger, William. "Pythagoras Meets Fibonacci." *Mathematics Teacher* 82 (April 1989): 277–82.

Hanson, David W. "On the Radii of Inscribed and Escribed Circles of Right Triangles." *Mathematics Teacher* 72 (September 1979): 462–64.

Nannini, Amos. "Geometric Solution of a Quadratic Equation." *Mathematics Teacher* 59 (November 1966): 464–67.

BIBLIOGRAPHY OF RECOMMENDED ARTICLES FOR STUDENTS

Akulich, Igor. "An Ant on a Tin Can." *Quantum* 8 (September/October 1997): 50–53.

Angelova, Yovka. "The Median Toward the Hypotenuse." *Mathematics and Informatics Quarterly* 2 (September 1992): 87–94.

Gerver, Robert K. *Writing Math Research Papers—Enrichment for Math Enthusiasts.* Berkeley, Calif.: Key Curriculum Press, 1997.

Kilmer, Jean. "Triangles of Equal Area and Perimeter and Inscribed Circles." *Mathematics Teacher* 81 (January 1988): 65–70.

Olson, Melfried. "Odd Factors and Consecutive Sums: An Interesting Relationship." *Mathematics Teacher* 84 (January 1991): 50–53.

Pritsker, Boris. "The Area of a Quadrilateral." *New York State Math Teachers Journal* 45 (Fall 1995): 176–80.

Sullivan, Mary, and Regina Panasuk. "Fibonacci Numbers and an Area Puzzle." *School Science and Mathematics* 97 (March 1997): 132–38.

Tabov, Jordan. "Simple Properties of the Orthodiagonal Quadrilaterals." *Mathematics and Informatics Quarterly* 1 (February 1991): 1–5.

Trask Frederick K. III. "Circular Coordinates: A Strange New System of Coordinates." *Mathematics Teacher* 64 (May 1971): 402–408.

18

Teaching and Assessing Statistical Reasoning

Joan B. Garfield

Iddo Gal

The Nature of Statistical Reasoning

STATISTICAL reasoning may be defined as the way people reason with statistical ideas and make sense of statistical information. This involves making interpretations based on sets of data, representations of data, or statistical summaries of data. Much of statistical reasoning combines ideas about data and chance, which leads to making inferences and interpreting statistical results. Underlying this reasoning is a conceptual understanding of important ideas, such as *distribution, center, spread, association, uncertainty, randomness,* and *sampling.*

This article begins by distinguishing statistical reasoning from mathematical reasoning, and then outlines goals for students studying statistics. Challenges in assessing statistical reasoning are described and information is provided on a unique paper-and-pencil instrument, the *Statistical Reasoning Assessment.* The final section suggests ways teachers may help students develop sound statistical reasoning skills.

Statistical Reasoning versus Mathematical Reasoning

Many people think of mathematics and statistics as the same thing, and therefore, confuse statistical reasoning with mathematical reasoning. Today's leading statistical educators see these disciplines and types of reasoning as quite distinct. There has been a recent shift from traditional views of teaching statistics as a mathematical topic (with an emphasis on computations, formulas, and procedures) to the current view that distinguishes between mathematics and statistics as separate disciplines. As Moore (1992) argues, statistics is a mathematical science but is not a branch of mathematics and has clearly emerged as a discipline in its own right, with characteristic modes of thinking that are more fundamental than either specific methods or mathematical theory. "Statistics has its own substance, its own distinctive concepts and modes of reasoning. These should be the heart of the teaching of statistics to beginners at any level ..." (Moore 1992, 14).

Gal and Garfield (1997) distinguish between the two disciplines in the following ways:

1. In statistics, data are viewed as numbers with a context. The context motivates procedures and is the source of meaning and basis for interpretation of results.

2. The indeterminacy or *messiness* of data distinguishes statistical investigations from the more precise, finite nature characterizing mathematical explorations.

3. Mathematical concepts and procedures are used as part of the attempt to manage or "solve" statistical problems, and some technical facility with the mathematics may be expected in certain courses and educational levels. However, the need for the accurate application of computations or execution of procedures is rapidly being replaced by the need for the selective, thoughtful, and accurate use of technological devices and increasingly more-sophisticated software programs.

4. The fundamental nature of many statistical problems is that they do not have a single mathematical solution. Rather, realistic statistical problems usually start with a question and culminate with the presentation of an opinion supported by certain findings and assumptions. Judgments and inferences expected of students (e.g., predictions about a population based on sample data students collected in a survey) very often cannot be characterized as "right" or "wrong," but rather evaluated in terms of quality of reasoning, adequacy of methods employed, and nature of data and evidence used. (p. 6)

What Students Should Understand and Do with Statistical Knowledge

In order to set a context for statistical reasoning in statistics education, it is helpful to examine concepts and procedures that are important for students to learn. Gal and Garfield (1997) outline several subgoals for statistics instruction. Some of these are described below.

Goal 1: Understand the Purpose and Logic of Statistical Investigations

We would like students to understand why statistical investigations are conducted and the *big ideas* that underlie approaches to data-based inquiries. Some important big ideas include the existence of variation, the need to describe populations by collecting data, and the need to reduce raw data by noting trends and main features through summaries and displays of the data. As students progress in carrying out statistical investigations, we would like them to understand the need to study samples instead of populations and to infer from samples to populations. We would also like them to understand the logic behind related sampling processes, the notion of error in measurement and inference, and the need to find ways to estimate and control errors. Some additional important ideas include the need to identify causal processes or factors and the logic behind methods (such as experiments) for determining causal processes.

Goal 2: Understand the Process of Statistical Investigations

It is important that students begin to understand the nature of and processes involved in a statistical investigation and considerations affecting the design of a plan for data collection. This includes recognizing how, when, and why existing statistical tools can be used to help an investigative process. Students need to become familiar with the specific phases of a statistical inquiry, which include; formulating a question; planning a study; collecting, organizing, and analyzing data; interpreting findings; and discussing conclusions, implications from the findings, issues for further study.

Goal 3: Master Procedural Skills

Students need to master the skills used in the process of statistical investigations: being able to organize data, to compute needed indices (e.g., median, average, confidence interval), or to construct and display useful tables, graphs, plots, and charts, either by hand or assisted by technology.

Goal 4: Understand Mathematical Relationships

We would like students to develop an understanding, intuitive and formal, of the main mathematical ideas that underlie statistical displays, procedures, or concepts. This includes understanding the connection between summary statistics, graphical displays, and the raw data on which they are based. For example, students need to be able to explain how the mean is influenced by extreme values in a data set and what happens to the mean and median when data values are changed.

Goal 5: Understand Probability and Chance

There are several types of understanding we would like students to develop as they study probability and chance. For example, they need to understand concepts and words related to chance, uncertainty, and probability that appear in our everyday lives, particularly in the media. Other important ideas include the understanding that probability is a measure of uncertainty, that models are useful for simulating events to estimate probabilities, and that sometimes our intuitions are incorrect and can lead us to the wrong conclusion regarding probability and chance events.

Goal 6: Develop Interpretive Skills and Statistical Literacy

In carrying out a statistical investigation, students learn to interpret results and be aware of possible biases or limitations on the generalizations that can be drawn from data. In carrying out this process, students need to learn how to interpret results from a statistical investigation and to pose critical and reflective questions about arguments that refer to summary statistics or to data.

Goal 7: Develop Ability to Communicate Statistically

We would like students to become effective communicators as they discuss or present results of statistical investigations or critique statistical or probabilistic arguments that claim to be based on some data. This involves being able to use statistical and probabilistic terminology properly, to convey results in a convincing way, and to construct reasonable arguments based on data or observations. As students become more knowledgeable about statistics, they should also be able to challenge the validity of other people's interpretations of data or graphical displays and generalizations made on the basis of a single study or a small sample.

Statistical Reasoning in Classroom Activities

Current mathematics curricula for students in elementary and secondary schools are designed to help students comprehend and deal with uncertainty, variability, and statistical information in the world around them and to participate effectively in an information-laden society (Gal and Garfield 1997). In order to demonstrate these outcomes successfully, students need to develop good statistical reasoning skills. The seven subgoals listed in the previous section directly relate to this broad, overarching goal of developing students' statistical reasoning skills, by enabling them to produce and communicate reasoned descriptions, judgments, inferences, and opinions about data.

Although statistical reasoning may be viewed as a broad goal, it is helpful to delineate some specific types of reasoning we would like students to develop as they learn statistics in elementary and secondary school. Several of these reasoning targets are described in the American Association for the Advancement of Science's (AAAS) publication, *Benchmarks for Science Literacy* (1993). These specific types of statistical reasoning include the following:

1. **Reasoning about data:** Recognizing or categorizing data as quantitative or qualitative, discrete or continuous, and knowing how the type of data leads to a particular type of table, graph, or statistical measure.
2. **Reasoning about representations of data:** Understanding the way in which a plot is meant to represent a sample, understanding how to read

and interpret a graph, knowing how to modify a graph to better represent a data set, and being able to see beyond random artifacts in a distribution to recognize general characteristics such as shape, center, and spread

3. **Reasoning about statistical measures:** Understanding what measures of center, spread, and position tell about a data set; knowing which are best to use under different conditions and how they do or do not represent a data set; knowing that using summaries for predictions will be more accurate for large samples than for small samples; knowing that a good summary of data includes a measure of center as well as a measure of spread; and knowing that summaries of center and spread can be useful for comparing data sets

4. **Reasoning about uncertainty:** Understanding and using ideas of randomness, chance, and likelihood to make judgments about uncertain events; knowing that not all outcomes are equally likely; knowing how to determine the likelihood of different events using an appropriate method (such as a probability tree diagram or a simulation using coins or a computer program)

5. **Reasoning about samples:** Knowing how samples are related to a population and what may be inferred from a sample; knowing that a larger, well chosen sample will more accurately represent a population and that there are ways of choosing a sample that can make it unrepresentative of the population; and being cautious when making inferences made on small or biased samples

6. **Reasoning about association:** Knowing how to judge and interpret a relationship between two variables, knowing how to examine and interpret a two-way table or scatterplot when considering a bivariate relationship, and knowing that a strong correlation between two variables does not mean that one causes the other

Assessing Statistical Reasoning

In light of the current goals for students and the differences between mathematics and statistics, an appropriate assessment of students' statistical reasoning is especially important. Traditional test questions involving statistical content too often lack appropriate context and tend to focus on accuracy of statistical computations, correct application of formulas, or correctness of graphs and charts. Questions and task formats that culminate in simple "right or wrong" answers do not adequately reflect the nature of students' thinking and problem solving, and therefore provide only limited information about the students' statistical reasoning processes and their ability to construct or interpret statistical arguments (Gal and Garfield 1997).

Just as mathematics educators of today realize that a range of different assessment methods is needed to provide broad information about the quality of students' thinking, communication, and reasoning processes in mathematics, appropriate assessment methods are needed for evaluating statistical reasoning that reveal students' thinking as they choose and apply statistical tools, make sense of data, interpret results, and draw conclusions. A student's ability to calculate the average of given data correctly, either manually or with the help of an electronic aid, for example, says little about her understanding of when the average is a reasonable way to summarize information or what other statistical tools may be better suited for the task of describing the data (Gal 1995).

Although statistical reasoning may best be assessed through one-to-one communication with students (e.g., interviews or observations) or by examining a sample of detailed, in-depth student work (e.g., a statistical project), carefully designed paper-and-pencil instruments can be used to gather some limited indicators of students' reasoning. One such instrument is the *Statistical Reasoning Assessment* (SRA).

The SRA was developed and validated as part of the ChancePlus Project (Konold 1990, Garfield 1991) to use in evaluating the effectiveness of a new statistics curriculum for high school students in achieving its learning goals. At that time, no other instrument existed that would assess high school students' ability to understand statistical concepts and apply statistical reasoning. There was a practical need to have an instrument that could easily be scored and captured students' thinking, reasoning, and application of knowledge, instead of a test where students *tell* the teacher what they remember or show that they can perform calculations and carry out procedures correctly.

The SRA is a multiple-choice test consisting of twenty items. Each item describes a statistics or probability problem and offers several choices of responses, both correct and incorrect. Most responses include a statement of reasoning, explaining the rationale for a particular choice. Students are instructed to select the response that best matches their own thinking about each problem. The SRA has been used not only with the ChancePlus project but with other high school and college students in a variety of statistics courses to evaluate the effectiveness of curricular materials and approaches as well as to describe the level of students' statistical reasoning. Items from this instrument have been adapted and used in research projects in other English-speaking countries such as Australia and the United Kingdom. This instrument has also been translated into French, Spanish, and Chinese versions.

The SRA provides sixteen scales, based on students' responses to the twenty multiple-choice items. These scores indicate the level of students' correct reasoning in eight different areas and the extent of their incorrect reasoning in eight related areas. Although the sixteen scales represent only a small subset of reasoning skills and strategies, they may provide a teacher with useful information regarding the thinking and reasoning of students when solving statistical problems. A sample of scales related to correct reasoning are listed below, followed by an example of one item from that scale.

Correct Reasoning Scales

Scale 1. Correctly Interprets a Probability

In this example, a correct response indicates that the student is able to interpret a probability as a ratio.

The following message is printed on a bottle of prescription medication:

> **WARNING:** For applications to skin areas there is a 15 percent chance of developing a rash. If a rash develops, consult your physician.

Which of the following is the best interpretation of this warning?

_____ a. Don't use the medication on your skin—there's a good chance of developing a rash.

_____ b. For application to the skin, apply only 15 percent of the recommended dose.

_____ c. If a rash develops, it will probably involve only 15 percent of the skin.

_____ d. About 15 of 100 people who use this medication develop a rash. (*correct response*)

_____ e. There is hardly a chance of getting a rash using this medication.

Scale 2. Understands How to Select an Appropriate Average

In this item, the student must recognize that one data value, an outlier, must actually be due to a measurement error, because it is too different from the other measurements.

A small object was weighed on the same scale separately by nine students in a science class. The weights (in grams) recorded by each student are shown below.

6.2   6.0   6.0   15.3   6.1   6.3   6.2   6.15   6.2

The students want to determine as accurately as they can the actual weight of this object. Of the following methods, which would you recommend they use?

_____ a. Use the most common number, which is 6.2.

_____ b. Use the 6.15 since it is the most accurate weighing.

_____ c. Add up the nine numbers and divide by 9.

_____ d. Throw out the 15.3, add up the other eight numbers and divide by 8. (*correct response*)

Scale 5. Understands Sampling Variability

This item assesses whether students understand the sampling process and the effect of large and small sample sizes by reasoning that a small sample is more likely to deviate from the population.

> Half of all newborns are girls and half are boys. Hospital A records an average of fifty births a day. Hospital B records an average of ten births a day. On a particular day, which hospital is more likely to record 80 percent or more female births?
>
> _____ a. Hospital A (with fifty births a day)
>
> _____ b. Hospital B (with ten births a day) (*correct response*)
>
> _____ c. The two hospitals are equally likely to record such an event.

Scale 6. Distinguishes between Correlation and Causation

This item determines whether students realize that a statistical relationship such as correlation does not mean that one variable causes another.

> For one month, 500 elementary students kept a daily record of the hours they spent watching television. The average number of hours per week spent watching television was twenty-eight. The researchers conducting the study also obtained report cards for each of the students. They found that the students who did well in school spent less time watching television than those students who did poorly.
>
> Listed below are several possible statements concerning the results of this research. Place a check by every statement that you agree with.
>
> _____ a. The sample of 500 is too small to permit drawing conclusions.
>
> _____ b. If a student decreased the amount of time spent watching television, his or her performance in school would improve.
>
> _____ c. Even though students who did well watched less television, this doesn't necessarily mean that watching television hurts school performance. (*correct response*)
>
> _____ d. One month is not a long enough period of time to estimate how many hours the students really spend watching television.
>
> _____ e. The research demonstrates that watching television causes poorer performance in school.
>
> _____ f. I don't agree with any of these statements.

Scale 7. Correctly Interprets Two-Way Tables

This item assesses whether students understand that in order to compare two groups within a two-way table, they need to compute and compare ratios or percents instead of comparing the total numbers in particular categories.

A new medication is being tested to determine its effectiveness in the treatment of eczema, an inflammatory condition of the skin. Thirty patients with eczema were selected to participate in the study. The patients were randomly divided into two groups. Twenty patients in an experimental group received the medication, whereas ten patients in a control group received no medication. The results after two months are shown below.

Experimental group (Medication)		Control group (No Medication)	
Improved	8	Improved	2
No Improvement	12	No Improvement	8

Based on the data, I think the medication was:

_____ 1. somewhat effective   _____ 2. basically ineffective

If you chose option 1, select the one explanation below that best describes your reasoning.

_____ a. Forty percent of the people (8/20) in the experimental group improved.

_____ b. Eight people improved in the experimental group while only 2 improved in the control group.

_____ c. In the experimental group, the number of people who improved is only 4 less than the number who didn't improve (12-8) although in the control group the difference is 6 (8–2).

_____ d. Forty percent of the patients in the experimental group improved (8/20), although only 20 percent improved in the control group (2/10). (*correct response*)

If you chose option 2, select the one explanation below that best describes your reasoning.

_____ a. In the control group, two people improved even without the medication.

_____ b. In the experimental group, more people didn't get better than did (12 versus 8).

_____ c. The difference between the numbers who improved and didn't improve is about the same in each group (4 versus 6).

_____ d. In the experimental group, only 40 percent of the patients improved (8/20).

Scale 8. Understands the Importance of Large Samples

This item determines whether students understand that it is more important to base decisions on large samples of data than on single cases or small samples, however compelling they might seem.

The Caldwells want to buy a new car, and they have narrowed their choices to a Buick or a Oldsmobile. They first consulted an issue of *Consumer Reports,* which compared rates of repairs for various cars. Records of repairs done on 400 cars of each type showed somewhat fewer mechanical problems with the Buick than with the Oldsmobile.

The Caldwells then talked to three friends, two Oldsmobile owners and one former Buick owner. Both Oldsmobile owners reported having a few mechanical problems but nothing major. The Buick owner, however, exploded when asked how he liked his car:

> *First, the fuel injection went out—250 bucks. Next, I started having trouble with the rear end and had to replace it. I finally decided to sell it after the transmission went. I'd never buy another Buick.*

The Caldwells want to buy the car that is less likely to require major repair work. Given what they currently know, which car would you recommend that they buy?

_____ a. I would recommend that they buy the Oldsmobile, primarily because of all the trouble their friend had with his Buick. Since they haven't heard similar horror stories about the Oldsmobile, they should go with it.

_____ b. I would recommend that they buy the Buick in spite of their friend's bad experience. That is just one case, whereas the information reported in Consumer Reports is based on many cases. And according to that data, the Buick is somewhat less likely to require repairs. (*correct response*)

_____ c. I would tell them that it didn't matter which car they bought. Even though one of the models might be more likely than the other to require repairs, they could still, just by chance, get stuck with a particular car that would need a lot of repairs. They may as well toss a coin to decide.

Incorrect Reasoning Scales

Kahneman, Slovic, and Tversky (1982) are well-known for their substantial body of research that reveals some prevalent ways of thinking about statistics that are inconsistent with a technical understanding. Their research suggests that even people who can correctly compute probabilities tend to apply faulty reasoning when asked to make an inference or judgment about an uncertain event, relying on incorrect intuitions (Garfield and Ahlgren 1988; Shaughnessy 1992). Other researchers have discovered additional misconceptions or errors of reasoning when examining students in classroom settings (e.g., Konold 1989, Lecoutre 1992). Several of the identified misconceptions or errors in reasoning were used to develop the eight scales on the SRA. These include the following:

1. *Misconceptions involving averages.* Averages are the most common number. To find an average, one must always add up all the numbers and divide by the number of data values (regardless of outliers). One should always compare groups by focusing exclusively on the difference in their averages.

2. *Outcome orientation.* This is an intuitive model of probability that leads students to make yes or no decisions about single events rather than looking at the series of events (Konold 1989). For example: A weather forecaster predicts the chance of rain to be 70 percent for ten days. On seven of those ten days it actually rained. How good were his forecasts? Many students will say that the forecaster didn't do such a good job, because it should have rained on all days on which he gave a 70 percent chance of rain. They appear to focus on outcomes of single events rather than being able to look at series of events—70 percent chance of rain means that it should rain. Similarly, a forecast of 30 percent rain would mean it won't rain. A 50 percent chance of rain is interpreted as meaning that you can't tell either way.

3. *Good samples have to represent a high percentage of the population.* It doesn't matter how large a sample is or how well it was chosen, it must represent a large percentage of a population to be a good sample.

4. *Law of Small Numbers.* Small samples should resemble the populations from which they are sampled, so small samples are used as a basis for inference and generalizations (Kahneman, Slovic, and Tversky 1982).

5. *Representativeness misconception.* People estimate the likelihood of a sample based on how closely it resembles the population. Therefore, a sample of coin tosses that has an even mix of heads and tails is judged more likely than a sample with more heads and fewer tails (Kahneman, Slovic, and Tversky 1982).

6. *Equiprobability bias.* Events tend to be viewed as equally likely. Therefore, the chances of getting different outcomes (e.g., three fives or one five on three rolls of a dice) are incorrectly viewed as equally likely events (Lecoutre 1992).

Helping Students Develop Good Statistical Reasoning Skills

The changes that have been taking place in mathematics education since publication of the NCTM *Curriculum and Evaluation Standards* (1989) are positive ones, such as the inclusion of statistical topics throughout the K–12 curriculum, a focus on exploratory data analysis, and the solution of statistical problems involving real data. The NCTM Standards are aligned with the following recommendations for helping students develop sound statistical reasoning.

1. Provide students with opportunities to work with real data, either solving interesting problems or posing problems of their own that involve going through the steps of a statistical investigation. Have students make decisions about data collection, coding, and analysis. Students should justify their decisions.

2. Provide students with practice articulating their reasoning by including written or oral communication as a regular part of statistical problem solving. Encourage students to go beyond providing an answer, and to explain the process and how the result is interpreted.

3. Encourage students to become aware of their thinking and reasoning by having them discuss and compare different solutions to statistical problems and their interpretations, assumptions, and explanations of those problems.

4. Provide students with opportunities to use technology to manage and explore data, so that they can focus more on the reasoning and less on the calculations and constructions.

5. Introduce software that helps students develop and support their statistical reasoning [e.g., allowing them to watch the sampling process and how it varies when different variables are changed, such as sample size or population shape, or allowing them to manipulate histograms to see how the relative size and position of the mean, median, and mode are affected (Rubin and Rosebery 1990)].

6. Allow students to make predictions and to test them so that they may become aware of and confront misconceptions and faulty reasoning. This type of challenge has to be handled very carefully, as research indicates that people, in general, are resistant to change and are very likely to find ways either to assimilate information or to discredit contradictory evidence rather than restructure their thinking in order to accommodate the contradictions (delMas, Garfield, and Chance 1997).

7. Build on students' prior knowledge or *real-world* knowledge, so that they are able to construct appropriate relationships with this knowledge as they extend it and apply it to new situations in order to develop good statistical understanding (Rubin and Rosebery 1990).

References

American Association for the Advancement of Science. *Benchmarks for Science Literacy.* New York: Oxford University Press, 1993.

delMas, Robert C., Joan Garfield, and Beth Chance. "Assessing the Effects of a Computer Microworld on Statistical Reasoning." Paper presented at the Joint Meetings of the American Statistical Association, Anaheim, Calif., 1997.

Gal, Iddo. "Statistical Tools and Statistical Literacy: The Case of the Average." *Teaching Statistics* 17, no. 3 (1995): 97–99.

Gal, Iddo, and Joan Garfield, eds. *The Assessment Challenge in Statistics Education.* Amsterdam: IOS Press, 1997.

Garfield, Joan. "Evaluating Students' Understanding of Statistics: Development of the Statistical Reasoning Assessment." In *Proceedings of the Thirteenth Annual Meeting of the North American Chapter of the International Group for the Psychology of Mathematics Education,* Vol. 2, pp. 1–7. Blacksburg, Va., 1991.

Garfield, Joan, and Andrew Ahlgren. "Difficulties in Learning Basic Concepts in Probability and Statistics: Implications for Research." *Journal for Research in Mathematics Education* 19 (January 1988): 44–63.

Kahneman, Daniel, Paul Slovic, and Amos Tversky. *Judgment Under Uncertainty: Heuristics and Biases.* Cambridge: Cambridge University Press, 1982.

Konold, Clifford. "Informal Conceptions of Probability." *Cognition and Instruction* 6 (1989): 59–98.

———. *ChancePlus: A Computer-Based Curriculum for Probability and Statistics.* Final Report to the National Science Foundation. Scientific Reasoning Research Institute, University of Massachusetts, Amherst, 1990.

Lecoutre, Marie-Paule. "Cognitive Models and Problem Spaces in 'Purely Random' Situations." *Educational Studies in Mathematics* 23 (1992): 557–68.

Moore, David. "Teaching Statistics as a Respectable Subject." In *Statistics for the Twenty-first Century,* edited by F. and S. Gordon, pp. 14–25. Washington, D.C.: Mathematical Association of America, 1992.

National Council of Teachers of Mathematics. *Curriculum and Evaluation Standards for School Mathematics.* Reston, Va.: National Council of Teachers of Mathematics, 1989.

Rubin, Andee, and Ann Rosebery. "Teachers' Misunderstanding in Statistical Reasoning: Evidence from a Field Test of Innovative Materials." In *Training Teachers to Teach Statistics,* edited by Anne Hawkins, pp. 72–79. Voorburg, Netherlands: International Statistical Institute, 1990.

Shaughnessy, J. Michael. "Research in Probability and Statistics: Reflections and Directions." *Handbook of Research on Mathematics Teaching and Learning,* edited by D. A. Grouws, pp. 465–94. New York: Macmillan, 1992.

19

Mathematical Reasoning and Educational Policy
Moving beyond the Politics of Dead Language

William F. Tate

Howard C. Johnson

> Language that is dead obscures fact, obscures history, obscures problems,
> obscures what needs to be learned and to be done; dead language succeeds only in
> "ringing the bells of response" among its devotees.
> —Edwin J. Delattre, "Psittacism and Dead Language"

THE statement, "We need students who can reason with mathematics," has widely appeared in education and business circles. Because mathematical reasoning is a product of opportunity to learn and policies that support learning, we are concerned that calls for increasing students' opportunities to reason with mathematics are being framed with "dead language." By dead language we do not mean ancient languages such as Latin and Attic Greek; rather we are referring to a language that ignores the realities of the inequalities that exist for many students of color or low socioeconomic status (SES). We refer to a modern, *standards-based* language-slogan system that fails to address the systemic nature of knowledge inequality and the noninclusion of students in college preparatory mathematics.

Many studies indicate that a disproportionate number of minority and low-SES students receive a mathematics education more closely associated with basic skills (Oakes 1990; Secada 1992). In the late 1960s and early 1970s, a mathematics reform movement, "back to basics," emerged that focused largely on elementary and middle schools (NCTM 1980). This movement was partly an outgrowth of efforts to achieve equality of opportunity through compensatory education. The back-to-basics effort called for teaching a core set of rudimentary mathematics procedures and facts, often to the exclusion of more advanced mathematical ideas. Although the basic skills movement influenced the entire U.S. educational system, it had a significant impact on the mathematics curriculum and pedagogy in low-income urban and rural schools (Strickland and Ascher 1992).

On the positive side, the basic skills movement did result in improved standardized test scores for students who were traditionally underserved (Secada 1992). It illustrated that when teachers and principals agreed on a common standard in mathematics, and received adequate institutional support to achieve that standard, students would learn the content.

On the negative side, the success of the basic skills movement has to do with teachers' beliefs and the fact that more of the basic skills philosophy is consistent with teachers' perceptions of minority and low-SES students' ability (Haberman 1995; Knapp and Woolverton 1995). As the vision of what it means to know and understand mathematics has shifted from the basic skills standard to a more demanding goal, the limits of past pedagogical practice have become obvious (Romberg 1992). Teaching elementary and middle grades students strictly low-level basic skills—absent of opportunities to reason with mathematics—will not adequately prepare them for the challenges of college preparatory mathematics. In fact, the practice of tracking students out of college-preparatory mathematics is akin to restricting them to the basic skills curriculum in most school districts.

Four interrelated forms of "knowledge policies" will be described in this article. They are course taking, teacher knowledge inequality, assessment, and fiscal adequacy. In general, the term *knowledge policy* can be used to describe the folkways of schooling, regulations of policymakers, and practices of teachers that influence student opportunity to learn. Linda Darling-Hammond (1995) provides a description of knowledge policies that is focused on teachers and their practice:

> [O]pportunities for minority students will rest in part on **policies** [our emphasis] that professionalize teaching by increasing the knowledge base for teaching, and on the mastery of this knowledge by all teachers permitted to practice. This means providing all teachers with a stronger understanding of how children learn and develop, how a variety of curricular and instructional strategies can address their needs, and how changes in school and classroom organization can support their growth and achievement. (p. 478)

Darling-Hammond's description of knowledge policies includes the specific knowledge policies addressed in this article. Each of these policies has a significant influence on the opportunities for mathematical reasoning by students of color or low SES. We argue that failure to directly address these policies is likely to result in no real opportunity to reason with mathematics.

Course Taking

Two of the most powerful predictors of student mathematics achievement in many large-scale assessments of mathematical reasoning have been (*a*) increased time on task in high level mathematics and (*b*) the number of advanced courses taken in mathematics. Generally, these two predictors are interrelated. Research indicates that African Americans, Hispanics, and low-SES students are less likely to be enrolled in higher level mathematics courses than middle-class white students (Oakes 1990; Secada 1992). Further, African American and Hispanic students, as demographic groups, are consistently outperformed by white students on national assessments of mathematics achievement and reasoning (Tate 1997). It should not be a surprise that a positive relationship between mathematics achievement and course taking exists across assessments (e.g., National Assessment of Educational Progress, SAT, and ACT).

Course-taking opportunities in U.S. schools are often subject to two forms of sorting mechanisms—curricular and ability tracking. Comprehensive high schools offer a wide range of mathematics courses associated with different employment opportunities in the world of work. No student could take all of the courses, and it is assumed that the school will regulate the selection process, matching students to offerings that reflect their ability and needs. To this end, students in most high schools are sorted into curricular tracks, each track involving a specific course sequence and, ultimately, different opportunities to reason with mathematics. Typically, three curricular tracks—college preparation, vocational, and general education—are offered within most traditional high schools. It is understood that the first track has higher status and provides greater opportunity to learn and to reason with mathematics. Curricular tracking has significant implications for the development of policies focused on mathematics reasoning.

Many high schools and middle schools also sort students into ability tracks. This form of sorting provides different levels of instruction to students across the various ability tracks. This version of tracking is more difficult to recognize because the process differs around the country. For example, schools may offer two different courses in Algebra I. Both may have the same title, however, the content covered in each course may vary dramatically. Another strategy is to offer students of different abilities entry into college-preparatory mathematics courses at different times (e.g., freshmen year versus junior year). Further, the organizational structure of the school may recognize many tracks or just a few; schools may have loosely or tightly coupled curricular and ability tracking; and schools may or may not link tracks to a block of subjects or to mathematics specifically.

Tracking is a serious impediment to mathematics achievement and opportunities to reason with mathematics. First of all, it doesn't work. In theory, tracking is designed to benefit all students, but evidence strongly suggests that this goal is not being accomplished (Hoffer, Rasinski, and Moore 1995). Instead, many studies have indicated that even when tracking systems have positive effects, those effects are largely associated with those assigned to high-status tracks (Oakes 1990; Rock and Pollack 1995). In contrast, when students are assigned to low tracks, they experience diminished cognitive and affective outcomes. One challenge for those serious about improving the mathematical reasoning skills of U.S. students is to address the knowledge policy of tracking.

Perhaps one solution is to constrain the curriculum options in mathematics at the secondary level. Currently, African American and Hispanic students are overrepresented in vocational programs. Despite a recent movement to redefine vocational education (now often called *school-to-work*) with high standards, typical vocational education still does not provide students with opportunities to engage in a rigorous mathematics curriculum. Lee, Croninger, and Smith (1997) found that students learn more mathematics in schools that offer them a narrow curriculum composed of college-preparatory academic courses. This research is suggestive, rather than definitive. Nevertheless, the findings provide direction for future discussions. Yet, as Cohen and Barnes (1993) noted, "Even if these problems of curriculum and course offerings were miraculously solved tomorrow, teachers still would find it very difficult to learn the pedagogy that recent reformers propose" (p. 248). Undoubtedly, teacher knowledge is linked to students' opportunities to reason with mathematics.

Teacher Knowledge Inequalities

It should be obvious to even the casual observer that high standards in mathematics education calling for more mathematical reasoning are not only indicators of what students should know but also of what teachers must understand. There is consensus across theories of instruction that teachers' content knowledge is a prerequisite to good teaching (Ladson-Billings 1995; Newman, Secada, Wehlage 1995; Shulman 1987). This is a serious system-wide challenge for U.S. public education. Although the qualifications of teachers—such as mathematics background and years of experience—are only indirect measures of the quality of teaching that students receive, teacher qualifications provide useful information about students' opportunities to reason with mathematics.

In thirty-four states, at least 30 percent of the public school districts do not require a college major or minor in the field to be taught when screening or considering teacher applicants (de Mello and Broughman 1996). According to a study by the U.S. Department of Education, about one-quarter (26.6 percent) of all public school students enrolled in mathematics classes in grades 7–12, or about 4 124 000 of the 15 510 000 students enrolled, were taught by teachers without at least a minor in mathematics or mathematics education (Ingersoll and Gruber 1996). Darling-Hammond (1995) noted: "Minority and low-income students in urban settings are most likely to find themselves in classrooms staffed by inadequately prepared, inexperienced, and ill-qualified teachers because funding inequities, distributions of local power, and labor market conditions conspire to produce teacher shortages of which they bear the brunt" (p. 470). Specifically, in mathematics, urban high school students have only a 50 percent chance of having a qualified math teacher (Education Trust 1996). This pattern persists even outside of urban centers. In 1990–91, 40 percent of high school mathematics courses in poverty schools were taught by teachers who were teaching "out of field." Similarly, although almost 70 percent of mathematics classes in low-minority schools were taught by mathematics majors, only about 42 percent of these classes in high-minority schools were taught by mathematics majors. Also in 1990–91, the amount of out-of-field teaching was not equally distributed across different types of classes and groups in schools. Both student achievement levels and type or track of class were related to access to qualified teachers (Ingersoll and Gruber 1996). In each case, the pattern was the same—low-track and low-achievement classes frequently had more out-of-field teaching than did high-track and high-achievement classes. However, teacher content knowledge is not the only indicator of teacher quality.

Teachers' knowledge of their students is another indicator of teacher quality. The CGI (cognitively guided instruction) studies support the idea that knowledge of students' reasoning, when it is integrated, robust, and a part of the established curriculum, can positively affect the teaching and learning of mathematics (Fennema and Franke 1992). It is important to point out that most content areas in mathematics lack this integrated set of knowledge. However, the general consensus in the mathematics education research community is that learning is dependent on the knowledge and reasoning skills the learner brings to the experience (Hiebert and Carpenter 1992; U.S. Department of Education 1994). Thus, one indicator of teacher quality is how well the teacher understands students' thinking and reasoning about mathematics and how best to extend their thinking and reasoning. A similar argument can be made for teachers' understanding of students' cultural backgrounds (Johnson 1990; Ladson-Billings 1997). For example, Knapp (1995, (pp. 199–200) found that teachers in high-poverty schools who placed the greatest emphasis on meaning in their mathematics instruction made two significant shifts in their thinking about learners,

> the first from a view of learners as passive recipients to one of learners as active participants in learning, and the second from a primary focus on the learners' deficits to an asset model of the learner that highlights the strengths and resources children bring to the learning situation. This shift was most visible in the way certain teachers responded to cultural diversity: By treating cultural background as a resource for learning and actively or proactively addressing cultural dimensions of instruction in mathematics, reading, or writing, teachers were able to sustain children's engagement with academic work and, more explicitly, connect the children's world of experience to the world of school-based learning. Not all teachers were successful in this regard, nor did all try to forge such connections; but those that did achieved a higher level of meaning in their work.

The policy implications of the current state of teacher knowledge inequality is clear. States and local school districts need more mathematically rigorous entry-level requirements for teaching. Further, real instructional change that includes mathematical reasoning—beyond basic skills objectives—will require targeted, continuous professional development in high poverty and minority schools. This professional development should focus on both mathematics and students' reasoning with mathematics. The latter has implications for assessment.

Assessment Policy

Students' opportunities to reason with mathematics are strongly associated with the assessment policies of the school district. Assessment policy often influences the nature of pedagogy and curriculum in a classroom. The influence of standardized testing is arguably greater in high-minority classrooms. In a nationwide survey, teachers of high-minority classrooms reported test-specific instructional practices more often than teachers of low-minority classrooms (CSTEEP 1992). For example, in high-minority classrooms, about 60 percent of the teachers reported teaching test-taking skills, teaching topics known to be on the test, increasing emphasis on tested topics, and starting preparation more than a month before the test. These practices were reported significantly less often in low-minority classrooms. Further, mathematics teachers with high-minority classes indicated more pressure from their districts to improve standardized test scores than teachers with low-minority classes.

In many cases, urban school districts with very large minority populations use standardized mathematics tests as vehicles to measure school and student progress. In essence, the standardized test is a mechanism of control—the control of teacher behavior. What type of curriculum and pedagogy is produced in this restrictive environment? Typically, mathematics pedagogy influenced by standardized assessment policy emphasizes teacher-centered lectures, with teachers offering one method for solving a problem—the most efficient method for the test—and students listening to the explanation. Generally, this lecture is followed by students working alone on a large set of problems from a textbook or worksheet (Porter 1989; Stodolsky 1988). This practice is repeated so often that it is a cultural artifact—a product of restrictive assessment policy in many cases. The intent of this assessment policy is to prepare students to produce correct answers to narrowly defined problems. The policy often includes a tracking system, with many students of color or low SES being selected to participate in basic skills mathematics programs and other remedial projects. In many instances, these programs portray mathematics as disconnected from the learner and void of real social context, thus limiting the opportunity to reason with mathematics (LeTrende 1991).

Woodson (1933, 1990) argued that the presentation of abstract and disconnected mathematical facts is a "foreign method" incapable of preparing the African American student for life in the United States. Secada (1996) and Stanic (1991) make a similar case for other traditionally underserved groups.

Many equity models of assessment in mathematics education borrow from opportunity-to-learn constructs employed in national and international testing programs (Tate 1995a). These models describe equity as the overlap of content taught and content tested. This is, without question, a serious equity consideration. However, these models ignore the narrow nature of mathematics defined by most standardized mathematics tests (Tate 1997). Moreover, these models fail to consider the limited opportunity to reason with mathematics on standardized tests. Future assessment policies in mathematics education should begin with recommendations found in the *Professional Standards for Teaching Mathematics* (NCTM 1991) and related research, which calls for pedagogy to build on (a) the influence of students' linguistic, ethnic, racial, gender, and SES backgrounds on their learning and reasoning; (b) the contribution that various cultures have made to mathematical reasoning; and (c) the realistic application of mathematics to authentic contexts and other subjects (see also Fuson, Smith, and Lo Cicero 1997; Silver, Smith, and Nelson 1995). These recommendations provide a different focus for mathematics assessment—a reasoning orientation.

Newmann, Secada, and Wehlage (1995) argued that opportunities to reason with mathematics on mathematics assessments should reflect authentic achievement. The authenticity of the assessment item depends on the extent to which it meets the following standards:

Standard 1. Organization of Information: The item/task requires students to organize, synthesize, interpret, explain, or evaluate complex information in addressing a concept or problem.

Standard 2. Consideration of Alternatives: The item/task requires students to explore alternative solutions, methods, or viewpoints in addressing a problem or concept.

Standard 3. Disciplinary Content: The item/task requires students to demonstrate understanding of perspectives, ideas, and theories central to the discipline of mathematics.

Standard 4. Disciplinary Process: The item/task requires students to use methods of analysis or communication characteristic of mathematics.

Standard 5. Elaborated Written Communication: The item/task requires students to express their explanations or conclusions through extended writing.

Standard 6. Problem Connected to World beyond the Classroom: The item/task requires students to address a problem or issue similar to one they have experienced or are likely to experience in life outside the classroom.

Standard 7. Audience beyond the School: The task requires students to communicate their knowledge, present a product or performance, or take some action for an audience beyond the school setting.

Perhaps an example of the pedagogy of a practicing teacher will illuminate how the authentic achievement framework can inform assessment of mathematics. The *war room* is occupied by ten middle school students (see Tate 1995b for more details). Their teacher, Sandra Mason (fictionalized name), is not a mathematics teacher but the head of the laureate program. The students have targeted twenty-five problems that they believe are adversely affecting their community, including the thirteen liquor stores within a mile radius of the school. Each student of the class has been affected by the presence of the liquor stores.

The students conducted legal research that revealed the disproportionate number of liquor establishments in their community was largely a product of a city code that relegates these stores to their largely African American neighborhood. To resolve the dilemma, the students reconstructed and proposed new tax incentives to entice the liquor stores to move away from their community—Standard 1. The process provided the students an opportunity to reason with mathematics for a purpose; it involved asking specific questions about the problem. What methods of mathematical analysis will best support our position? What are the limitations of our analysis? What variables should be included in our analysis to strengthen our position? What variables will the city government and the liquor store owners include in their thinking and analysis? Thus, the students considered alternative methods and viewpoints as they worked through the problem-solving process—Standard 2. Resolving this problem required the students to reason with ratios, proportions, graphs, charts, and tables. They also created mathematical algorithms and employed basic statistical reasoning to gain further insight into possible solutions—Standards 3 and 4.

For Ms. Mason's students, mathematics became an important tool to communicate with others and an agent of persuasion. For example, each student was able to present a three-minute sound bite about the issues (or about his or her position) to local reporters. The construction of the sound bites required a great deal of thinking about communicating and reasoning with mathematics—Standards 5 and 7. Many important questions emerged from this process. Will percents, fractions, or raw numbers make a more striking impression? How can we minimize the appearance of variables that may weaken the public's perception of our position? These questions are integral aspects of reasoning with mathematics in the public domain. Unfortunately, such questions are rarely found in discussions of mathematical reasoning.

We need a change in the vision of mathematics assessment to support authentic achievement. If supported, this shift in assessment practice will undergird reasoning opportunities more consistent with social practice.

FISCAL ADEQUACY

Limited course-taking opportunities, teacher knowledge, and narrow assessment practices are compounded by the inequitable distribution of resources (Rury and Mirel 1997; The Education Trust 1996). The Council of Great City Schools (1992) reported that the average per-pupil expenditure in 1990–91 was $5 200 in a large urban school district compared with $6 073 in suburban public school systems. Although urban public schools allocated the same percentage of their budget (62 percent) to classroom instruction as suburban schools, they spent about $506 less per child on instruction. This discrepancy is especially problematic given that the call for mathematics standards will increase the burden on the fiscally stressed systems of urban education.

The call for more mathematical reasoning represents an epistemological shift in school mathematics from a shopkeeper (basic skills) philosophy of mathematics pedagogy to a constructivist, technology-driven vision of mathematics instruction (Romberg 1992). The fiscal appeal of the basic skills curriculum is low implementation costs. There is rarely a need for new books, calculators, computers, and other instructional materials in the basic skills curriculum. However, a standards-based reasoning curriculum will require urban and rural schools to (a) reallocate funds, seek additional funding for professional development of teachers, or both, and (b) update instructional materials (e.g., textbooks, laboratories, and computer facilities) and enhance the quality of other resources (Darling-Hammond 1995; Knapp 1995; Clune 1997).

Clune (1997) argued that the standards-based approach to educational policymaking requires a new vision for fiscal policy. He posited that funding should shift from fiscal equity to fiscal adequacy and from debates for financial inputs to a focus on standards-based outcomes as the goal of both curriculum policy and school finance strategy. For example, in mathematics education, implementing a policy of fiscal adequacy would require a school district to (a) adopt a set of mathematics standards (where reasoning is central), (b) identify resources needed for achieving the standards, (c) formulate a long-term plan that aligns the standards and resources, (d) develop the plan before the money is spent, and (e) adopt the necessary structural changes to maximize cost-effectiveness.

A call for more reasoning in the mathematics curriculum is linked to fiscal adequacy. The authors of the *Curriculum and Evaluation Standards for School Mathematics* (NCTM 1989) recognized the new costs associated with preparing students to use mathematics in authentic contexts. Romberg (1992) provided insight into the thinking of the *Standards'* authorship team:

> As the *Standards* were being developed, we were aware that change is costly. In fact, we felt that the primary costs would occur in the professional reeducation of teachers. Our strategy was to create a demand for new products (text materials, software, tests, teacher preparation programs, and in-service programs). (p. 435)

Higher mathematics standards require strategic financial planning. School districts must decide whether existing fiscal resources are sufficient for meeting tougher educational goals.

SUPPORT IS ESSENTIAL

One thing that is missing from most reform proposals that call for greater emphasis on mathematical reasoning is a discussion of the knowledge policies required to support the proposed curriculum goals. Four questions that emerged from our analysis are relevant to administrators and policymakers interested in adopting reasoning-based mathematics standards: (*a*) Do course-taking options impede or increase students' opportunity to reason? (*b*) Are opportunities for teacher professional development consistent with the demands of a reasoning-oriented curriculum? (*c*) Are assessment policies consistent with a reasoning-oriented curriculum? (*d*) Does the fiscal plan adequately support a reasoning-oriented curriculum?

It is very important to develop educational policy that supports proposed curriculum reform. The dearth of curriculum reform is a product of many different factors. One factor is political language that does not incorporate arguments for supporting relevant knowledge policies. Not caring enough about the realities of education in urban and rural settings exacts a dreadful cost to the reform effort.

REFERENCES

Center for the Study of Testing, Evaluation, and Educational Policy (CSTEEP). *"The Influence of Testing on Teaching Math and Science in Grades 4–12.* Boston, Mass.: Boston College, 1992.

Clune, William H. "The Empirical Argument for Educational Adequacy, the Critical Gaps in the Knowledge Base, and a Suggested Research Agenda." In *Selected Papers in School Finance 1995,* edited by William J. Fowler, pp. 101–24. Washington, D.C.: National Center for Education Statistics, 1997.

Cohen, David, and Carol Barnes. "Conclusion: A New Pedagogy for Policy." In *Teaching for Understanding: Challenges for Policy and Practice,* edited by David K. Cohen, Milbrey W. McLaughlin, and Joan E. Tolbert, pp. 240–75. San Francisco, Calif.: Jossey-Bass, 1993.

Council of Great City Schools. *National Urban Education Goals: Baseline Indicators, 1990–1991.* Washington, D.C.: Council of Great City Schools, 1992.

Darling-Hammond, Linda. "Inequality and Access to Knowledge." In *Handbook of Multicultural Education*, edited by James A. Banks and Cherry A. McGee Banks, pp. 465–83. New York: Macmillan, 1995.

de Mello, Victor, and Stephen Broughman. *1993–1994 Schools and Staffing Survey: Selected State Results*. Washington D.C.: National Center for Education Statistics, 1996.

Fennema, Elizabeth, and Megan Franke. "Teachers' Knowledge and its Impact." In *Handbook of Research on Mathematics Teaching and Learning*, edited by Douglas A. Grouws, pp. 147–64. New York: Macmillan, 1992.

Fuson, Karen, Steven Smith, and Ana Maria Lo Cicero. "Supporting Latino First Graders' Ten-Structured Thinking in Urban Classrooms." *Journal for Research in Mathematics Education* 28, no. 6 (December 1997): 733–60.

Haberman, Martin. *Star Teachers on Children in Poverty*. West Lafayette, Ind.: Kappa Delta Pi, 1995.

Hiebert, James, and Thomas Carpenter. "Learning and Teaching with Understanding." In *Handbook of Research on Mathematics Teaching and Learning*, edited by Douglas A. Grouws, pp. 65–100. New York: Macmillan, 1992.

Hoffer, Thomas, Kenneth Rasinski, and Whitney Moore. *Social Background Differences in High School Mathematics and Science Coursetaking and Achievement*. Washington D.C.: National Center for Education Statistics, 1995.

Ingersoll, Richard, and Kerry Gruber. *Out-of-Field Teaching and Educational Equality*. Washington D.C.: National Center for Education Statistics, 1996.

Johnson, Howard C. "How Can the *Curriculum and Evaluation Standards* Be Realized for All Students." *School Science and Mathematics* 90 (October 1990): 527–43.

Knapp, Michael S. *Teaching for Meaning in High Poverty Classrooms*. New York: Teachers College Press, 1995.

Knapp, Michael, and Sara Woolverton. "Social Class and Schooling." In *Handbook of Research on Multicultural Education*, edited by James A. Banks and Cherry A. McGee Banks, pp. 548–622. New York: Macmillan, 1995.

Ladson-Billings, Gloria. "Making Mathematics Meaningful in Cultural Contexts." In *New Directions for Equity in Mathematics Education*, edited by Walter S. Secada, Elizabeth Fennema, and Lisa Byrd, pp. 126–45. Cambridge: Cambridge University Press, 1995.

———. "It Doesn't Add Up: African American Students' Mathematics Achievement." *Journal for Research in Mathematics Education* 28, no. 6 (December 1997): 697–708.

Lee, Valerie, Robert Croninger, and Julia Smith. "Course-Taking, Equity, and Mathematics Learning: Testing the Constrained Curriculum Hypothesis in U.S. Secondary Schools." *Educational Evaluation and Policy Analysis* (Summer 1997): 99–121.

LeTendre, Mary J. "The Continuing Evolution of a Federal Role in Compensatory Education." *Educational Evaluation and Policy Analysis* (Winter 1991): 328–34.

National Council of Teachers of Mathematics. *An Agenda for Action: Recommendations for School Mathematics of the 1980s.* Reston, Va.: National Council of Teachers of Mathematics, 1980.

———. *Curriculum and Evaluation Standards for School Mathematics.* Reston, Va.: National Council of Teachers of Mathematics, 1989.

———. *Professional Standards for Teaching Mathematics.* Reston, Va.: National Council of Teachers of Mathematics, 1991.

Newmann, Fred, Walter Secada, and Gary Wehlage. *A Guide to Authentic Instruction and Assessment: Vision, Standards and Scoring.* Madison. Wis.: Wisconsin Center for Education Research, 1995.

Oakes, Jeannie. "Opportunities, Achievement, and Choice: Women and Minority Students in Science and Mathematics." In *Review of Research in Education*, edited by Courtney B. Cazden, pp. 143–222. Washington, D.C.: American Educational Research Association, 1990.

Porter, Andrew C. "A Curriculum Out of Balance: The Case of Elementary School Mathematics." *Educational Researcher* (June/July 1989): 9–15.

Rock, Donald, and Judith Pollack. *Mathematics Course-Taking and Gains in Mathematics Achievement.* Washington, D.C.: National Center for Education Statistics, 1995.

Romberg, Thomas A. "Further Thoughts on the Standards: A Reaction to Apple." *Journal for Research in Mathematics Education* (November 1992): 432–37.

Rury, John, and Jeffery Mirel. "The Political Economy of Urban Education." In *Review of Research in Education*, edited by Michael W. Apple, pp. 49–110. Washington, D.C.: American Educational Research Association, 1997.

Silver, Edward, Margaret Smith, and Barbara Nelson. "The QUASAR Project: Equity Concerns Meet Mathematics Education Reform in the Middle School." In *New Directions for Equity in Mathematics Education*, edited by Walter S. Secada, Elizabeth Fennema, and Lisa Byrd, pp. 9–56. Cambridge: Cambridge University Press, 1995.

Shulman, Lee. "Knowledge and Teaching: Foundations of a New Reform." *Harvard Educational Review* (February 1987): 1–22.

Secada, Walter G. "Race, Ethnicity, Social Class, Language, and Achievement in Mathematics. In *Handbook of Research on Mathematics Teaching and Learning*, edited by Douglas A. Grouws, pp. 623–60. New York: Macmillan, 1992.

———. "Urban Students Acquiring English and Learning Mathematics in the Context of Reform." *Urban Education* 30 (January 1996): 422–48.

Stanic, George M. A. "Social Inequality, Cultural Discontinuity, and Equity in School Mathematics." *Peabody Journal of Education* 66 (Winter 1991): 57–71.

Stodolsky, Susan S. *The Subject Matters: Classroom Activity in Mathematics and Social Studies.* Chicago: University of Chicago Press, 1988.

Strickland, Dorothy, and Carol Asher. "Low Income African-American Children and Public Schooling." In *Handbook of Research on Curriculum*, edited by Philip W. Jackson, pp. 609–25. New York: Macmillan, 1992.

Tate, William F. "School Mathematics and African American Students: Thinking Seriously about Opportunity-to-Learn Standards." *Educational Administration Quarterly* 31 (August 1995a): 424–48.

———. "Mathematics Communication: Creating Opportunities to Learn." *Teaching Children Mathematics* 1 (February 1995b): 344–49, 368–69.

———. "Race-Ethnicity, SES, Gender, and Language Proficiency Trends in Mathematics Achievement: An Update." *Journal for Research in Mathematics Education* 28, (December 1997): 652–79.

The Education Trust. *The 1996 Education Trust State and National Data Book*. Washington, D.C.: The Education Trust, 1996.

United States Department of Education. *Issues of Curriculum Reform in Science, Mathematics, and Higher Order Thinking Across the Disciplines*. Washington, D.C.: U.S. Government Printing Office, 1994.

Woodson, Carter G. *The Miseducation of the Negro*. 1933. Reprint, Trenton, N.J.: African World Press, 1990.

20

Adventures in Mathematics Inquiry

Gail Boldt

Aaron Levine

FOUR years ago, we came to the conclusion that we had to create a mathematics curriculum for our third- and fourth-grade students that called for the students to create and investigate their own mathematics projects. Before that, we posed the problems for the whole class to solve or gave exercises so students could sharpen their numbers-sense skills. However, we found that because this approach did not make use of the prior knowledge and interests of individual students, many students did poorly in this curriculum. Some students found the problems too easy and were bored. In group situtations, the group often solved a given problem but was not committed to seeing that all group members understood the reasoning that was used to produce a solution. In fact, many group members found the problems too difficult and gladly surrendered the responsibility for solving them to others. These students often expressed negative feelings about mathematics and themselves as mathematicians.

In the former curriculum, students rarely made connections between developing number-sense skills and solving complex problems, and many struggled in problem-solving situations. We discovered that our students thought that both complex problems and number-sense problems could be translated into steps to be memorized, rather than viewed as problem situations about which they could reason. Students rarely saw the connections among different areas of mathematics, seeing each problem situation as separate from anything done earlier. There was little discussion about the logic of mathematics or how to reason from one set of understandings to another. Mathematics was something that others initiated and reasoned about; the students were technicians carrying out the procedures of others.

In the updated curriculum, we drew upon the success we had achieved with student-initiated projects in writing, social studies, and science. We felt confident that when students proposed their own problems and devised their own methods, they would reason about and understand their own work. We referred to the steps of our writing workshop (Atwell 1987; Short et al. 1996) to devise a process for student self-initiated mathematics projects. We called the process "Choose Your Own Math Adventures" or "Math Adventures" for short. (The title comes from the *Choose Your Own Adventure* book series, published by Bantam Books. These books are popular with elementary school students.) Over the past four years of using this process, we have been thrilled by what we feel is a transformation of our students into mathematicians. The purpose of this article is to give an overview of the Math Adventure process and to show how it has facilitated our students' greatly improved abilities to work and reason as mathematicians.

MATH ADVENTURES

The guidelines from which we and our students work are under constant review and revision. Our goal is to give the students a structure that encourages them to work as a collaborative community of mathematicians and elicits the best possible mathematics reasoning from each student.

Guidelines for Math Adventures	
Step	Procedure
1	Write Math Adventure proposal. Review with teacher.
2	Work on Adventure. Research and record notes and calculations every day. Conference with peers/teachers if stuck.
3	Write presentation. Conference with teacher; revise.
4	Present at Mathematician's Chair. Revise if necessary. Have final discussion with teacher.
5	Make poster or Web page.

In our new mathematics curriculum, students are proposing, researching, and solving their own personal math problems. Here are few examples of problems successfully solved by individual students:

- How many seconds old am I?
- How long would it take for a turtle to swim around Oʻahu?
- If the polar ice caps melted completely, how much water would this add to the oceans and what would the new topographical map of Hawaiʻi look like?
- How do I make a scale drawing of the Titanic?

- Is there a relationship between a state's geological location or average yearly temperature and its leading causes of death by disease?
- How many lines of symmetry are in different geometric shapes? Can I find rules for predicting this?

In creating this process, we took certain ideas as axiomatic. First, to ensure that students understand what they are doing and that they build a sense of the logic of mathematics, we believe that students can and should invent for themselves means to solve problems, both complex reasoning problems and meaningful algorithms. The teaching of rote algorithms has been overemphasized, and often students cannot apply them to problem-solving situations. We believe that students benefit from learning number-sense and algorithm skills within a context that holds meaning for them, such as through Math Adventure projects. Finally, we believe that having a process that can be used to work through any kind of mathematical problem is an invaluable resource that allows our students to experience mathematics as a process of reasoning and encourages each student to develop mathematical self-confidence.

A Closer Look

Each step in our guidelines exists because it has proven successful in helping students and teachers stay organized and on track and, more important, because it has helped the students be more explicit about their mathematical reasoning. In the following sections we will discuss each step in greater detail.

Step 1: Presenting the Proposal

Each student begins by coming up with a problem proposal and talking it through with a teacher. This is a student's first chance to articulate his or her thoughts and possible approaches to working on the selected problem. Sometimes, these student-teacher discussions help the students understand their own work more clearly and, at other times, cause them to change or modify their problems. For example, Maile proposed to figure out how many paper towels would cover the area of the classroom floor. Maile had already shown a sophsisticated understanding of area in a previous problem, so the teacher asked her, "Do you already know how to do this? Will it challenge you?" Maile decided that a more challenging problem would be to find how many paper towels would fill the entire space (volume) of the room.

Step 2: Working on the Math Adventure

When the children are working on solving their problems, they are encouraged to employ any method they can think of, such as using calculators or computers, building models, working with pencil and paper, and talking with their peers, parents, and teachers. The students are in e-mail contact with university mathematics education professors who serve as resources to the children. (Mahalo [thank you] to Dr. Neil Pateman and Dr. Joseph Zilliox from the University of Hawaii at Manoa, College of Education, Department of Teacher Education and Curriculum Studies, for their enthusiam and support.) For example, Gina had four e-mail exchanges with one of these professors when she was trying to discover who came up with the idea of zero and how cultures before ours recorded numbers.

We require the students to record their ideas, findings, and calculations daily. This helps them keep track of where they are in their work. We review the students' notebooks with them, discussing and introducing mathematical language, and helping them to be more cognizant of their own thought processes and how to communicate those processes clearly.

Step 3: Writing the Presentation

When a student thinks the solution to the problem is complete, he or she has a brief meeting with a teacher. The purpose of the meeting is *not* to ensure that the child has reached a satisfactory answer—we leave that up to the audience during the presentation. Rather, it is to check that the child has written a clear presentation, including all necessary charts, diagrams, and explanations.

Finishing a problem does not always mean that the student will come up with a final solution. Some Adventures would take too long to finish, given the number of necessary calculations or steps required. Carlie, for example, wanted to find out which numbers between 1 and 100 were prime. She came to us after she had worked on the first fifty numbers saying that she knew how to determine if a number was prime, that she had discovered several patterns that helped her decide, and that she didn't think it was worthwhile to continue to 100. We agreed.

Other children realize part way through the Adventure that they've chosen a problem to do that is simply too difficult for them to solve. Once we and the children agree that they have given a problem their best shot, we have them write up a presentation that explains what they have figured out. The emphasis here is on mathematics as a process, a way of thinking about solving problems, and not necessarily on correct solutions. When Billy wanted to find the volume of Earth in units of cubic "Billies," he soon realized that the problem was too difficult for him. He was able to find the circumference of Earth in Billies, and during his presentation, he explained his ideas for solving the volume problem and also his understanding about why those ideas would not work.

Step 4: Making the Presentation

Discussion during *Mathematician's Chair* is the most lively and dynamic part of the process for the classroom community. During the presentations, the student audience has the opportunity to finally learn what classmates have been doing for the last weeks or months. There is a sense of excitement as students anticipate hearing the strange and wonderful problems and solutions posed by their peers. Students present their work without being interrupted. A discussion following each presentation typically lasts up to thirty minutes and gives students and teachers the opportunity to have significant conversations about mathematics.

Initially, we had to give the students some firm direction to help them learn to really listen to one another. We felt early on that the students did not expect to understand one another or to participate in real discussions about another child's work in mathematics. We found it productive to require the students to take notes during presentations and then to sit quietly for some time after the presentation and prior to beginning the discussion, writing notes about what they didn't understand, possible errors, and alternative solutions. Once students began to jot down notes and participate spontaneously, it was not necessary to always require note taking. We talked about and modeled good questioning skills and sometimes asked the presenter to question the audience about parts of the presentation that may have been difficult to understand. We tell the children that some of them may not be able to understand every aspect of every presentation, but we know there are things each student can learn from any presentation. Our goal is that the students come to expect that they can reason together about the process, the outcomes, and even how the presentations relate to other things the audience members are thinking about. For example, when Jeff figured out a method for converting fractions into decimals, his classmates were not able to understand his method, but several students articulated new things they understood about fractions following his presentation.

During presentations, students often recognize a mistake in their own or in one another's work. When this occurs, it is generally possible for the student to complete the presentation with the audience understanding that a certain step or the final answer is incorrect and needs to be revised. When Nalani was trying to figure out the weight of the water in the community pool, her classmates pointed out to her that she had figured out the weight for only one "layer" (area) rather than for the entire depth of the pool (volume). Because Nalani's classmates recognized her error and because she showed us in a follow-up conference that she understood her error, we left it up to her whether she wanted to make a second presentation. Sometimes, however, a student's initial work is too far off and requires a second presentation, or the student simply wants to present the revised work. Whether or not the students present their revised work, the opportunity to receive input during the Mathematician's Chair session and to revise his or her work means that each child experiences success in mathematics.

Step 5: Making a Poster or Web Page

When the child finally completes the Math Adventure, the finished work may be displayed either on a poster or Web page. Posters and Web pages include graphics and written explanations of the students' work. In these formats, students must once again consider how to represent their thinking. They also allow others (parents, other students and teachers in the school, and anyone who browses our Web site, www.epiphany_hi.org.) to interact with the child about the math project, thus extending the conversation beyond the classroom.

FINDINGS

We believe that the Math Adventure structure has resulted in several important mathematical developments in our classroom. Among the most significant of these developments are:

1. Students have a rich understanding of mathematics that connects to previous discussions and work that continues through the two years they are with us;

2. Students experience improved enthusiasm and confidence as they are able to work successfully at an appropriate level;

3. Students know that they can reason about mathematics.

As we considered examples of student work to use for highlighting the strengths of Math Adventures, we realized that each example truly illustrates all of the mathematical developments cited above. Nevertheless, we will use different examples of student work in the remainder of this section to illustrate each development more clearly.

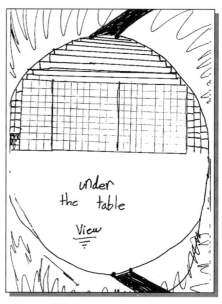

Fig. 20.1. Jenny's project

Building Connections

In the children's mathematics projects, we have seen them making connections across their own projects as well as from the projects of others. Early in the year, Jenny was presenting how she had figured out the the area of a circle. (fig. 20.1) She had covered the surface of a round table with centimeter blocks, a technique she had used previously with rectangular surfaces. However, the uncovered spaces around the edge of the round table presented a new challenge to Jenny. She realized she could see the spaces as triangles, except that each had a slightly curved side. She then discovered that if she ignored the curve, these triangles could be seen as right triangles, a concept she had learned about in other students' presentations. When she put two of the triangles together, she figured out that they had an area of 1 square centimeter. She was then able to add up all the halves and divide by two to help her obtain a final answer. Jenny's presentation elicited discussion of the idea that shapes can be seen as combinations of other shapes.

Jared was fascinated by Jenny's discovery. Later, as he attempted to measure the volume of the school's chapel (fig. 20.2), he realized that he could imagine the room as an *isosceles triangle* set on top of a *rectangle*. Jared easily calculated the volume of the rectangular portion of the building. Next, to help him figure out the *ceiling*, he got out paper, cut out an isosceles triangle and, after folding it, realized that it could be seen as two right triangles which, in turn, could be seen as a rectangle. He was able to use that information to figure out the volume of the ceiling and get his final answer.

As Jared was explaining his work, his peers asked him again and again to explain how he got the ceiling. All at once, a collective gasp arose from several students. They realized at the same moment that Jared had found the volume of the ceiling by visualizing it as half of a rectangular solid, equivalent to the volume of the triangular portion. This, in turn, inspired several other students to undertake related Math Adventure projects.

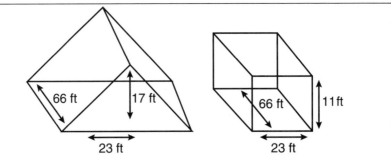

And then I had to figure out how to measure the ceiling, which was an isosceles triangle. I drew a triangle on the graph paper, and Mr. Levine helped me figure out that if you split the triangle in half and flip one end over, you will get a rectangle from the two right triangles. So I took the original measurements from the rectangle I had on the bottom of the chapel. I found out that the measurements for the ceiling would be 11.5 ft × 17 ft × 66 ft if it were a rectangle. 21 + 462 is the cubes for 11.5 ft = 483. 6 × 462 = 3816. 462 + 252 for the 17 feet = 714. 714 × 3816 × 483 = 955,957,464 cubes.

Fig. 20.2. Jared's work

Success for a Variety of Students

Math Adventures accommodate students regardless of their strength as mathematicians. All students experience success as they move at their own pace and work on projects they understand and find interesting. Jamie, a student who dreaded mathematics to the point of tears and was far behind her peers in her mathematical understanding, showed immediate improvement in her feelings toward mathematics. For her first project, Jamie chose to research the birthdays of her classmates (fig. 20.3).

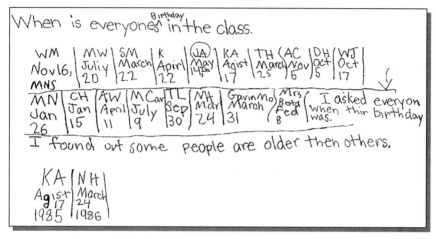

Fig. 20.3. Jamie's birthday project

This project was challenging but not overwhelming for her. Jamie decided on her own to extend the project when she discovered that the year in which people were born was important. She redid the project a second time and organized it by birth order. Jamie began exhibiting enthusiasm about her work. The tears subsided, and the frustrations she encountered were met with more confidence that she could and would figure out an answer. This newfound confidence clearly translated into Jamie's later mathematical endeavors, as she challenged herself with problems such as finding the volume of a large bookshelf in cubic centimeters (fig. 20.4).

Jeff is clearly our most remarkable mathematician. For one of his Math Adventures, Jeff set out to discover what πr^2 means and how it is derived (fig. 20.5, p. 242). He created diagrams of circles to help him look for the relationships between different attributes of a circle. Jeff remembered a Math Adventure from last year that involved an inquiry into pi (π). At home, his father explained the concept of theta (θ) as it pertains to a circle. For several days, Jeff played around with various concepts and equations, trying different approaches to derive the equation πr^2. Jeff finally came up with a diagram and explanation for one of his approaches. He explained that the circle could

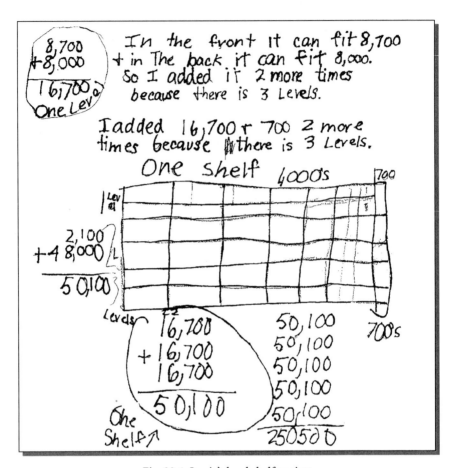

Fig. 20.4. Jamie's bookshelf project

actually be thought of as 360 tiny right triangles, each with an area of $r\theta/2$, the area for a right triangle. Jeff derived the area for a right triangle by drawing a diagonal across a rectangle, thereby getting $1/2(a \times b/2)$, where $a =$ length and $b =$ width (see step 1 on Jeff's diagram). The entire area of the circle could be expressed as $r\theta \times 360/2$ or $r\theta \times 180$ (see steps 2 and 3). Remembering the equations for the circumference of a circle, $2\pi r = C$ and $\theta \times 360 = C$, Jeff was able to derive the standard formula for the area of a circle by making several simultaneous substitutions (see steps 3, 4, and 5).

As the above examples illustrate, Math Adventures give all our mathematicians the opportunity to go as far as their interest, ability, and ambition will take them. Students bring a sense of playfulness, exploration, and reasoning to Math Adventures. They know that they have the time to toy around with various ideas and see where different tactics take them. They are becoming fearless about mathematics.

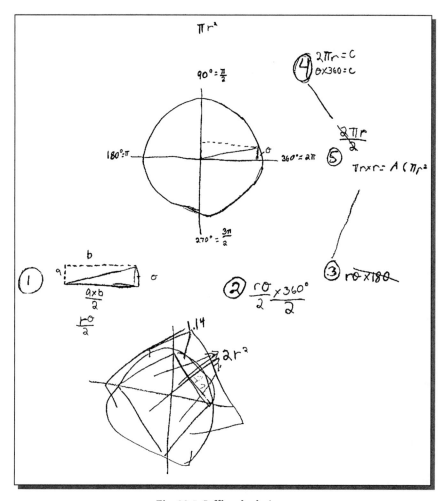

Fig. 20.5. Jeff's calculations

But What about Number Skills?

We are often asked if Math Adventures makes up our entire mathematics curriculum. While we devote most of our math time to Math Adventures, we also engage the children in mental mathematics; teacher-generated problem-solving activities; mini-lessons on a variety of strategies, concepts, and skills; and whole class inquiries related to our larger, integrated curriculum, such as doing scale drawings of their bodies as part of our study of Indonesian shadow puppetry.

Along with many others, we have been concerned about the children's development of number skills in this curriculum and, therefore, decided to explore the issue specifically. We began looking at the algorithms that the children were developing to help them solve their Math Adventure problems. What we noticed delighted us and confirmed our expectation that Math Adventures can help the children to develop powerful mathematical reasoning skills in relation to number sense.

We found that when challenged to develop ways to work with large numbers, most of the students were able to master a method with just a few hours of effort. In some instances, it took students only minutes. The students were able to think about the meaning of what they were doing and the value of numbers. Many of them liked using a method such as this to multiply:

$$26 \times 15: 5 \times 6 = 30, 5 \times 20 = 100, 10 \times 6 = 60,$$
$$10 \times 200; 26 \times 15 = 200 + 100 + 60 + 30 = 390.$$

A popular means of division looked like this:

$$687 \div 17 = 17 \times 10 = 170, 17 \times 20 = 340, 17 \times 40 = 680.$$

Answer: 40, 7 left over.

In both cases, much of the children's work was done mentally, with some written notation to help them keep track of the more difficult computations.

We have two hypotheses about the ease with which the children were able to develop number skills. First, we think that this reflects the habit they developed of thinking about mathematics as something that makes sense and not simply as a series of operations. The children reasoned about the meaning of numbers and how they can be broken down to determine a total. Second, we feel that because we did not rush the children to master this kind of work, most of them were more than ready to tackle and understand what they were being asked to do. The few students who were not able to develop an understanding of these kinds of number operations were, we felt, simply not ready yet. In any case, these students were still quite capable of solving Math Adventure questions that involved large numbers by calculating in ways that they did understand.

In spite of the relative ease with which the children were able to develop computational methods, we do not spend much time working on number skills outside of meaningful contexts. We have had too many experiences like Jared, who had worked with us on division, having no sense of using division when trying to figure out how many hours it would take a rocket to travel to the moon. A teacher asked him, "Have you thought about using division?" to which he replied, "What's division?" The teacher then asked him to solve a problem like 175 ÷ 6, which he solved with no difficulty, but he then had no idea how that related to the problem he was facing. He went back and solved his rocket problem through repeated addition and number doubling.

We decided to look at computational skills that students were developing while they were working on Math Adventures. For instance, Joseph was

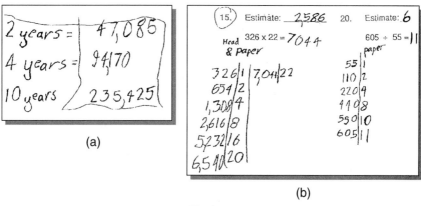

(a)

(b)

Fig. 20.6

trying to figure out how long it would take to ride a bike to the moon (fig. 20.6a). After he figured out that he could travel about 129 miles every two days, he used a calculator to figure out how far he could go in one year. From there, Joseph added on paper, combining answers to get the necessary information to solve what could have been solved with large number multiplication or division.

A short time later, we presented Joseph with a couple of large number multiplication and division problems (fig. 20.6b). He had never before been asked by us to do these kinds of problems, but he had no difficulty with solving them using the same addition and recording processes he used in Math Adventures. For Joseph and our other students, number skills developed in the context of their own Math Adventures could be used successfully in problem solving. It was very often the case, however, that students who learned computation number skills outside a meaningful context did not know when to apply them.

FINAL THOUGHTS

In their self-evaluations at the end of a recent school year, our students reported that good mathematicians are people who undertake mathematics projects that are more difficult than they knew how to solve when they began. They are people who are organized and record their processes carefully. The students wrote that mathematicians stick with their work for a long time; they revise their work over and over until they understand it and get it right; they discuss their work with others when they get stuck; and they can explain and represent their work to others. Many of the students said that mathematics is their favorite subject and that it is fun and challenging. Even those students who said that they were "okay" mathematicians, rather than "good" or "great" mathematicians, described math as something they usually like. They said that their work in math was "successful" because they were able to stay with their projects until they solved them or came to some reasonable conclusion.

As teachers, we understand that talent may figure significantly in what a person excels at. Some of us are better artists, some better athletes, some better writers, some better mathematicians. We don't expect all our students to end up in science-and mathematics-related fields. However, we think that the Math Adventures curriculum we have developed is helping all of our students to come to a broader, more powerful view of what mathematics is. It is helping them to succeed with mathematics, to appreciate the beauty and fun of mathematics, and to understand its value in their lives.

REFERENCES

Atwell, Nancie. *In the Middle: Writing, Reading and Learning with Adolescents.* Portsmouth, N.H.: Boynton/Cook Publishers, Heinemann Education Books, Inc., 1987.

Choose Your Own Adventure. 83 vols. New York: Bantam Books, 1982–1998.

Short, Kathy G., Jerome C. Harste, Carolyn Burke, et al. *Creating Classrooms for Authors and Inquirers,* 2nd ed. Portsmouth, N.H.: Heinemann, Reed Elsevier, Inc., 1996.

21

Using Short Questions to Develop and Assess Reasoning

William M. Carroll

Teacher: Today we will be investigating how to construct some different types of rectangles. Let's see if we remember how rectangles are different from other geometric shapes. What is your definition of a rectangle, Gilbert?

Gilbert: I think that a rectangle is a polygon that has parallel sides.

Teacher: Hmm. Do you mean like this? (*Teacher sketches a regular hexagon on the board.*) Latrice?

Latrice: No, that figure is a hexagon. It has six sides. A rectangle is a 4-sided figure with all of its sides parallel.

Teacher: (*Looks perplexed, then draws four unconnected parallel line segments*) Four parallel lines. Is this what she means, Sarah?

Sarah: No, it's got to be closed. A rectangle has four sides with only the opposite ones parallel.

Teacher: (*Sketches a parallelogram with no right angles*) Like this?

Alberto: No. For a rectangle, all four of the angles have to be right angles.

Teacher: (*Draws a rectangle*). So this is a rectangle. Let's see if we can put this all together. What would be a clear and complete definition for rectangle?

IN CONTRAST to more traditional instruction where students might memorize definitions provided by the text or teacher, students in the brief vignette above engaged in an active discussion of mathematical ideas. In this particular sixth-grade class, where reasoning is a regular part of mathematics, students felt comfortable attempting an answer, moving towards a solution, and building on each other's ideas. Although the correct answer (developing a clear definition for *rectangle*) was the one goal of the activity, an overarching objective was to involve students actively in reasoning about mathematics. Because these students were accustomed to reasoning with mathematics—making hypotheses, building on prior ideas, and moving toward a correct answer—they were not intimidated by errors. Rather, the errors provided guidelines for refining the definition and thinking about mathematical properties.

Promoting students' reasoning helps the teacher assess students' understanding and plan appropriate instruction. For example, figure 21.1 illustrates two fifth graders' responses to a "mystery graph" question, involving a bar graph representing temperatures of four months during the year. The question was constructed to assess students' understanding of bar graphs and their application to real data. Although the question itself requires reasoning ("What is a typical pattern of temperatures in the midwestern United States?" and "How would that look graphically?"), the written part

Max was making a graph of the average temperatures in January, April, July, and October for St. Paul, Minnesota.

Which one of the graphs below do you think shows this best? Circle the best graph. Then explain why you chose that graph.

Average temperature for St. Paul, Minnesota

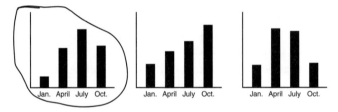

Jan. April July Oct.   Jan. April July Oct.   Jan. April July Oct.

(a) Mystery graph question with correct answer

Explain why you chose that graph: because I have been there before.

(b) Chris's explanation

Explain why you chose that graph: after July things should start to get cooler! Also July should be warmer than April

(c) Juan's explanation

Fig. 21.1.

offers a window into the students' thinking. Both students correctly circled the first graph, but only the second student, Juan, shows evidence of understanding the concept by explaining how the graph relates to the temperatures during different seasons. Although Chris may have an understanding of this relationship, she shows no evidence here.

A balanced instructional approach incorporates reasoning throughout whole-class discussions, small-group interactions, students' interviews, and extended projects. However, the purpose of this article is to examine how short, written explanations can be used to facilitate and assess reasoning. Larger projects and more detailed explanations provide deeper insight into students' thinking, but short, open-ended questions provide quick checks into students' thinking and conceptual understanding and are generally no more time-consuming to correct than simple correct-incorrect questions. Regular use of these types of problems also helps students develop the skills of reasoning and communication in words, diagrams, or pictures. (See also article 14, by Peressini and Webb, in this volume.)

Most of the examples are drawn from classrooms using one of the current *Standards*-based elementary curricula that implement the NCTM Standards for teaching, learning, and assessment (NCTM 1989, 1991, 1995). (The curriculum is the University of Chicago School Mathematics Project's elementary school curriculum, Everyday Mathematics. Observations and data in this article come from evaluations funded by the National Science Foundation as part of the development and field testing of this program.) Along with problem solving and discussions, activities often focus on reasoning about mathematical situations. Although teachers often find that students initially have difficulty expressing their thinking, especially in writing, they report that students' performance improves with practice. This is especially true when students see good examples of written explanations.

Three examples of short-answer questions and students' responses are presented in this article. The second question provides a rubric that was developed to help assess the students' understanding. All the questions are meant to be prototypes on which teachers can improve.

EXAMPLE 1: COMPARING TWO FRACTIONS

At the beginning of the year, fourth graders were asked to compare 1/2 and 1/3. In particular students were told that one child reasoned that 1/2 was larger because each piece of a half was larger than each piece of a third. Another child argued that 1/3 was larger than 1/2 because three is larger than two. Students were asked to decide which of the two children were correct and to justify their reasoning in pictures and words. Figure 21.2 gives three of the answers. Clearly, if students were only asked, "Which fraction is bigger, 1/2 or 1/3," Warren's and Ana's responses would have been scored as

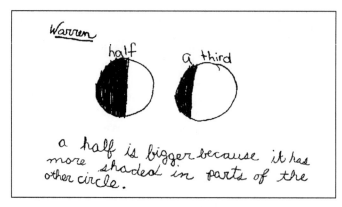

(a) Warren's explanation

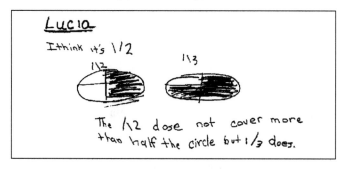

(b) Lucia's explanation

(c) Ana's explanation

Fig. 21.2

correct. However, only Ana shows a correct understanding of the meaning of fraction in her picture, although she does not give full written justification. Although Warren answered that 1/2 was larger, he showed underlying misconceptions about illustrating fractions. Lucia's picture also provides an insight into her error—interpreting one-third as a ratio of one part to three parts (see fig. 21.2c). Both incorrect drawings suggest the students would benefit from work on representing unit fractions.

This simple question provides information to the teacher about what course fraction work may take. Ana's response, linking the fractions to a meaningful situation—pizzas—suggests that the student might benefit from this context. A nice follow-up question might be, "If you want the biggest pieces of pizza, would you rather have 1/2, 1/3, or 1/4 of a pizza? Explain your reasoning, using words *and* pictures." The errors that the other students made on the original question can be discussed productively, and any exemplary responses can be used to illustrate how good reasoning is expressed. The answers also indicate that students have no difficulty illustrating 1/2, but do not have a good understanding of 1/3 or lack the ability to represent it correctly.

EXAMPLE 2: GEOMETRIC PROPERTIES

Because geometry has been underrepresented in the elementary school mathematics curriculum, research has often found that many junior high school and secondary school students have trouble reasoning about geometric properties and relationships (e.g., Fuys, Geddes, and Tischler 1988). However, as illustrated in the vignette that opened this chapter, middle school students who have had regular exposure to geometric explorations are quite capable of thinking about and discussing relationships.

As part of a field test and evaluation of the *Standards*-based fifth- and sixth-grade curricula, the following problem was used to assess students' reasoning about geometric properties.

> Sheila said, "I can draw a triangle with 2 right angles." Do you agree with Sheila? Explain your reasoning.

Ten classes using the *Standards*-based curriculum and ten classes using a more traditional mathematics curriculum were presented this problem. Students' responses included a wide range of answers, from those that seemed to lack the basic vocabulary of geometry, especially right angle, to those that clearly recognized that the sum of two right angles leaves a measure of 0 degrees for the third angle. These responses, and those to similar questions, provided a good picture of the geometric understandings and misconceptions of students and the types of activities that would be appropriate for them.

In order to assess more fully the reasoning and communication of these students, a rubric based on expectations of strong responses was developed and refined using examples from the students. Students' responses that were used to determine the rubric can be found in table 21.1.

TABLE 21.1
Rubric and Sample Responses to Sheila's Triangle

Level	Description and sample of students' responses
0	No response or off task. Geometric language is not used. "I agree with Sheila because you can do it."
1	Incorrect response, but some reasoning is attempted: "Yes, because all triangles have a right angle and a left angle." "Yes. You make one at the top and one at the bottom." Partially correct response but reasoning is weak or incorrect: "No, because all triangles have right angles."
2	Correct response, but reasoning is not complete or clear: "No, because you can only put 1 right angle in a triangle." "No, it would have to be a square or rectangle."
3	Correct response and good reasoning. Explanation goes beyond Level 2, but relies on concrete or visual understanding rather than abstract knowledge of properties: "Because if you put 2 right angles together, you already have 3 sides, and the sides are not closed." "No, because if you draw 2 right angles and try to connect them, you get a square or a rectangle. Two right angles is already 3 sides."
4	Exemplary response. Student applied knowledge of triangles and angles. "Triangles have 3 angles and 180°. If there are 2 right angles, then it would equal 180°. But that is only 2 angles." "How could you possible have 2 right angles equaling 180° when you only have 2/3 of a triangle done?" "You would have 2 parallel sides."

Our results showed that 30 percent of the fifth graders and 53 percent of the sixth graders in the *Standards*-based curriculum scored at Level 3 or 4 (see table 21.1 for level descriptors). In contrast, only 4 percent of the fifth graders and 13 percent of the sixth graders in the more traditional programs scored at these levels. (We tested 76 fifth graders and 109 sixth graders from *Standards*-based classes and 91 fifth graders and 137 sixth graders from traditional classes.) Given the emphasis on geometric explorations in the *Standards*-based curriculum, these results are not surprising. Furthermore, the results probably reflect students' experience explaining their reasoning in oral, pictorial, or written form. The scores of the classes in traditional instruction resemble results from the Sixth National Assessment of Educatiional Progress (NAEP) (Kouba, Zawojewski, and Strutchens 1997), which found low scores when students were asked to provide an explanation or drawing to support their thinking. The higher scores of the *Standards*-based classes indicate how students benefit from the use of reasoning in writing and class discussions.

While this rubric was useful to our research, classroom teachers may find it more useful to devise simpler methods for categorizing responses to reasoning and problem-solving questions. One simple three-point rubric is: Little understanding, Making progress, and Good understanding.

EXAMPLE 3: TURNING CLOSED-RESPONSE QUESTIONS INTO OPEN-ENDED REASONING QUESTIONS

One way of engaging students in the reasoning process is to have them examine and explain an error. This can be especially useful for students who are reluctant to write about or discuss their own reasoning but not so reluctant to explain an error made by someone else. Looking for, and analyzing, an error can be as motivating as solving a puzzle. Because understanding is the goal, good questions should focus on conceptual errors rather than simple procedural mistakes, thus building a better understanding of mathematical ideas while developing communicating and reasoning skills. For example, the question in figure 21.3 is based on an eighth-grade item taken from the Second NAEP (Carpenter, Corbitt, Kepner, Lindquist, and Reys 1981). Although the original question only asked eighth graders to estimate the sum of the two fractions, the revised problem has two parts (fig. 21.3b). First, fifth-, and sixth-grade students analyzed and explained the mistake that most students made. Second, they gave their best estimate and explained their reasoning. The two answers given in figure 21.3 indicate the quality of responses that can develop when reasoning and communication are a part of the mathematics classroom. For example, Marsha's answer (figure 21.3c) shows an exemplary understanding of fractions—that 12/13 is 1/13 away from 1. As shown, reasoning questions can encourage students to go beyond the minimal answers to integrating their mathematical knowledge in clear statements.

Not only can questions involving conceptual errors be used to engage individual students in communicating their reasoning processes, they also promote class discussion. For example, an overhead of some of the incorrect responses in figure 21.2, or potential errors the teacher knows the students might make, can be used to spark class or group discussions. Thus students might be asked to work in small groups to analyze the errors and provide a correct explanation.

The new focus on reasoning reflects a major change in how we think about mathematics learning. This is characterized by a shift from practicing isolated skills toward developing a rich network of conceptual understanding. Although there is often a strong tendency for students to see mathematics as algorithmic activities, the inclusion of reasoning questions on a regular basis is a reminder that understanding and explanation are crucial aspects of mathematics. The information obtained from these questions also provides

Estimate the answer to 12/13 + 7/8. You will not have enough time to solve the problem using paper and pencil.

1   2   19   21   I don't know

(a) Original question from NAEP

Read the question and then answer parts (a) and (b) below.
Eighth-grade students were given the question below:

Estimate the answer to 12/13 + 7/8. You will not have enough time to solve the problem using paper and pencil.

1   2   19   21   I don't know

a. The most common answer chosen was 19. This is wrong. What mistake do you think was made by the students who chose 19?

I think they just added the numerators and forgot that they numbers were part of a fraction.

b. What is the correct answer? Explain how you got it. 2 is the correct answer. The way I got this was simple. 12/13 and 7/8 are both almost one so if you add them they would be very close to 2.

(b) Extension question and Jim's explanation

a. The most common answer chosen was 19. This is wrong. What mistake do you think was made by the students who chose 19?

The students who chose 19, only added the numerators and just forgot about the denominators.

b. What is the correct answer? Explain how you got it. I think the correct answer is 2, because 12/13 is only 1/13 away from 1, and 7/8 is only 1/8 away from 1. And so if you couod them both up to 1, your answer will be 2.

(c) Marsha's explanation

Fig. 21.3

direction for the teacher as to what activities, remediation, and discussions might be most fruitful for the class.

Often the goal of assessing reasoning sounds complex and formidable. As illustrated by the examples in this article, relatively short questions can assess and promote reasoning without placing a huge burden on the teacher. In fact, these types of questions can facilitate teaching and planning because they identify strengths and weaknesses in students' mathematical thinking. As opposed to more in-depth problems and projects, which can be used periodically, shorter items are easy to develop and evaluate.

Teachers often report that their students seem to lack the reasoning skills they would like. It has been my experience that many students have difficulty giving meaningful explanations initially if this has not been part of their mathematics preparation in previous years. With experience, however, students' reasoning develops quite well, as do other higher-order skills such as planning, reflecting, making mathematical connections, and communicating.

REFERENCES

Carpenter, Thomas P., Mary Kay Corbitt, Henry S. Kepner, Jr., Mary Montgomery Lindquist, and Robert Reys. *Results from the Second International Assessment of the National Assessment of Educational Progress.* Reston: Va.: National Council of Teachers of Mathematics, 1981.

Fuys, David, Dorothy Geddes, and Rosamond Tischler. *The van Hiele Model of Thinking in Geometry among Adolescents.* Journal for Research in Mathematics Education Monograph No. 3, Reston, Va.: National Council of Teachers of Mathematics, 1988.

Kouba, Vicky L., Judith S. Zawojewski, and Marilyn E. Strutchens. "What Do Students Know About Numbers and Operations?" In *Results from the Sixth Mathematics Assessment of the National Assessment of Educational Progress,* edited by Patricia A. Kenney and Edward A. Silver, pp. 87–140. Reston, Va.: National Council of Teachers of Mathematics, 1997.

National Council of Teachers of Mathematics. *Assessment Standards for School Mathematics.* Reston, Va.: National Council of Teachers of Mathematics, 1995.

————. *Curriculum and Evaluation Standards for School Mathematics.* Reston, Va.: National Council of Teachers of Mathematics, 1989.

————. *Professional Standards for Teaching Mathematics.* Reston, Va.: National Council of Teachers of Mathematics, 1991.

22

Helping Elementary- and Middle-Grades Preservice Teachers Understand and Develop Mathematical Reasoning

George W. Bright

ALTHOUGH teachers need to be able to reason mathematically as they "do" mathematics themselves, it is probably more important for them to be able to understand the mathematical reasoning of students in the classroom. It is well known that novices do not think like experts, and indeed, children are not simply miniature adults; their thinking is qualitatively different than that of adults. In order to help all students achieve mathematical power, teachers need to know a lot about the thinking of students (i.e., mathematical novices) and know how to understand students' reasoning as it evolves. One goal, then, of helping all teachers, and in particular preservice teachers, develop mathematical reasoning is to give them the tools necessary to understand students' thinking in the classroom.

Preservice teachers enter the professional education sequence in a teacher preparation program with a variety of mathematical experiences in a variety of types of classrooms that incorporate a variety of pedagogical approaches. Often these preservice teachers are successful mathematics students, but they may not be completely confident in their personal mathematics knowledge. When they are asked to demonstrate competent mathematical reasoning skills by solving a particular problem, they can do that. If they are asked to solve a problem in more than one way, or to paraphrase the way that one of their peers explains a solution, they may not be so successful. In addition, they are often surprised that their peers (or the students they expect to teach) do not think about problems in the same ways that they do. It is as if their personal reasoning about mathematics acts as a set of blinders that prevent them from being able to see multiple approaches to problems. (See also article 15, by House, in this volume)

There are many strategies that might be used to help preservice teachers develop better mathematical reasoning, but here we will discuss three: (*a*) learn mathematics differently, (*b*) study curriculum materials designed for students, and (*c*) interact with students. These three strategies will be discussed as if they might be used in isolation from each other when, in fact, most preservice (and in-service) teacher development programs incorporate various combinations of these strategies. Although there is some evidence to support the effectiveness of each type of intervention, most teacher educators probably suspect that combinations will be more effective than any one strategy individually.

LEARN MATHEMATICS DIFFERENTLY

Intuitively, it makes sense to believe that if you want people to know mathematics better, you should teach them in a different way. Indeed, this argument is often made by people who want to align mathematics instruction with NCTM's *Standards* (1989, 1991, 1995), so it ought to apply also to preservice teachers and the way they learn mathematics. In order to make these changes, however, it is necessary to coordinate the efforts of many different mathematics teachers, from the early primary grades through university level. The people involved may or may not be members of NCTM and may or may not be completely familiar with the *Standards* or other attempts to reform mathematics instruction. When all of the players *can* develop a coordinated consensus about how to help preservice teachers develop better mathematical reasoning, then this approach has great potential to be effective. However, the mixed messages that are sometimes sent by mathematics teachers across grades and across courses may act to inhibit the mathematical development that is possible for some preservice teachers.

One of the most obvious ways to teach mathematics differently is through the use of manipulatives. Many preservice teachers claim that they did not have manipulatives available when they learned mathematics. They are often surprised at how clearly what they know is modeled with materials, and they incorrectly assume that "If I had been taught this way, I would know mathematics better." That is, they generalize that it is the materials themselves that carry meaning and support the development of reasoning skills. They usually overlook the fact that they already have learned automatized procedures, perhaps in a rote fashion, and that they do not have to think about which step in a procedure to do next. They see the materials as a tactile illustration of what they know, but they cannot really imagine how learning might be different if a student did not already know the steps to perform. So, although use of manipulatives seems to help many preservice teachers attach some meaning to the procedures they already know, it is not clear how this approach really enhances their ability to reason about *new* mathematics that might not be familiar to them.

The following two examples illustrate some of the ways that preservice teachers' reasoning can be influenced. Either example could occur in a content or methods course, but the focus in each case is understanding mathematics rather than pedagogy.

Earlier in my career, I used to demonstrate how manipulatives modeled mathematics concepts, and I expected students to use manipulatives in the fairly limited ways that I more or less prescribed. More recently, however, I have let students explore the materials themselves to develop personal connections between those materials and the mathematics that they think they know. One class, working in six groups of four or five students per group, was asked to use base-ten materials to show numbers in a variety of ways. Everything was going smoothly for two- and three-digit numbers. Then I asked them to show 1524. Three of the groups agreed that the proper way to show this was with two large cubes (what I thought of as one thousands cubes), three flats, two rods, and four small cubes. I had never seen students do this before, so I am sure there was a puzzled look on my face, but in my typical way, I asked why their representation worked. They told me that the large cubes were 600 each for a total of 1200, the three flats were 300, the two rods were 20, and the four small cubes were 4, for a total of 1524. Of course, I followed up with "Why does the large cube represent 600?" to which they pointed to each face and counted by hundreds to 600. Other groups disagreed, claiming the large cube represented 1000, and this prompted a class discussion, at the end of which we agreed that, for the sake of mathematical consistency in modeling place value, 1000 was a better choice.

However, one lesson that I learned from this incident is that reasoning is frequently bound by concrete knowledge. Part of the difficulty seems to have been that most of the large cubes in our particular collection of base-ten materials were hollow plastic cubes; they were not the solid wooden cubes of days gone by. In the discussion, one student even commented on the fact that the large cubes "didn't have anything inside" and wondered, "How can this be 1000?" There were a few solid wooden versions of the large cubes, however, and these were pointed out by students during the discussion as evidence supporting the interpretation of the large cube as 1000.

In most cases, students did not reason from the logic of three dimensions. Rather, they reasoned solely from their perceptions of the objects. That is, they reasoned from concrete experience rather than generalized knowledge. In some sense, the large cube ought to have been viewed in an *ideal* way, but it was not.

Use of calculators can also help challenge preservice teachers' reasoning about mathematics concepts. It is not unusual for preservice teachers to have an implicit notion that multiplying always makes a number bigger and dividing always makes a number smaller, though they are frequently not this explicit about their beliefs. These students are often surprised when they are asked to use calculators to find answers to computations like these:

$32 \div 16$, $32 \div 8$, $32 \div 4$, $32 \div 2$, $32 \div 1$, $32 \div 0.5$, $32 \div 0.25$. Although everything seems to be going well for the first five examples, the answers of 64 and 128 for the last two examples are unexpected. Follow-up discussion about the meaning of division, including the difference between measurement and partitive models, helps allay their concerns, but re-creation of understanding does not come easily or quickly. Preservice teachers need to tie the calculator examples to manipulative and diagrammatic models.

It seems clear from these examples that it is not just the use of manipulatives or technology that helps preservice teachers reconstruct their reasoning. In both cases, there was significant dialogue about the underlying meaning for the models and solutions. Discourse about mathematics seems essential in the process of helping preservice and in-service teachers reflect on what they think they know in order for them to decide if what they think they know is correct. Discourse is also the vehicle for raising alternative views, so that when preservice teachers decide that what they know is wrong, they have some other options to consider.

One of the difficulties that we will increasingly face is that developing reasoning of preservice teachers through instruction in content and methods courses will work only if preservice teachers identify themselves soon enough to enroll in these courses. It is projected that over the next decade there will be a serious teacher shortage (e.g., The Public School Forum of North Carolina 1996, p. 6), so many states will expand their *nontraditional* teacher licensure programs to allow more and more new teachers to bypass university-based teacher preparation programs. Most of these alternatively-licensed teachers will not take mathematics courses especially designed for preservice teachers. More and more responsibility for improving the mathematical reasoning abilities of preservice teachers will fall on people who provide the professional education components of these nontraditional programs.

STUDY CURRICULUM MATERIALS

Russell (1997) has suggested that curriculum materials themselves might be designed to help teachers learn more mathematics and, by extension, learn better mathematical reasoning. This appears to be an approach that has received little study, but stories about it suggest it is effective. Indeed, it may provide a means for helping not only preservice teachers but also in-service teachers. There are several ways that curriculum materials might accomplish this task.

Used Numbers, for example, uses "Dialogue Boxes" to provide a sense of how students might respond to key mathematical questions. An example is given in figure 22.1 (Russell and Corwin 1989, p. 53). Preservice teachers could be asked to analyze the thinking of students in the dialogue with their teacher. Discussion questions could help focus attention on the children's reasoning.

DIALOGUE BOX
What good is knowing the median?

Now you've found the median height for our class and the median height of the All-Star team. So you know *how to find* a median. But what good is knowing the median? Why do you think statisticians or other scientists are interested in knowing the median of a set of data?

DAVE: It's the middle number.

Yes, it is the middle number; for example, the middle height in our class is 58 inches. But if you knew that the median height of some other class was 58 inches, too, what would you know about that other class?

SARAH: Well, if they lined up, the middle kid would be 58 inches tall.

Uh-huh, what else?

CATHY: I don't agree with Sarah, because it might not be the middle kid. It might be between the two kids in the middle.

OK, so you're both saying that 58 inches is the middle value either way. How does that help us know something about the height of the class?

IRENA: You know that half the kids are below 58 and half the kids are taller.

ALAN: They're like our class, about the same height.

They're like our class. What does that mean?

ALAN: The middle of their heights is 58 inches, and so is ours.

What else could you say about whether they're like us or not?

BEN: They wouldn't have to be exactly alike. They could have some kids who were much taller than kids in our class.

How would that work?

BEN: The middle kid could still be 58 inches, but the kids taller than 58 inches could reach all the way up to 80 inches.

So the top half could be more spread out. What do other people think?

CARMEN: I don't think it would be that spread out. Fifth graders aren't 80 inches tall.

OTHERS: Yeah, that's silly. That's as tall as a basketball player.

So you're saying that you have some experience that tells you that another class with a median height of 58 inches wouldn't be as drastically different from ours as Ben was saying. What do you think, Ben?

BEN: They probably wouldn't be all the way up to 80 inches, but there still could be some kids who would be taller.

SUE: Yeah, or shorter.

Shorter? How would that work? …

[Later] …

It seems to me you've been saying that the median tells you some things about data but not everything. So, now, let's pretend again that there's another class with the same median height as we have. What would that tell us about how we're the same?

ANNIE: The middle is the same.

CHRIS: Well, it's kind of that we're clustered around the same height. It's, like, we're kind of the same, but not exactly.

Who can add something or say it differently?

CARMEN: Maybe the typical kid is around 58 inches in both classes, but there could still be things that are different. Like our tallest kid might be taller than their tallest kid.

KYLE: The middle is the same but the ends might be different.

(In this dialogue, the teacher attempts to move the students away from *how to find the median* to an explanation of what the median is good for—what it does and does not tell you about the data it represents. Students need to be able not only to *find* a median, but also to interpret one. Often a median will be stated with no surrounding context; for example, "The median age in the United States is 31.5 years." Understanding what the median tells you about the data as a whole depends in part on the prior knowledge of the context that you bring to interpreting this statistic. For example, students in this class have some knowledge about a reasonable range of fifth-graders' heights, and this helps them interpret a given median height.)

Fig. 22.1

1. What kinds of reasoning are evident?
2. What evidence is there that the children have correct or incorrect understandings of the median?
3. How do the children connect median with other statistics concepts?
4. What responses do you think have been omitted from this dialogue, and what reasoning would those responses illustrate?
5. How did the teacher's questioning promote reasoning about the median as opposed to just knowing how to find the median of a set of data?
6. What other questions might help expand students' connections between median and other concepts?

Analysis of dialogue boxes is clearly different from interacting directly with students, but it seems like a reasonable way to introduce the reasoning of children to preservice teachers. In this setting, preservice teachers have as long as they need to think about what the children have said and to try to make sense of the underlying mathematics. It also demonstrates that children (i.e., mathematical novices) reason differently from teachers (i.e., mathematical experts) and that it might be necessary for them to rethink their own mathematical thinking. When they reach real classrooms and work with real children, they will have to think at a much more rapid pace.

Preservice teachers can also expand their mathematical reasoning by examining the strategies used to model concepts (e.g., the addition of fractions) across different textbooks for children. The assignment here would be to explain the underlying mathematics of each model and to determine whether the representations are equivalent. For example, some textbooks approach the addition of fractions symbolically in *pieces* by first adding only fractions with like denominators, then fractions for which one denominator is an exact multiple of the other denominator, and then fractions with unlike denominators. Writing the sum in lowest terms becomes an exercise in finding common factors of the numerator and denominator. Addition is approached only as a symbolic game without providing much conceptual support. The implicit reasoning inherent in this approach is somewhat like the development of axiomatic systems. As such, it might be relatively comfortable for the adult preservice teachers but not quite so comfortable for elementary- or middle-grades students.

Other textbooks approach the addition of fractions through the use of some variation of fraction bars. The sum of two fractions is represented by the length of the appropriate bars, and expressing the sum in lowest terms becomes a puzzle of finding the largest-sized piece of a bar that can be iterated to match the length exactly. A symbolic algorithm can be developed through finding a pattern by comparing fractions, their representations, and the sum. The implicit reasoning inherent in this approach is the symbolism of concrete situations. As such, it might not be terribly comfortable for the preservice teachers, but it might be more accessible to elementary- or middle-grades students than an approach built on symbolic reasoning.

Further exploration of alternatives (e.g., fraction as part of a whole, or ratio, or operator) could lead to an assignment of designing a presentation for children that would illustrate the addition of fractions that might call on more than one representation or type of reasoning. The payoff in such assignments is having preservice teachers make sense of multiple views of mathematical ideas so that they develop better connections among these ideas. If these assignments involve group work, the analysis of the mathematics underlying the models and representations tends to be richer than when the analysis is done by individuals.

Interact with Students

Many in-service projects, such as cognitively guided instruction (Carpenter, Fennema, Peterson, Chiang, and Loef 1989), Project IMPACT (Campbell and Robles 1997), and QUASAR (Silver and Smith 1996), are trying to help teachers understand the thinking of students in much greater depth so that teachers can make better instructional decisions. The evaluation of these projects suggests that this is an effective strategy for in-service teachers; indeed, teachers' mathematical reasoning skills seem to improve. Few of these projects, however, have explicitly tried to move their approach into preservice teacher education.

One exception is cognitively guided instruction (CGI). In 1991, the Primary Preservice Teacher Education Project was begun (e.g., Vacc and Bright 1994). The goal of the project was to help preservice teachers understand children's thinking better and then to learn to use that increased knowledge about children to provide better instruction so that children learned more mathematics. Project preservice teachers were expected to master some background information about the structure of mathematics and the solution strategies that children might employ in solving problems. Then, interactions with children (e.g., interviews, instruction in small and large groups) provided the data for validating the background information as accurate for describing what children really do as they solve mathematics problems. That is, the preservice teachers were expected to improve their ability to reason about children's mathematical reasoning. In all cases, this process was spread out across multiple semesters and across multiple courses and internship experiences, though the amount of *spread* varied across the sites.

Since the incorporation of CGI into the preservice program was initially through the mathematics methods course, the main goal was to help the preservice teachers provide better instruction for children. It was not primarily to improve the preservice teachers' mathematical reasoning, though that appears to have been an important extra outcome. The discussion of mathematics in this context was primarily to understand what children were thinking so that instruction could be adapted to meet the needs of the children. This points to the importance of the connection between content and pedagogical knowledge for preservice teachers.

For example, children sometimes use negative numbers to keep track of partial difference in subtraction, as shown in the composite example in figure 22.2. Most preservice teachers think that work with negative numbers is not within the grasp of third graders, so when they see a student reasoning like this, their mind-set seems to discount what is happening. The explanation catches them by surprise, so their initial reaction is, "I don't understand what this student is doing." Through group discussion, however, most preservice teachers can eventually follow the logic behind this strategy, and they finally agree that it is an accurate solution to this example.

When asked to compute 423 − 157, Pat (a third-grader) wrote the following:

$$4 -$$
$$30 -$$
$$34 -$$
$$300$$
$$266$$

"You can't take 7 from 3; it's 4 too many, so that's negative 4. You can't take 50 from 20; it's 30 too many, so that's negative 30, and with the other 4, it's negative 34. 400 minus 100 is 300, and then you take the 34 away from the 300, so it's 266."

Fig. 22.2. A third grader's solution to a subtraction problem

The discussion then turns to whether this student's reasoning will work for all subtraction problems. This is a more difficult question, and it is one that has only rarely been asked of most preservice teachers. Yet, for learning about teaching, it is probably the more important consideration. The initial reaction of many preservice teachers is, "No one ever taught me about this technique, so it must not be an accurate procedure for solving all subtraction problems." This reaction is, of course, disappointing for a couple of reasons. First, it reflects the view that mathematical ideas can only be handed down from one person to another and that learners are not capable of inventing new mathematics themselves. If teachers believe this, then they are likely to limit the experiences that students have only to those ideas that are understood by the teacher; there will be little opportunity for exploring novel situations. Second, it reflects a view that children are not capable of doing original mathematics. The more we study children's approaches to problem solving, the more we realize that this is a much too restricted view.

To explore the generalizability of Pat's procedure, preservice teachers can be challenged to try more examples. They discover that Pat's procedure works in all of the examples, but very few of them can present a logical argument for why it works. It is certainly not automatic that they will attempt to symbolize any of the solutions to particular examples, so it is sometimes useful to show the symbolic manipulation for one or two examples.

$$423 - 157 = (400 + 20 + 3) - (100 + 50 + 7) = (400 - 100) + (20 - 50) + (3 - 7)$$
$$= 300 + (-30) + (-4) = 300 + (-34) = 300 - 34 = 266$$

It is easy at this point, to drop in variables to show that the particular digits are not important, though it is impossible to complete the justification just with these symbols.

$$abc - xyz = (100a + 10b + c) - (100x + 10y + z) = (100a - 100x) + (10b - 10y) + (c - z)$$

Preservice teachers begin to see that some of the differences in the last expression might be negative, so writing down negative numbers would be one way to keep track of the "partial differences" in the problem.

In the context of a mathematics content course, developing ways to write down logical arguments justifying or refuting children's procedures might be a useful way to help improve preservice teachers' mathematical expertise. If there is too much emphasis on this in a methods course, however, there may be a negative impact on preservice teachers' pedagogical knowledge. It may reinforce preservice teachers' procedural (rather than conceptual) orientation to mathematics and may implicitly, and incorrectly, suggest that teachers ought to teach children the same symbolic manipulations. Preservice teachers' content and pedagogical knowledge are intertwined, and instructors need to keep in mind the interactions between these two parts of developing knowledge of teaching. Techniques for improving the personal mathematical reasoning of preservice teachers may interfere with the development of their techniques for helping children develop mathematical reasoning.

Not surprisingly, the Primary Preservice Teacher Education Project met with varying success at getting preservice teachers to understand children's thinking and then to use that knowledge in planning instruction. Although there were no direct measures of preservice teachers' mathematical reasoning, it is clear from some preservice teachers' journal entries that they did not always reason accurately or easily. Further, as evidenced by transcripts of videotapes of their instruction, typically made during student teaching, they often did not understand the mathematical reasoning of their students. As noted by Vacc and Bright (1999) some preservice teachers seemed to make progress toward the goal but showed evidence of backsliding, whereas other preservice teachers seemed not to attend to the differences in their students' reasoning.

Another example is built on the work of the Teach-Stat project (Friel and Bright 1998). Although Teach-Stat has not directly been incorporated into preservice education, some of the materials developed have proven useful.

As teachers examine children's thinking, there need to be judgments made about both the accuracy and the generalizability of what is being said. Because children often reason in ways that are different from ways that adults reason, it is sometimes a challenge to see the world from a child's perspective in order to understand that child's reasoning. Discussion about children's solution techniques forces preservice teachers to confront their conceptual deficiencies and to give them a reason for expanding their understanding.

For example, middle-grades students seem to confuse the conventions of making and reading graphs (e.g., Bright and Friel 1998), but these confusions do not surface uniformly across all types of questions that might be asked about a graph. In recent studies, students in grades 6 and 8 were presented with a graph of the lengths of cats (fig. 22.3) and asked several questions about the data in the graph (Friel and Bright 1995), both before and after instruction about graphing. For the first question, performance was quite good; 84 percent (pretest) and 93 percent (posttest) of the students

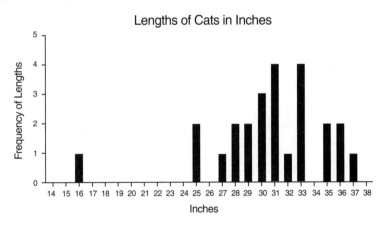

A group of students has been investigating information about their pets. Several students have cats. They decided to collect some information about each of the cats. One set of data they collected was the length of the cats measuring from the tips of the cats' noses to the tips of their tails. Here is a bar graph showing the information they found:

1. How many cats are 30 inches long from nose to tail? How can you tell?
2. How many cats are there in all? How can you tell?
3. If you added up the lengths of the three shortest cats, what would the total of those lengths be? How can you tell?
4. What is the typical length of a cat from nose to tail? Explain your answer.

Fig. 22.3. Graph of data on lengths of cats

answered correctly. Students seemed to be able to read information directly off the graph. By contrast, performance on the third question was poor; only 28 percent (pretest) and 37 percent (posttest) of the students answered correctly. Of most interest was the variety of confusions that seemed to surface in the students' answers (fig. 22.4): adding the values of the two left-most bars without taking into account the frequencies associated with those bars (answer: 41), adding the values of the three left-most bars (answer: 68), focusing on some subset of the four shortest bars (answers: 75, 96, 112), or using the frequencies of bars as lengths of cats (answers: 1, 3, 4).

3. If you added up the lengths of the three shortest cats, what would the total of those lengths be? How can you tell?

68. You take the last 3 legths that have a bar/on them and add.

75, You take the three shortest black bars and add there inches up

Becase 3 they shortest have 1 + that how much it added up to

Fig. 22.4

When preservice teachers are presented with the students' responses to these questions, their challenge is to make some sense of what students said. This task is typically difficult, since they have not frequently considered what mathematics underlies the construction of graphs. Question 1 is quite common in mathematics instruction; students are often asked to "read the data" (Curcio, 1989). Question 3 is less common, however; it asks students to "read between the data." Understanding what is involved in reading between the data forces preservice teachers to rethink how students might reason about data in ways that would produce the wide variety of incorrect answers. The importance of interpreting students' responses comes when preservice teachers think about what the bars might represent for students and how students might be applying procedures learned rotely in other contexts.

Children learn about bar graphs initially in elementary school. In these settings they often draw one bar for each piece of data (i.e., a bar graph of ungrouped or unreduced data), so each bar might represent a cat and the height of the bar might represent the length of that cat. The graph in figure 22.3, in contrast, is a bar graph of grouped or reduced data; the bars represent one or more cats, depending on the frequency associated with a bar, and the height of the bar is not associated with the length of a cat. Obviously, when the processes (e.g., the reasoning) for graphs of ungrouped data are applied inappropriately to graphs of grouped data, incorrect answers can result. Students sometimes act as if they do not realize the situations are different. For example, the confusions of (*a*) focusing on the three left-most bars or the shortest bars and (*b*) using heights of bars (e.g., frequencies) as lengths of cats can be explained if we assume that students are interpreting the bars as representing individual cats. Discussion of these confusions can lead preservice teachers to begin to understand the importance of multiple representations of mathematical concepts to reasoning skills and making connections among different concepts. If students deal with only one representation (e.g., bar graphs of ungrouped data) over a long period of time, then they begin to interpret visually similar representations (e.g., bar graphs of grouped data) from that single perspective. Flexible reasoning can be inhibited if too much is prescribed for students by teachers.

Examining children's thinking, especially unusual thinking, forces preservice teachers to evaluate approaches to solving problems with which they might not be familiar. It is hoped that this will help them make more connections among the things that they do know so that, as they think about how to teach mathematics to children, they will think about ways to make connections among mathematical ideas.

DISCUSSION

In this era of mathematics reform, the importance of improving the mathematical reasoning of preservice teachers cannot be overstated. If new teachers do not enter teaching with firm reasoning skills, they are not likely to be able to pull off the instruction envisioned by the *Standards*. Teacher educators have multiple opportunities to work with preservice teachers (e.g., in content courses, in methods courses, and during internships and student teaching), and there are many tools available to use (e.g., engaging in problem solving, examining children's reasoning, becoming familiar with curriculum materials, analyzing instruction on videotape). It is crucial, however, that the messages communicated in these settings and with these tools be at least moderately consistent about the importance of mathematical reasoning in the development of mathematical power. This means that teacher educators need to engage in their own professional development to learn how to use the tools successfully to highlight reasoning and how to take advantage of the limited opportunities we have to work with preservice teachers.

References

Bright, George W., and Susan N. Friel. "Graphical Representations: Helping Students Interpret Data." In *Reflections on Statistics: Agendas for Learning, Teaching, and Assessment in K–12*, edited by Susanne P. Lajoie, pp. 63–88. Mahwah, N.J.: Lawrence Erlbaum Associates, 1998.

Campbell, Patricia F., and J. Robles. "Project IMPACT: Increasing the Mathematical Power of All Children and Teachers." In *Reflecting on Our Work: NSF Teacher Enhancement in K–6 Mathematics*, edited by Susan N. Friel and George W. Bright, pp. 179–86. Lanham, Md.: University Press of America, 1997.

Carpenter, Thomas P., Elizabeth Fennema, Penelope L. Peterson, C-P. Chiang, and Megan Loef. "Using Knowledge of Children's Mathematics Thinking in Classroom Teaching: An Experimental Study." *American Educational Research Journal* 26 (1989): 499–531.

Curcio, Frances R. *Developing Graph Comprehension: Elementary and Middle School Activities*. Reston, Va.: National Council of Teachers of Mathematics, 1989.

Friel, Susan N., and George W. Bright. *Assessing Students' Understanding of Graphs: Instruments and Instructional Module*. Chapel Hill, N.C.: The University of North Carolina at Chapel Hill, UNC Mathematics and Science Education Network, 1995.

———. "Teach-Stat: A Model for Professional Development in Data Analysis and Statistics for Teachers K–6. In *Reflections on Statistics: Agendas for Learning, Teaching, and Assessment in K–12*, edited by Susanne P. Lajoie, pp. 89–117. Mahwah, N.J.: Lawrence Erlbaum Associates, 1998.

National Council of Teachers of Mathematics. *Assessment Standards for School Mathematics*. Reston, Va.: National Council of Teachers of Mathematics, 1995.

———. *Curriculum and Evaluation Standards for School Mathematics*. Reston, Va.: National Council of Teachers of Mathematics, 1989.

———. *Professional Standards for Teaching Mathematics*. Reston, Va.: National Council of Teachers of Mathematics, 1991.

The Public School Forum of North Carolina. *A Profession in Jeopardy: Why Teachers Leave and What We Can Do about It*. Raleigh, N.C.: The Public School Forum of North Carolina, 1996.

Russell, Susan J. In "The Role of Curriculum in Teacher Development." *Reflecting on Our Work: NSF Teacher Enhancement in K–6 Mathematics*, edited by Susan N. Friel and George W. Bright, pp. 247–54. Lanham, Md.: University Press of America, 1996.

Russell, Susan J., and Rebecca B. Corwin. *Statistics: The Shape of the Data*. Palo Alto, Calif.: Dale Seymour Publications, 1989.

Silver, Edward A., and Margaret S. Smith. "Building Discourse Communities in Mathematics Classrooms: A Worthwhile but Challenging Journey." In *Communicating in Mathematics, K–12 and Beyond*. 1996 Yearbook of the National Council of Teachers of Mathematics, edited by Portia C. Elliott and Margaret J. Kenney, pp. 20–28. Reston, Va.: National Council of Teachers of Mathematics, 1996.

Vacc, Nancy N., and George W. Bright. "Changing Preservice Teacher-Education Programs." In *Professional Development for Teachers of Mathematics*. 1994 Yearbook of the National Council of Teachers of Mathematics, edited by Douglas Aichele and Arthur Coxford, pp. 116–27. Reston, Va.: National Council of Teachers of Mathematics, 1994.

——— . "Elementary Preservice Teachers' Changing Beliefs and Instructional Use of Children's Mathematical Thinking." *Journal for Research in Mathematics Education* 30, no.1 (January 1999): 89–110.

23

Twenty Questions about Mathematical Reasoning

Lynn Arthur Steen

WE BEGIN with two warm-up questions. First, *Why is mathematics an integral part of the K–12 curriculum?* The answers are self-evident and commonplace: to teach basic skills, to help children learn to think logically, to prepare students for productive life and work, and to develop quantitatively literate citizens.

Second, and more problematic, *How does mathematical reasoning advance these goals?* This is not at all self-evident since it depends greatly on the interpretation of "mathematical reasoning." Sometimes this phrase denotes the distinctively mathematical methodology of axiomatic reasoning, logical deduction, and formal inference. Other times, it signals a much broader quantitative and geometric craft that blends analysis and intuition with reasoning and inference, both rigorous and suggestive. This ambiguity confounds any analysis and leaves room for many questions.

1. Is Mathematical Reasoning Mathematical?

Epistemologically, reasoning is the foundation of mathematics. As science verifies through observation, mathematics relies on logic. The description of mathematics as the "science of drawing necessary conclusions," given over a century ago by the philosopher C. S. Peirce, still resonates among mathematicians of today. For example, a contemporary report by mathematicians on school mathematics asserts that "the essence of mathematics lies in proofs" (Ross 1997).

Yet mathematics today encompasses a vast landscape of methods, procedures, and practices in which reasoning is only one among many tools (e.g., Mandelbrot 1994; Thurston 1994; Denning 1997). Computation and computer graphics have opened new frontiers of both theory and application that could not have been explored by previous generations of mathematicians. This frontier has revealed surprising mathematical insights; for example, that deterministic phenomena can exhibit random behavior, that repetition can be the source of chaos as well as accuracy, and that uncertainty is not entirely haphazard since regularity always emerges (Steen 1990).

It took innovative mathematical methods to achieve these insights—methods that were not tied exclusively to formal inference. Does this mean that mathematical reasoning now includes the kind of instinct exhibited by a good engineer who finds solutions that work without worrying about formal proof? Does it include the kinds of inferences from "noisy" data that define the modern practice of statistics? Must mathematical reasoning be symbolic or deductive? Must it employ numbers and algebra? What about visual, inductive, and heuristic inferences? What about the new arenas of experimental mathematics and computer-assisted problem solving? What, indeed, is distinctively *mathematical* about mathematical reasoning?

2. Is Mathematical Reasoning Useful?

For most problems found in mathematics textbooks, mathematical reasoning is quite useful. But how often do people find textbook problems in real life? At work or in daily life, factors other than strict reasoning are often more important. Sometimes intuition and instinct provide better guides; sometimes computer simulations are more convenient or more reliable; sometimes rules of thumb or back-of-the-envelope estimates are all that is needed.

In ordinary circumstances, people employ mathematics in two rather different ways: by applying known formulas or procedures to solve standard problems or by confronting perplexing problems through typically mathematical strategies (e.g., translating to another setting, looking for patterns, reasoning by analogy, generalizing and simplifying, exploring specific cases, or abstracting to remove irrelevant detail). Rarely do they engage in the rigorous deduction characteristic of formal mathematics. At work and in the home, sophisticated multistep calculations based on concrete measurement-based mathematics are far more common than are chains of logical reasoning leading to mathematical proof (Forman and Steen 1995). It is not the methodology of formal deduction that makes mathematics useful for ordinary work so much as the mathematical habits of problem solving and the mathematical skills of calculation (Packer 1997).

Can people do mathematics without reasoning? Many certainly do—using routine methods ingrained as habit. Can people reason without using mathematics? Obviously so, even about situations (e.g., gambling, investing) that mathematicians would see as intrinsically mathematical. Those few people who employ advanced mathematics necessarily engage in some forms of mathematical reasoning, although even for them the role played by reasoning may be unconscious or subordinate to other means of investigation and analysis. But how much mathematical reasoning is really needed for the kinds of mathematics that people do in their lives and work? Does ordinary mathematical practice really require much mathematical reasoning?

3. Is Mathematical Reasoning an Appropriate Goal of School Mathematics?

Mathematics teachers often claim that all types of critical thinking and problem solving are really examples of mathematical reasoning. Nevertheless, employers have a different view, rooted in a paradox: Graduates with degrees in mathematics or computer science are often less successful than other graduates in solving the kinds of problems that arise in real work settings. Often students trained in mathematics tend to seek precise or rigorous solutions regardless of whether the context warrants such an approach. For employers, this distinctively mathematical approach is frequently *not* the preferred means of solving most problems arising in authentic contexts. Critical thinking and problem solving about the kinds of problems arising in real work situations is often better learned in other subjects or in integrative contexts (Brown 1995).

The goals of school mathematics seem to shift every decade, from "conceptual understanding" in the new math '60s to "basic skills" in the back-to-basics '70s, from "problem solving" in the pragmatic '80s to "mathematical power" in the standards-inspired '90s. Will "mathematical reasoning" be next? Not likely. In its strict (deductive) meaning, mathematical reasoning is hardly sufficient to support the public purposes of school mathematics. Everyone needs the practice of mathematics. But who really needs to understand mathematics? Who really needs mathematical reasoning? Can one make the case that every high school graduate needs to be able to think mathematically rather than just perform mathematically?

4. Can Teachers Teach Mathematical Reasoning?

The Third International Mathematics and Science Study (TIMSS) documented that U.S. mathematics teachers focus on teaching students how to do mathematics and not on understanding what they do (NCES 1996). There are many reasons for this, including teachers' image of mathematics as a set of skills, parental demands that children master the basics before advancing to higher-order tasks, and the constraining environment of state-mandated tests that emphasize routine calculations.

Many believe that curricular reform based on mathematical reasoning will never succeed since there are far too few teachers prepared to do justice to such a goal. Even if enough willing and able teachers can be found (or educated), will the public allow them to teach mathematical reasoning in school? Might the fear of "fuzzy mathematics" (Cheney 1997) constrain even those teachers who might want to stress understanding?

5. Can Mathematical Reasoning Be Taught?

Just as we do not really know what mathematical reasoning is, so we also do not know very much about how it develops. Research does support a few general conclusions. First, successful learners are mathematically active (Anderson, Reder, and Simon 1997). Passive strategies (memorization, drill, templates) are much less likely than active tasks (discussion, projects, teamwork) to produce either lasting skills or deep understanding. Second, successful mathematics learners are more likely to engage in reflective (or "metacognitive") activity (Resnick 1987). Students who think about what they are doing and why they are doing it are more successful than those who just follow rules they have been taught.

We also know that students differ: No single strategy works for all students, nor even for the same student in all circumstances. Howard Gardner's theory of multiple intelligences (Gardner 1983, 1995) supports the practice of experienced teachers who create multiple means for students to approach different topics. Diverse experiences provide implicit contexts in which mathematical reasoning may emerge. But can we be sure that it will eventually emerge? Might some students, or some types of reasoning, require explicit instruction? Are there some types of mathematical reasoning that can only develop through students' construction and reflection? If some types of mathematical reasoning cannot be taught explicitly, is it appropriate to require it of all high school graduates?

6. Do Skills Lead to Understanding?

Although mathematical performance generally involves a blend of skills, knowledge, procedures, understanding, reasoning, and application, the public mantra for improving mathematics education focuses on skills, knowledge, and performance—*what* students "know and are able to do." To this public agenda, mathematics educators consistently add reasoning and understanding—*why* and *how* mathematics works as it does.

Experienced teachers know that knowledge and performance are not reliable indicators of either reasoning or understanding. Deep understanding must be well-connected. In contrast, superficial understanding is inert, useful primarily in carefully prescribed contexts such as those found in typical mathematics classrooms (Glaser 1992). Persons with well-connected understanding attach importance to different patterns and are better able to engage in mathematical reasoning. Moreover, students with different levels of skills may be equally able to address tasks requiring more sophisticated mathematical reasoning (Cai 1995).

Nonetheless, the public values (and hence demands) mathematics education not so much for its power to enhance reasoning as for the quantitative skills that are so necessary in today's world. It is not that adults devalue understanding but that they expect basic skills first (Wadsworth 1997). They believe in a natural order of learning—first skills, then higher order reasoning. But, do skills naturally lead to understanding? Or is it the reverse—that understanding helps secure skills? Does proficiency with mathematical facts and procedures necessarily enhance mathematical reasoning? Conversely, can mathematical reasoning develop in some students even if they lack a firm grasp of facts and basic skills? Might the relation of skills to reasoning be like that of spelling to writing—where proficiency in one is unrelated to proficiency in the other?

7. Can Drill Help Develop Mathematical Reasoning?

Critics of current educational practice indict "drill and kill" methods for two crimes against mathematics: disinterest and anxiety. Both cause many students to avoid the subject as soon as they are given a choice. Yet despite the earnest efforts to focus mathematics on reasoning, one out of every two students thinks that learning mathematics is mostly memorization (Kenney and Silver 1997).

And they may have a point. Research shows rather convincingly that real competence comes only with extensive practice (Bjork and Druckman 1994). Nevertheless, practice is certainly not sufficient to ensure understanding. Both the evidence of research and the wisdom of experience suggest that students who can draw on both recalled and deduced mathematical facts make more progress than those who rely on one without the other (Askew and William 1995).

However, children who can recite multiplication facts may still not understand why the answers are as they are or recognize when multiplication is an appropriate operation, much less understand how ratios relate to multiplication. High school students who memorize proofs in a traditional geometry course may show good recall of key theorems but be totally unable able to see how the ideas of these proofs can be used in other contexts. Is there, indeed, any real evidence that practiced recall leads to reasoning and understanding?

8. Is Proof Essential to Mathematics?

Despite the dominance of proof as the methodology of advanced mathematics courses, contemporary advances in applied, computer-aided, and so-called "experimental" mathematics have restored to mathematical practice much of the free-wheeling spirit of earlier eras. Indeed, these recent innovations have led some to proclaim the "death" of proof—that although proof is still useful in some contexts, it may no longer be the *sine qua non* of mathematical truth (Horgan 1993). Although this claim is hotly disputed by many leading mathematicians, it resonates with diverse pedagogical concerns about the appropriateness (or effectiveness) of proof as a tool for learning mathematics. Uncertainty about the role of proof in school mathematics caused NCTM in its *Standards* (NCTM 1989) to resort to euphemisms— "justify," "validate," "test conjectures," "follow logical arguments." Rarely do the *Standards* use the crystalline term "proof."

In fact, most people understand *proof* in a pragmatic rather than a philosophical way: provide just enough evidence to be convincing. For many people, proof is tantamount to the civil legal test of "preponderance of evidence"; others require the stricter standard of "beyond reasonable doubt." In routine uses of mathematics, what works takes precedence over what is provable. So how much understanding of formal proof is necessary for the routine practice of mathematics? Probably not very much. But how much is needed for advanced study of mathematics? Undoubtedly a great deal.

9. Does Learning Proofs Enhance Mathematical Reasoning?

Nothing divides research mathematicians and mathematics educators from each other as do debates about the role of proof in school mathematics. Proof is central to mathematical reasoning, yet there is precious little agreement on how, when, why, or to whom to teach it. Its suitability for school mathematics has always been open to question, both on the grounds of pedagogy and relevance.

The vocabulary of mathematical truth, rigor, and certainty is not a natural habitat for most students. Their world is more empirical, relying on modeling, interpretation, and applications. Only a very few students in high school comprehend proof as mathematicians do—as a logically rigorous deduction of conclusions from hypotheses (Dreyfus 1990). Students generally have very little comprehension of what proof means in mathematics, nor much appreciation of its importance (Schoenfeld 1994). Might early introduction of proof actually do more to hinder than enhance the development of mathematical reasoning?

Although mathematicians often advocate including proof in school curricula so students can learn the logical nature of mathematics (Ross 1997), the most significant potential contribution of proof in mathematics education may be its role in communicating mathematical understanding (Hanna and Jahnke 1996). The important question about proof may not be whether it is crucial to understanding the nature of mathematics as a deductive, logical science, but whether it helps students and teachers communicate mathematically. Is, perhaps, proof in the school classroom more appropriate as a means than as an end?

10. Does "Math Anxiety" Prevent Mathematical Reasoning?

Mathematics is perhaps unique among school subjects in being a major cause of anxiety. Many students believe deeply that they cannot do mathematics and so learn to avoid it; a few are so paralyzed by the prospect that they exhibit physiological evidence of acute anxiety (Buxton 1991; Tobias 1993). It may seem obvious that anyone suffering even mildly from "math anxiety" would not engage in much mathematical reasoning. But this is not at all the case. Many students (and adults) who fear mathematics are, in fact, quite capable of thinking mathematically, and do so quite often—particularly in their attempts to avoid mathematics! What they really fear is not mathematics itself, but school mathematics (Cockcroft 1982).

Both research and common sense say that anxiety is reduced when individuals can control uncertainties (Bjork and Druckman 1994). When percentages and ratios appear as impossible riddles, panic ensues. But, when self-constructed reasoning—under the control of the individual—takes over, much valid mathematical reasoning may emerge, often in a form not taught in school. How can schools respect each student's unique approach to mathematical reasoning while still teaching what society expects (and examines)? Would reduced panic result in improved reasoning? Is this a case where less may be more—where reduced instruction might yield deeper understanding?

11. Do Cooperative Activities Enhance Individual Understanding?

Arguments for cooperative learning and teamwork come from two rather different sources: first, from those (primarily in the education world) who view these activities as effective strategies for learning mathematical reasoning and, second, from those (primarily in the business world) who view cooperative activities as essential for productive employees (SCANS 1991). Advocates envision mathematics classes as communities where students engage in collaborative mathematical practice with each other and with their teachers (Silver, Kilpatrick, and Schlesinger 1990). In such classes students would regularly engage in authentic forms of mathematical practice by inventing strategies, arguing about approaches, and justifying their work.

Parents often object to educators' rationale for teamwork since they view mathematics as an ideal subject in which individual accomplishment can be objectively measured and rewarded. They worry both that children who are above average will be held back by slower students and that those who are behind will be instructed, not by teachers, but by other children. Ironically, despite their distrust of teamwork in subjects like mathematics, most parents and students admire teamwork in sports and musical organizations. (Of course, in sports and music—as in the workplace—success accrues not to individuals but to the team as a whole.) Despite these objections, there is considerable evidence that cooperative learning is effective, especially for children (Bjork and Druckman 1994). For high school students and adults, however, the evidence is more mixed. Older students bring to cooperative groups stronger individual motivations, complex experiences in social interactions, and often some defensiveness or embarrassment about learning.

Employers value teamwork because it produces results that no individual can accomplish alone. But can teamwork in the classroom also produce reasoning at a higher level than could be accomplished by any single member of a team? Will individual members of a team learn more mathematics as a result? Just how do group activities promote mathematical reasoning in individuals? Even more difficult and important: How can mathematics educators gain public support for cooperative activities?

12. Can Calculators and Computers Increase Mathematical Reasoning?

At home and at work, calculators and computers are "power tools" that remove human impediments to mathematical performance. For example, spreadsheets and statistical packages are used by professionals both to extend the power of mind as well as to substitute for it—by performing countless calculations without error or effort. Students certainly need to learn these empowering uses of technology.

But, in addition, calculators and computers are responsible for a "rebirth of experimental mathematics" (Mandelbrot 1994). They provide educators with wonderful tools for generating and validating patterns that can help students learn to reason mathematically. Computer games can help children master basic skills; intelligent tutors can help older students master algebraic procedures. Many educators have argued that since programming enforces logical rigor, computer languages such as Logo and ISETL can help students learn to reason.

Calculators and computers hold tremendous potential for mathematics. Depending on how they are used, they can either enhance mathematical reasoning or substitute for it, either develop mathematical reasoning or limit it. However, judging from public evidence, the actual effect of calculators in school is as often negative as positive: For every student who learns to use spreadsheets, there seem to be several who reach for a calculator to add single digit numbers or to divide by 10. Why are the consequences of calculators in school mathematics so mixed? Why is there such a big gap between aspirations and accomplishment?

13. Why Do So Many Students Feel That Mathematics Is a Foreign Culture?

A substantial number of children find school mathematics opaque. Part of children's difficulty in learning school mathematics lies in their failure to reconcile the rules of school-math with their own independently developed mathematical intuition (Freudenthal 1983; Resnick 1987). Too often, entrenched assumptions—like regular grammar applied in contexts where irregularity rules—impede learning.

To what extent does the mathematical environment in a child's home affect how the child responds to mathematics in school? Many people believe that certain peoples or cultures are better suited to mathematics than others.

The thriving—and controversial—specialty of ethnomathematics documents beyond reasonable doubt that all societies have developed some form of mathematics and that these forms reflect the cultures in which they emerge. Historically alert mathematicians can recognize similarities and differences in the mathematics of different cultures and can trace the influence of cultures on one another in the evolution of mathematics (Joseph 1992). Thus, there are undeniable cultural differences in mathematics.

But are there cultural differences in the development of mathematical reasoning? Here the evidence is less definitive. World-class mathematicians have emerged from societies all around the globe, yet certain cultures put greater emphasis on the kinds of rigor and reasoning that give mathematics its special power. Students growing up in these cultures are more likely to recognize a zone of comfort in school mathematics, whereas students growing up in cultures that view the world through other lenses may feel as if school mathematics is a foreign culture. Why do some students see mathematics as the only welcoming subject in school, whereas others see it as the most foreign of cultures? Why, indeed, do some children find mathematics so unreasonably hard?

14. Is Context Essential for Mathematical Reasoning?

For at least a decade, both educational researchers and reformers have been preaching the message of *situated cognition* or *contextualized learning.* For much longer, scientists and engineers have fussed at mathematicians for persisting with context-free instruction (Rutherford 1997). Recently vocational educators have joined the chorus, citing persistent lack of context in mathematics courses as one of the chief impediments to student learning (Bailey 1997; Hoachlander 1997). Yet, according to a National Research Council report, there is no consistent evidence that performance is enhanced when learning takes place in the setting in which skills will be performed (Bjork and Druckman 1994).

Context can affect learning in two opposing ways: Generally, it enhances motivation and long-term learning, but it can also can limit the utility of what is learned. Knowledge often becomes context-bound when it is taught in just one context. Anyone who has ever taught mathematics has heard complaints from teachers in other subjects that students don't appear to know any of the mathematics they were supposed to have learned in mathematics class. The pervasive problem of compartmentalized knowledge has led many educators to assume that transfer of knowledge from one subject to another is atypical. In fact, transfer does occur, but not nearly as systematically or as predictably as we would like.

Just how situated is mathematical cognition? Does instruction in context facilitate learning mathematics? Does it limit or enhance the likelihood of transfer to other domains? When, if ever, does mathematical reasoning transfer to other domains?

15. Must Students Really Construct Their Own Knowledge?

One of the most widely accepted goals of the mathematics community is that students should understand the mathematics they perform. For centuries, educators have known that understanding grows only with active learning. This has led, in the argot of mathematics educators, to a widespread belief that students *construct* their own understanding (Davis, Maher, and Noddings 1990; Hiebert and Carpenter 1992). In this view, understanding cannot be delivered by instructors, no matter how skillful, but must be created by learners in their own minds.

The constructivist posits that children learn as they attempt to solve meaningful problems. In this view, understanding emerges from reflection catalyzed by questions (Campbell and Johnson 1995). The teachers primary role is not to instruct but to pose problems and ask questions that provoke students to reflect on their work and justify their reasoning. In this way, activities such as explaining, justifying, and exemplifying not only demonstrate understanding but also help create it.

According to supporters, constructivism focuses education on the learner (what happens in students' minds), on inquiry (seeking the right questions, not just the right answers), on relevance (questions of natural interest to children), and on activity (learning with both hand and mind) (Brooks and Brooks 1993). Yet critics (e.g., Anderson et al. 1996; Wu 1996) contend that constructivist methods too easily slight the importance both of didactics (systematic instruction) and drill (systematic practice). What is the appropriate balance between teacher-directed and student-inspired learning? Do students need to construct everything for themselves? What should be memorized and what constructed?

16. How Many Mathematics Are There?

Mathematics lives in many environments—home math, school math, street math, business math, work math—and many students who succeed in one mathematical world fail in another. Even though these are all mathematics, these environments offer fundamentally different contexts in which students learn and use mathematics. One might well imagine that, like multiple intelligences (Gardner 1983), there may be multiple mathematics (Grubb 1997).

Evidence of multiple mathematics abounds. Research documents what parents and teachers know from rueful experience—that many children see school mathematics as disconnected from sense-making and the world of everyday experience (Silver, Kilpatrick, and Schlesinger 1990; Schoenfeld 1991). The widespread separation of symbols from meaning and of calculation from reasoning is an inheritance of an educational system whose historic purpose was to separate the practical from the abstract and workers from scholars (Resnick 1987). Only for the elite was abstract or higher-order reasoning a goal (much less an accomplishment) of education. School has helped foster the public's view of different mathematics for different purposes.

This history encourages a pervasive myth about mathematics learning—that mathematical reasoning is appropriate only for the ten percent of students who are destined for mathematically rich careers in science and engineering. Yet in today's workplace, mathematical thinking is needed by more students than ever before. Nonetheless, some students learn mathematics better in mathematics classes, some in science or shop courses, and some on the job or at home. Do these settings offer different mathematics? In what circumstances is abstract mathematics appropriate? When is concrete mathematics better? Can we trust students to know which type of mathematics is best for them in particular contexts? Do teachers know enough to decide? Does anyone?

17. How Does Our Brain Do Mathematics?

Recent research in neuroscience has begun to open a window into what has heretofore been largely beyond the reach of science: the neural mechanism of cognition. Intriguingly, this research suggests a Darwinian mechanism of diversity and selection that operates within the brain just as it does among species in an ecosystem (Edelman 1992; Abbott 1994; Changeux and Connes 1995). Such a mechanism may help explain the stages of mathematical creativity noted in the classic work of Jacques Hadamard (1945) of preparation (trial and error), incubation (often subconscious), illumination (frequently sudden), and verification (requiring reasoning). According to this theory, mathematical reasoning depends on the same two forces as the evolution of species: a mechanism for generating diversity (alternatives) and a strategy for selection that stabilizes optimal choices among this diversity.

What, indeed, is the neural mechanism of mathematical thought? This is now a researchable question, and the implications of such research are profound. For the first time, we may be able to connect mathematical thinking to the biology of the brain. We now know, for instance, that memory involves several anatomically different structures. As improved understanding of physiology has moved athletes' performances to the edge of human potential, might we soon be able to scientifically improve individuals' mathematical performance? Can we identify the biochemistry of mathematical reasoning? Might neuroscience help educators understand the vexing problem of transfer—or of the relation of skills to reasoning?

18. Is Our Brain Like a Computer?

We tend naively to think of the brain as a computer—especially when it is engaged in mathematical activity. Store basic facts in memory; provide key algorithms for calculation; then push a button. Much of the drill-oriented pedagogy of traditional mathematics education is rooted in this metaphor. In fact, as contemporary neuroscience reveals, the brain is less like a computer to be programmed or a disk to be filled than like an ecosystem to be nourished (Abbott 1996; ECS 1996, 1997).

Although the evidence against the brain-as-computer metaphor is overwhelming (e.g., recovery patterns of stroke victims), the paradigm persists in large measure for lack of a compelling alternative. But that may be about to change. Research in the intersection of evolutionary genetics and neuroscience suggests potentially important neurological differences between those cognitive capacities that are evolutionarily primitive (e.g., counting) and those such as arithmetic (not to mention algebra!) that are more recent social constructs (Geary 1995). Capacity for reasoning is created by a continually changing process of natural selection of neuronal groups responding to an individual's goals (called "values" by Edelman [1992]). Thus both the processes of cognition and the elements on which these processes act—if you will, procedures and facts—are subject to the evolutionary pressures of diversity and selection within the living brain.

19. Is The Capacity for Mathematics Innate?

For years, linguists and neuroscientists have studied the way babies learn language in an effort to understand the relation of human language to the genetic endowment of our species. As children naturally develop their own rules of grammar—regularizing irregular verbs, for example—so they also invent rules to explain patterns they see around them. To the extent that making patterns is a mathematical activity (Steen 1988; Devlin 1994), young children learning language are doing mathematics!

There is abundant evidence that young children, on their own, develop simple mathematical rules that they use to solve problems in their environment (Resnick 1987). Yet these patterns often lead to mathematical misconceptions—e.g., that multiplication makes things bigger—that persist despite subsequent contrary evidence and instruction (Askew and Willliam 1995). Does this mean that young children have the same innate capacity to learn mathematics as they have to learn language? How might mathematical reasoning be enhanced if babies were bathed in an environment as rich in mathematical patterns as it is in natural language?

20. Is School Too Late?

Although certain aspects of the brain are determined by genetics and by the environment in the womb, both neurons and synapses grow and change rapidly during the early years of life. How they grow is determined by the environment of the infant. What they become—after five or six years— determines to a considerable degree the cognitive capacity of the child and adult. Although much of the brain is formed at birth, much remains plastic, amenable to being shaped by experience. The capacity for abstract thinking is particularly plastic. Synapse growth occurs at a phenomenal rate until age two or three and then gradually diminishes for the rest of life (ECS 1997). "Use it or lose it" is a fitting description of the early brain.

Everyone knows the importance of aural stimulation for the learning of language in the first years of life. Recent research has provided rather firm evidence that musical stimulation in these early years enhances capacity for spatial and mathematical abstraction later in life (Rauscher and Shaw 1997). (Whether early musical stimulation enhances musicality is less clear.) Apparently the acoustical bath of aural structure provided by classical music does for the abstract centers of the brain what hearing phonemes does for language learning.

This research leads to many questions that are hardly touched on in mathematics education. Are there "windows" for learning arithmetic or algebra, or for mathematical reasoning, as there surely are for learning language? What, besides music, can enhance the young brain's capacity for mathematical thinking? How sensitive is mathematical ability to the sensory environment of a baby? Just how does learning change the brain's physiology? Might we someday be able to sculpt children's capacity for mathematical reasoning?

References

Abbott, John. "The Search for Next-Century Learning." *AAHE Bulletin* 48, no. 7 (March 1996): 3–6.

———. *Learning Makes Sense: Recreating Education for a Changing Future.* Letchworth, U.K.: Education 2000, 1994.

Anderson, John R., Lynne M. Reder, and Herbert A. Simon. "Applications and Misapplications of Cognitive Psychology to Mathematics Education." Carnegie Mellon University Web Site, <sands.psy.cmu.edu/ACT/papers/misapplied-absja.html> (1997).

Askew, Michael, and Dylan William. *Recent Research in Mathematics Education 5–16.* London: Her Majesty's Stationery Office, 1995.

Bailey, Thomas. "Integrating Vocational and Academic Education." In *High School Mathematics at Work.* Washington, D.C.: National Academy Press, 1997.

Bjork, Robert A., and Daniel Druckman, eds. *Learning, Remembering, Believing: Enhancing Human Performance.* Washington, D.C.: National Research Council, 1994.

Brooks, Jacqueline G., and Martin G. Brooks. *In Search of Understanding: The Case for Constructivist Classrooms.* Alexandria Va.: American Society for Curriculum Development, 1993.

Brown, Patricia, ed. *Promoting Dialogue on School-to-Work Transition.* Washington, D.C.: National Governors' Association, 1995.

Buxton, Laurie. *Math Panic.* Portsmouth, N.H.: Heinemann Educational Books, 1991.

Cai, Jinfa. "A Cognitive Analysis of U.S. and Chinese Students' Mathematical Performance on Tasks Involving Computation, Simple Problem Solving, and Complex Problem Solving." *Journal for Research in Mathematics Education*, Monograph No. 7. Reston, Va.: National Council of Teachers of Mathematics, 1995.

Campbell, Patricia F., and Martin L. Johnson. "How Primary Students Think and Learn." In *Prospects for School Mathematics*, edited by Iris M. Carl, pp. 21–42. Reston, Va.: National Council of Teachers of Mathematics, 1995.

Changeux, Jean-Pierre, and Alain Connes. *Conversations on Mind, Matter, and Mathematics*. Princeton, N.J.: Princeton University Press, 1995.

Cheney, Lynne. "Creative Math or Just 'Fuzzy Math'? Once Again, Basic Skills Fall Prey to a Fad." *The New York Times* (11 August1997): A13.

Cockcroft, Sir Wilfred. *Mathematics Counts*. London: Her Majesty's Stationery Office, 1982.

Davis, Robert B., Carolyn A. Maher, and Nel Noddings, eds. "Constructivist Views on the Teaching and Learning of Mathematics." *Journal for Research in Mathematics Education*, Monograph No. 4. Reston, Va.: National Council of Teachers of Mathematics, 1990.

Denning, Peter J. "Quantitative Practices." In *Why Numbers Count: Quantitative Literacy for Tomorrow's America*, edited by Lynn Arthur Steen, pp. 106–17. New York: The College Board, 1997.

Devlin, Keith. *Mathematics: The Science of Patterns*. New York: W. H. Freeman, 1994.

Dreyfus, Tommy. "Advanced Mathematical Thinking." In *Mathematics and Cognition*, edited by Pearla Nesher and Jeremy Kilpatrick, pp. 113–34. Cambridge U.K.: Cambridge University Press, 1990.

Edelman, Gerald. *Bright Air, Brilliant Fire*. New York: Basic Books, 1992.

Education Commission of the States. *Bridging the Gap Between Neuroscience and Education*. Denver, Colo.: Education Commission of the States, 1996

———. *Brain Research Implications for Education* 15, no. 1 (Winter 1997).

Forman, Susan L., and Lynn Arthur Steen. "Mathematics for Life and Work." In *Prospects for School Mathematics*, edited by Iris M. Carl, pp. 219–41. Reston, Va.: National Council of Teachers of Mathematics, 1995.

Freudenthal, Hans. "Major Problems of Mathematics Education." In *Proceedings of the Fourth International Congress on Mathematical Education*, edited by Marilyn Sweng, et al., pp. 1–7. Boston, Mass.: Birkhäuser, 1983.

Gardner, Howard. *Frames of Mind: The Theory of Multiple Intelligences*. New York: Basic Books, 1983.

———. "Reflections on Multiple Intelligences: Myths and Messages." *Phi Delta Kappan* (November 1995): 200–209.

Geary, David C. "Reflections on Evolution and Culture in Children's Cognition: Implications for Mathematical Development and Instruction." *American Psychologist* 50, no. 1 (1995).

Glaser, Robert. "Expert Knowledge and the Processes of Thinking." In *Enhancing Thinking Skills in the Sciences and Mathematics*, edited by Diane. F. Halpern, pp. 63–75. Hillsdale, N.J.: Lawrence Earlbaum Associates, 1992.

Grubb, Norton. "Exploring Multiple Mathematics." Project EXTEND Web Site <www.stolaf.edu/other/extend/Expectations/grubb.html> (1996).

Hadamard, Jacques. *The Psychology of Invention in the Mathematical Field.* Princeton, N.J.: Princeton University Press, 1945.

Hanna, Gila, and H. Niels Jahnke. "Proof and Proving." In *International Handbook of Mathematics Education*, edited by Alan J. Bishop, et al., pp. 877–908. Dordrecht: Kluwer Academic Publishers, 1996.

Hiebert, James, and Thomas P. Carpenter. "Learning and Teaching with Understanding." In *Handbook of Research on Mathematics Teaching and Learning*, edited by Douglas A. Grouws, pp. 65–97. New York: Macmillan, 1992.

Hoachlander, Gary. "Organizing Mathematics Education Around Work." In *Why Numbers Count: Quantitative Literacy for Tomorrow's America*, edited by Lynn Arthur Steen, pp. 122–36. New York: The College Board, 1997.

Horgan, John. "The Death of Proof." *Scientific American* 269 (April 1993): 93–103.

Joseph, George Ghevergheze. *The Crest of the Peacock: Non-European Roots of Mathematics.* London: Penguin Books, 1992.

Kenney, Patricia Ann, and Edward A. Silver, eds. *Results from the Sixth Mathematics Assessment of the National Assessment of Educational Progress.* Reston, Va.: National Council of Teachers of Mathematics, 1997.

Mandelbrot, Benoit. "Fractals, the Computer, and Mathematics Education." In *Proceedings of the 7th International Congress on Mathematical Education*, edited by Claude Gaulin, et al. pp. 77–98. Sainte-Foy, Que.: Les Presses de l'Université Laval, 1994.

National Center for Educational Statistics. *Pursuing Excellence.* Washington, D.C.: U.S. Department of Education, 1996.

National Council of Teachers of Mathematics. *Curriculum and Evaluation Standards for School Mathematics.* Reston Va.: National Council of Teachers of Mathematics, 1989.

Packer, Arnold. "Mathematical Competencies that Employers Expect." In *Why Numbers Count: Quantitative Literacy for Tomorrow's America*, edited by Lynn Arthur Steen, pp. 137–54. New York: The College Board, 1997.

Rauscher, Frances, and Gordon Shaw. "Music Training Causes Long-Term Enhancement of Preschool Children's Spatial-Temporal Reasoning." *Neurological Research* 19 (February 1997): 2–8.

Resnick, Lauren B. *Education and Learning to Think.* Washington, D.C.: National Research Council, 1987.

Ross, Kenneth A. "Second Report from the MAA Task Force on the NCTM Standards." Mathematical Association of America Web Site <www.maa.org/past/nctmupdate.html> (1997).

Rutherford, F. James "Thinking Quantitatively about Science." In *Why Numbers Count: Quantitative Literacy for Tomorrow's America*, edited by Lynn Arthur Steen, pp. 60–74. New York: The College Board, 1997.

Schoenfeld, Alan H. "On Mathematics as Sense-Making." In *Informal Reasoning and Education*, edited by J. F. Voss, D. N. Perkins, and J. W. Segal, pp. 311–43. Hillsdale, N.J.: Lawrence Earlbaum Associates, 1991.

———. "What Do We Know About Curricula?" *Journal of Mathematical Behavior* 13 (1994): 55–80.

Secretary's Commission on Achieving Necessary Skills (SCANS). *What Work Requires of Schools: A SCANS Report for America 2000*. Washington, D.C.: U.S. Department of Labor, 1991.

Silver, Edward A., Jeremy Kilpatrick, and Beth Schlesinger. *Thinking Through Mathematics*. New York: College Entrance Examination Board, 1990.

Steen, Lynn Arthur. "The Science of Patterns." *Science* 240 (29 April 1988): 611–16.

———. ed. *On the Shoulders of Giants: New Approaches to Numeracy*. Washington, D.C.: National Academy Press, 1990.

Thurston, William P. "On Proof and Progress in Mathematics." *Bulletin of the American Mathematical Society* 30 (1994): 161–77.

Tobias, Sheila. *Overcoming Mathematics Anxiety* (rev. ed.). New York: W. W. Norton, 1993.

Wadsworth, Deborah. "Civic Numeracy: Does the Public Care?" In *Why Numbers Count: Quantitative Literacy for Tomorrow's America*, edited by Lynn Arthur Steen, pp. 11–22. New York: The College Board, 1997.

Wu, Hung-Hsi. "The Mathematician and the Mathematics Education Reform." *Notices of the American Mathematical Society* 43, no. 12 (December 1996): 1531–37.

Index